Global Perspectives on Dissociative Disorders

Dissociative disorders are one of the psychiatric consequences of childhood psychological trauma. While oppression is an aspect of traumatic conditions, dissociation undermines resistance to oppression throughout a person's lifespan. Neither oppression nor dissociation are restricted to particular cultures, and both can affect individuals as well as societies.

This collection engages with the universality of dissociative disorders and their close relationship to oppression. The chapters cover extreme examples such as ongoing incest in adulthood, children and adults forced to kill others, and abusive states in interrogation. Further subjects examined include the utilization of dissociation to maintain societal oppression, the oppressive conditions of asylum seekers and the consequences of oppression as they are dealt with in psychotherapy. The final chapter considers how a paedophile pandering network employed multi-layered oppression to prevent the public becoming aware of the widespread and organised abuse of children.

This book will engender interactions between trauma investigators – those whose approach is close clinical observation, those who use instruments to survey groups of individuals, those whose research takes the form of investigative journalism and those who examine the truth embedded or hidden in documents created for multiple, and at times, disturbing political purposes.

Portions of this book were originally published as a special issue of the *Journal of Trauma & Dissociation*. It also includes material from other sources.

Vedat Şar, MD, is a Professor of Psychiatry in Istanbul University, Turkey. He has previously been president of the International Society for the Study of Trauma and Dissociation (ISSTD) and is currently president of the European Society for Traumatic Stress Studies (ESTSS). He has published numerous studies on adult psychiatric consequences of childhood trauma covering diagnosis, epidemiology, neurobiology and treatment. He has been awarded the Cornelia Wilbur Award and Morton Prince Award for Scientific Achievement for his work on dissociative disorders.

Warwick Middleton, MBBS, FRANZCP, MD, is Adjunct Professor at La Trobe University, Melbourne, Australia, at the University of New England, Armidale, USA, and at the University of Canterbury, Christchurch, New Zealand. He is Associate Professor at the School of Medicine, University of Queensland, Australia. Professor Middleton has made substantial and ongoing research contributions to the fields of bereavement, trauma, dissociation and psychotherapy. He currently chairs the Cannan Institute and is Director of the Trauma and Dissociation Unit, Belmont Hospital, Brisbane, Australia, and is a Board member and Fellow of the International Society for the Study of Trauma and Dissociation.

Martin Dorahy, PhD, DClinPysch, is Associate Professor of Psychology, University of Canterbury, Christchurch, New Zealand. He is on the Board of Directors of the International Society for the Study of Dissociation. He has published widely on dissociative disorders and complex trauma. He maintains a private practice focused on adult outcomes of complex childhood trauma.

Global Perspectives on Dissociative Disorders

Individual and Societal Oppression

Edited by
Vedat Şar, Warwick Middleton and Martin Dorahy

Routledge
Taylor & Francis Group
LONDON AND NEW YORK

First published 2014
by Routledge
4 Park Square, Milton Park, Abingdon, Oxon OX14 4RN
605 Third Avenue, New York, NY 10017

Routledge is an imprint of the Taylor & Francis Group, an informa business

British Library Cataloguing in Publication Data
A catalogue record for this book is available from the British Library

ISBN13: 978-0-415-71807-3 (hbk)

Typeset in Garamond
by Taylor & Francis Books

Publisher's Note
The publisher accepts responsibility for any inconsistencies that may have arisen during the conversion of this book from journal articles to book chapters, namely the possible inclusion of journal terminology.

Disclaimer
Every effort has been made to contact copyright holders for their permission to reprint material in this book. The publishers would be grateful to hear from any copyright holder who is not here acknowledged and will undertake to rectify any errors or omissions in future editions of this book.

Contents

Citation Information

The chapters in this book were originally published in the *Journal of Trauma and Dissociation*, volume 14, issues 2 and 3 (2013). When citing this material, please use the original page numbering for each article, as follows:

Chapter 1
Stimulus Deprivation and Overstimulation as Dissociogenic Agents in Postmodern Oppressive Societies
Vedat Şar and Erdinc Ozturk
Journal of Trauma and Dissociation, volume 14, issue 2 (2013) pp. 198–212

Chapter 2
The Role of Abusive States of Being in Interrogation
Frank W. Putnam
Journal of Trauma and Dissociation, volume 14, issue 2 (2013) pp. 147–158

Chapter 4
Ongoing Incestuous Abuse During Adulthood
Warwick Middleton
Journal of Trauma and Dissociation, volume 14, issue 3 (2013) pp. 251–272

Chapter 5
Dissociation and Symptoms of Culture-Bound Syndromes in North America: A Preliminary Study
Colin A. Ross, Elizabeth Schroeder and Laura Ness
Journal of Trauma and Dissociation, volume 14, issue 2 (2013) pp. 224–235

Chapter 6
Ethnic Syndromes as Disguise for Protest Against Colonialism: Three Ethnographic Examples
Elizabeth Hegeman
Journal of Trauma and Dissociation, volume 14, issue 2 (2013) pp. 138–146

Chapter 7
Dissociation and Identity Transformation in Female Survivors of the Genocide Against the Tutsi in Rwanda: A Qualitative Research Study
Denise H. Sandole and Carl F. Auerbach
Journal of Trauma and Dissociation, volume 14, issue 2 (2013) pp. 127–137

Chapter 8
Transference-Focused Psychotherapy with Former Child Soldiers: Meeting the Murderous Self
Nel Draijer and Pauline Van Zon
Journal of Trauma and Dissociation, volume 14, issue 2 (2013) pp. 170–183

Chapter 9
Boundary Modifications in the Treatment of People with Dissociative Disorders: A Pilot Study
Adah Sachs
Journal of Trauma and Dissociation, volume 14, issue 2 (2013) pp. 159–169

Chapter 10
Seeking Asylum—Trauma, Mental Health, and Human Rights: An Australian Perspective
Louise Newman
Journal of Trauma and Dissociation, volume 14, issue 2 (2013) pp. 213–223

Please direct any queries you may have about the citations to
clsuk.permissions@cengage.com

Notes on Contributors

Carl F. Auerbach, Department of Psychology, Yeshiva University, Bronx, New York, USA

Nick Bryant, Investigative Journalist, New York, New York, USA

Martin Dorahy, Department of Psychology, University of Canterbury, Christchurch, New Zealand

Nel Draijer, Department of Psychiatry, VU University Medical Center/GGZinGeest, Amsterdam, The Netherlands

Elizabeth Hegeman, John Jay College of Criminal Justice, City University of New York, New York, New York, USA

Warwick Middleton, The Cannan Institute, Australia; La Trobe University, Melbourne, Australia; University of New England, Armidale, USA; University of Canterbury, Christchurch, New Zealand; University of Queensland, Australia

Laura Ness, The Colin A. Ross Institute for Psychological Trauma, Richardson, Texas, USA

Louise Newman, Centre for Developmental Psychiatry & Psychology, Monash University, Clayton, Victoria, Australia

Erdinc Ozturk, Department of Psychiatry, Istanbul University, Istanbul, Turkey

Frank W. Putnam, Department of Psychiatry, University of North Carolina at Chapel Hill, Chapel Hill, North Carolina, USA

Colin A. Ross, The Colin A. Ross Institute for Psychological Trauma, Richardson, Texas, USA

Adah Sachs, Clinic for Dissociative Studies and The Bowlby Centre, London, UK

Denise H. Sandole, Department of Psychology, Yeshiva University, Bronx, New York, USA

Vedat Şar, Department of Psychiatry, Istanbul University, Istanbul, Turkey

Elizabeth Schroeder, The Colin A. Ross Institute for Psychological Trauma, Richardson, Texas, USA

Pauline Van Zon, Psychotraumacentrum Zuid-Nederland/Reinier van Arkel Groep, s'Hertogenbosch, The Netherlands

INTRODUCTION

Global Perspectives on Dissociative Disorders: Individual and Societal Oppression

VEDAT SAR, MD
Department of Psychiatry, Istanbul Faculty of Medicine, Istanbul University, Istanbul, Turkey

WARWICK MIDDLETON, MBBS, FRANZCP, MD
The Cannan Institute, La Trobe University, University of Queensland, University of New England, University of Canterbury

MARTIN DORAHY
Department of Psychology, University of Canterbury, Christchurch

> 3RD FISHERMAN: "Master, I marvel how the fishes live in the sea."
> 1ST FISHERMAN: "Why, as men do a-land—the great ones eat up the little ones."
> [William Shakespeare (1564–1616) Pericles (1606–08), Act 2, Scene 1].

Frans de Waal (2000), in his masterful study of the relational dynamics of a chimp colony, identified power, sex and food as primary motivating factors in the organization of chimpanzee society. Literacy, education, scientific progress, economic improvement, advances in public health, disease prevention, life expectancy and the increasingly accessible mechanisms of mass communication have combined to progressively expose a world where individuals and hierarchical human organizations operate using—and are also characteristically reluctant to relinquish—power. Many individuals are owned, exploited or abused in the operation of individual and social power, and typically accounting of the practices which maintain power structures and dynamics comes only with extreme reluctance. Despite the temptation to impose an ethnocentric Western viewpoint on the nature of oppression, such practices are not absent from "advanced" Western democracies, an example being Bryant's (2009) extensive investigation of the Franklin saga (see Bryant, Chapter 11, this volume). Even within established democracies there are frequently groups or organizations that have power structures worthy of the most totalitarian state, and although such entities may include orphanages, churches, cults and organized criminals, globally the most commonly encountered abusive totalitarian structure is based on the family.

Prilleltensky (2003) defines *oppression* as a "state of asymetric power relations characterized by domination, subordination, and resistance, whereby the controlling person or group exercise [sic] its power by processes of political exclusion and violence and by psychological dynamics of depreciation" (p. 195). Oppression is argued to be most accurately understood as a psychopolitical process where subjugation occurs both outside the person (political; e.g., forced economic, social, material and legal obstructions to liberties, freedom and justice) and also within the person (psychological; e.g., internalized images of self-rejection, helplessness, obedience and inferiority; Naidoo & Rajab, 2005). A simple construction of the nature of oppression is that it represents a misuse of power such that individual rights are not respected. Excessive power and force that evoke fear and motivate subjugation are not the only tools of the oppressor. In many cases, more subtle operations to undermine character, identity and sense of self by heightening shame, activate the sanction of silence and compliance, such that external force is rarely needed because resistance is eroded by internal decrees of inferiority, helplessness and lack of worth. The term oppression is being used in this book to reflect contexts in which these external and internal forces operate to enslave, subdue and suppress groups (e.g., subject to dictatorial rule) and individuals (e.g., subject to an incestuous abuser). Oppression does not respect boundaries, and in dealing with the consequences of it often draws us to reassess our own (see Sachs, Chapter 9, this volume).

The civil wars, class conflicts and societal struggles against oppression that have paved the way for individual freedoms (including sexual equality) have been hard fought. Yet there is no room for complacency or for harboring belief that even in the richest, most stable or democratic societies, there are not many examples of the human rights of individuals being chronically ignored or actively suppressed. Politics represents the mechanisms by which power is gained and distributed within groups, organizations and societies. Although political democracy does not stop oppression, it does offer hope that widespread subjugation can be reduced. However, one of the most challenging aspects of oppression in postmodern times is that it may be invisible (see Sar & Ozturk, Chapter 1, this volume); that is, with an outward shape of democracy (e.g., voting rights, etc.) but lacking the essence of democracy.

Time and again we find that extreme oppression has occurred in our very midst, whether it be what happens inside an outwardly unremarkable house, or what happens inside an international organization, where the protection of reputation is given a higher priority than the protection of individuals. D'Antonio (2013) recounts the progressive waves of revelations that left the Catholic Church the focus of global judgment:

> Scattered outbreaks of accusation became a firestorm that consumed huge portions of the Church's resources and reputation. The Vatican's claim to moral supremacy, the basis for all of its influence after the fall of Rome, became the standard by which it was judged and found wanting. In the course of the continuous scandal, more than 6,100 priests were deemed by the Church itself to be 'not implausibly' or 'credibly' accused of sexual crimes against more than 16,000 underage victims in the United States alone. More than five hundred American priests were arrested and prosecuted. Of these, more than four hundred were convicted and imprisoned. As of 2012, the worldwide church had paid about $3 billion to settle civil suits, but countless claims remained unresolved (p. 4).

Generally similar revelations of the oppressive use of religious authority played out in multiple countries. As of April 29, 2013, a total of 60 Catholic bishops from 20 different countries had either been convicted of sexual offences or have had to resign because of complicity and/or scandal (BishopAccountability.org, 2013).

Paralleling the wider reporting of child sex abuse within church settings, which has been gathering pace since the early eighties, has been a congruent reporting of similar types of abuse in sporting organizations, in the scouting movement, in orphanages and reform schools, as well as an emergent focus on exploitation and abuse (frequently sexual) that occurs when boundaries are violated in therapy settings. The case perhaps more than any other which demonstrated that whatever the dynamic is that allows the powerful to silently abuse the vulnerable, and was very much a part of the mental health landscape, was the one involving Jules H. Masserman. He was past president of both the American Academy of Psychoanalysis and the American Psychiatric Association, and the author of a score of books and over 400 articles. Masserman reached financial settlements in 1986 with four women who stated they had been drugged and sexually molested by him (see Noël & Watterson, 1992). After Masserman surrendered his medical licence, the American Psychiatric Association Appeals Board voted to suspend him for five years rather than expel him (Landers, 1992; Pace, 1994). For further discussion on therapeutic boundaries, see Sachs, Chapter 9, this volume.

Herman and Chomsky (2002) argue that indocrination is the essence of democracy (i.e., a way of controlling what people think when force cannot be used to control them). Thus, oppression can be justified and legitimized. *Indoctrination works best on a substrate of unprocessed trauma.* Samuel Oliner was only 12 years old when his entire extended family, save for one cousin and his wife, were murdered by the Nazis in Poland, part of the 60% of the Jewish population of Europe to perish at the hands of the Nazis. Oliner and Oliner (1988) interviewed 406 authenticated rescuers of Jews, compared them with 126 nonrescuers and found that their education, religion, economic class, political involvement, employment profile and other social characteristics were all similar. Only their child rearing experiences were significantly different. Altruistic personalities, they found, had families that showed them more respect, more love, more concern for fairness and had less emphasis on obedience and more on individuality. Growing up they were more likely to have friends from outside their own religious grouping. As children, they were almost never sent out to others to be cared for, and if as children they received corporal punishment, their parents often apologized. In reflecting on the comparisons between those who risked their lives to rescue Jews and those who were primarily concerned with their own survival, the Oliners conclude,

> If we persist in defining ourselves as doomed, human nature as beyond redemption, and social institutions as beyond reform, then we shall create a future that will inexorably proceed in confirming this view. Rescuers refused to see Jews as guilty or beyond hope and themselves as helpless, despite all the evidence that could be marshaled to the contrary. They made a choice that affirmed the value and meaningfulness of each life in the midst of a diabolical social order that repeatedly denied it (Oliner & Oliner, 1988, p. 260).

Altruism, a defining feature of well-developed self-hood (see Middleton, 2005) and a strong counter force to the dynamics that define oppression, remains too rare a feature of human affairs. At the Evian conference in 1938, delegates from 32 countries spent nine days discussing the plight of refugees from Germany and Austria, but little was done. Samuel Oliner, in a later work (2003), reflects,

> When the German government heard about talk of sympathy for Jewish refugees in Germany, it replied that foreign countries criticized Germany for their treatment of the Jews, but none of them wanted to open their doors when the opportunity presented itself (p. 61).

Yet genocide, ethnic cleansing and the displacement of large populations by religious or racial divisions remain outcomes of contemporary oppression. The United Nations estimates that in 1994 some 800,000 ethnic Tutsis and moderate Hutus died in around 100 days in Rwanda, the fastest genocide in human history. Most of the victims were killed in their villages by their neighbors or fellow villagers. Hutus who refused to kill were often murdered on the spot. "Either you took part in the massacres or you were massacred yourself" (New World Encyclopedia). Between 250,000 and 500,000 Rwandan women and girls were raped (Jacobs, 2009), with between 2,000 and 5,000 pregnancies resulting. Political leaders in France, Belguim and the USA were aware of preparations for the genocide but failed to take steps to prevent it; indeed they shunned the use of the "g-word", fearing that it would trigger calls for intervention (United Human Rights Council). Paul Rusesabagina, who saved over 1,200 people by sheltering them at the Hôtel des Mille Collines, has reflected: "In a sense things got better after the peacekeepers left . . . People realized no one was going to help them and took matters into their own hands" (Zakaria, 2004). An independent report on the UN failures in Rwanda commissioned by Secretary-General Kofi Annan criticized the major political powers for "deplorable inaction" (People Pledge Union Information). President Bill Clinton was to reflect that his failure to deal effectively with the emergent genocide in Rwanda was the "biggest regret" of his presidency (Myer, 2012). Clinton opined in 2013 that if the USA had gone into Rwanda sooner following the start of the genocide in 1994, at least a third of the lives lost could have been saved (Moodley, 2013).

In July 1995, more than 8,000 ethnic Muslim men and boys were massacred near Srebrenica, the worst massacre in Europe since World War II. Another 25,000–30,000 individuals were subjected to mass expulsion as part of a campaign of ethnic cleansing in Bosnia carried out by forces under the direct command of General Ratko Mladic, who in turn took orders from the Bosnian-Serb leader, Radovan Karadžić (GoreGrish.com, 2011). Prior to perpetrating genocide and being prosecuted for war crimes, Karadžić, a published poet, had practiced as a psychiatrist at the psychiatric treatment centre of the main Sarajevo hospital. When finally arrested in Belgrade in July 2008, Karadžić was working under an alias, that of "Dr Dragan Dabić, 'Spiritual Explorer'", in a private clinic specializing in alternative medicine and psychology in Belgrade, Serbia. He wrote a column for the magazine *Healthy Life* which focused on the art of meditation (Todorovic & de Quetteville, 2008). Karadžić gave lectures in front of hundreds of people on alternative medicine and he even had his own website offering his assistance in the treatment of sexual problems via the use of what he called Human Quantum Energy (Reuters, 2008). Such a breathtaking transformation from genocidal nationalist leader to fugitive/personal therapist reinforces the need to maintain vigilance—that so frequently people are not what they seem to be.

White (2011) noted that it was a relatively new theory among political scientists that deadly famines don't occur in democracies. Amartya Sen (2000), who won the Nobel Prize in 1999, observed: "[n]o famine has ever taken place in the history of the world in a functioning democracy" (p. 16). While it might be assumed that democracies are usually rich countries where food is plentiful, Sen noted that a nation's wealth didn't matter, be it a rich Western Europe or North American country or relatively poor nations such as post-independence India, or Botswana. "The deciding factor seems to be that elected governments have to keep the voters happy, and letting citizens starve to death results in a loss of votes in addition to the obvious loss of voters" (White, 2011, p. 309).

Chapters within this volume examine different aspects of political and psychological oppression and various manifest merges between them (e.g., Newman, Chapter 10; Sandole & Auerbach, Chapter 7; Sar & Ozturk, Chapter 1). The general themes are now elucidated.

ORGANIZED ABUSE

Abuse and exploitation will occur in any society or in any societal structure in which it *can* occur. We can have no confidence that in any substantive grouping, no matter how well credentialled or respectable the members, there won't be individuals who engage in various forms of oppression. They will economically exploit, commit incest, sexually abuse children, indulge in sadism, directly or indirectly support sex trafficking and thus ignore the human rights of the vulnerable and powerless. Given particular circumstances, there will be individuals, in all societies, who will actively participate in torture (see Putnam, Chapter 2, this volume), ethnic cleansing or genocide, mass rapes, the enslavement of children, forcing children to be soldiers (see Draijer & Van Zon, Chapter 8, this volume) and, in effectively being a party to murder, to remove witnesses to crimes that would result in public disgrace and imprisonment.

Repeated evidence of high-level sex abuse rings impacts on the national consciousness of all countries where it is detected. Yet, the actions of government and/or its security apparatus/police have repeatedly been evident globally in compromising investigations into sex abuse rings. A prominent example being the enormously bungled investigation into the Belgian case involving Marc Dutroux (a serial killer and pedophile) and his accomplices which resulted in a protest march (the "White March") of 300,000 citizens in Brussels in October 1996. Protesters were not only distressed at the apparent incompetence of police, the slowness in the investigation and the removal of the original presiding judge from the case, but were very disturbed by Dutroux's claim that he was part of a sex ring that included high ranking members of the police force and government. The original presiding judge in the case, Jean-Marc Connerotte, broke down in tears in the witness stand when he described how:

> the bullet-proof vehicles and armed guards needed to protect him against the shadowy figures determined to stop the full truth coming out. Never before in Belguim has an investigating judge at the service of the king been subjected to such pressure. We were told by police that [murder] contracts had been taken out against magistrates (Evans-Pritchard, 2004).

Judge Connerotte testified that the investigation was seriously hampered by the protection of suspects by people in government. He said that the "dysfunctional judiciary" was breaking down and that mafia groups were taking control of the "key institutions in the country" (Evans-Pritchard, 2004). Belgium is not alone in high profile sex abuse claims and alleged cover-ups.

The Portugese Judiciary Police in 1981 first accused the caretaker of a Casa Pia state-run children's home of raping dozens of children over a 30-year period. No legal action resulted and it wasn't for another generation that in September 2002 there was renewed focus on allegations brought forward by children that politicians, diplomats and media celebrities were part of a pedophile ring that had operated for decades. A trial finally started in 2004. Critics expressed concern that the excruciatingly slow justice system was vulnerable to corrupting external influences. In September 2010, six individuals were finally convicted on charges of pedophilia and other crimes occurring in the late 1990s and early 2000s. They included Carlos Cruz (a famous Portuguese television presenter), Manuel Abrantes (former Casa Pia governor) and Jorge Ritto (former UNESCO ambassador) (BBC, 2010b).

Allegations of political interference in the repeated attempts to investigate a pedophile ring in north Wales are matters of recent reporting. In 2012, the British Home Secretary, Theresa May, announced a new police inquiry into allegations of child abuse in north Wales in the 1970s and 1980s, one of eight inquiries launched in the wake of the Jimmy Savile revelations (BBC, 2012). The Metropolitan Police's Operation Yewtree is investigating claims from 450 potential victims of Savile which date from 1955 to 2009 (Rankin, 2013). Savile maintained a close relationship with Prince Charles, cultivated an image as a tireless charity worker, had friendships with senior members of the government and avoided any serious examination of his crimes during his lifetime, despite the fact that many who worked with him were aware of his pedophilia. Prime Minister David Cameron in the House of Commons wondered, "How did he get away with it for so long?" (London 24, 2012). Similar questions were asked about Jerry Sandusky, assistant coach at Pennsylvania State University from 1969 to 1999, who was finally arrested in 2011. In June 2012, he was found guilty on 45 charges relating to the sexual abuse of ten boys and sentenced to 30 to 60 years in prison (Thompson, 2013). In 1977, Sandusky had established The Second Mile, a non-profit charity serving underprivileged and at-risk youth. Sandusky met his young victims via The Second Mile, (whose motto is "Providing Children With Help and Hope").

In December 2012, there was national outrage and widespread protest across Argentina following the Tucuman court acquiting 13 defendants accused of trafficking women. Argentine President, Christina Kircher, and other political leaders were among the many who publicly expressed anger at the verdict. Susan Trimarco became an activist, having searched for a decade for her daughter, Marita, who vanished at the age of 23. Trimarco and fellow campaigners believe that Marita had been kidnapped and trafficked by an alleged sex ring located in Tucuman province in northern Argentina. Trimarco's relentless search for her daughter and her political activicism exposed an underworld of organized crime, including individuals who were operating brothels with protection afforded by authorities across Argentina. While hundreds of trafficked women have been saved by the foundation Trimarco created in her daughter's name, its lawyers have found proving sex slavery difficult in the absense of full support from police—who are often paid to protect the prostitution rings (Aljazeera, 2012).

Other examples of alleged organized sex abuse rings include the grouping of politicians and clergymen centered on Wollongong, Australia, which featured prominently in the Wood Royal Commission in the late 90s (Brown, 1996; Kidd, 2013); the Haut de la Garenne children's home scandal in Jersey, which has recently been linked to Jimmy Savile (Halliday et al., 2012); and what has become known as the Franklin

Scandal, centered on Omaha, Nebraska, and Washington DC (see Bryant, Chapter 11, this volume, for an investigative journalist's account).

In March 2011, in the largest operation of its kind ever undertaken, it was reported that police in 30 countries had arrested 184 suspects and identified 486 others as members of a large-scale international child pornography ring centered in the Netherlands. The ring was linked to an internet forum Boylover.net moderated by Amir Ish-Hurwitz and which at its peak had more than 70,000 members around the world. Police were able to trace 71,000 IP addresses in 109 countries from Ish-Hurwitz's computer (Tyler, 2011).

WARFARE

Jacob Bronowski (2011) observed that *in reality most wars are about stealing*. By late 2011, there were 24 different countries affected by ongoing wars, 13 of them by protracted wars (systemicpeace.org, 2013). As of mid-2013, there are at least 12 global conflicts associated with at least 1,000 deaths per year (Chesser, 2012; Black, 2013; necrometrics.com). Perhaps the most deadly is the Syrian civil war which dates back to March 2011. By April 2013, the official death toll was nearing 100,000, over 6,000 being children (Black, 2013). Also included is the enduring civil war in Afghanistan that dates from the communist military coup of 1978. This ongoing conflict incorporates the Russian invasion of 1979, the withdrawal of the Russians in 1989, the fall of Kabul in 1992 and the establishment of an Islamic state, the emergence of the Taliban which succeeded in taking Kabul in 1996 and which was supported in its ongoing fight with the Northern Alliance by Pakistan's Army and several thousand Al Qaeda fighters from Arab countries and central Asia, as well as receiving financial backing from Saudi Arabia.

The tangled web of tribal conflict and associated religious and political oppression, the reality of ever shifting alliances and the impact of geo-political forces on a poor, corruption-driven, but strategically positioned country, reached something of a zenith in Afghanistan. Prominent leaders of the Northern Alliance, which controlled around 30% of the country, were former foes Ahmad Shan Massoud and Abdul Rashid Dostum. From 1996 to 2001 the Taliban Ministry of Defense or the Taliban leader himself, Mullah Omar, ordered 15 massacres of civilians. When the Taliban took Mazar-i-Sharif in 1998 around 4,000 Hazaras civilians were executed. This massacre was seen as a reprisal for the 1997 killing of 2,000 surrendered Taliban fighters (Gargan, 2001).

After Abdul Rashid Dostum's forces were defeated in 1998, the only remaining leader who was able to defend vast areas against the Taliban was Ahmad Shan Massoud. Massoud signed the Women's Right's declaration. He opposed forced marriages and women and girls in areas under his administration did not have to wear the Afghan burqa. Massoud stated that men and women were equal and that through education a culture of equality would be achieved (Escobar, 2001). Human Rights Watch cited no evidence of any human rights crimes for forces controlled by Massoud. In early 2001 he addressed the European Parliament in Brussels seeking humanitarian help for the people of Afghanistan. He told his listeners that without the support of Pakistan and Al Qaeda the Taliban would not be able to sustain their military campaign for a year. On September 9, 2001, Massoud was killed as a result of a suicide bomb attack by two Arabs. Hundreds of thousands attended his funeral. Two days after Massoud's assassination the twin towers were destroyed and the Pentagon was hit in Al Qaeda suicide attacks. The destruction of the Capital Building or the White House was averted by the bravery of passengers on the fourth plane hi-jacked that morning and which crashed into a field in Pennsylvania. The NATO invasion of Afghanistan shortly followed. In June 2013, NATO handed over security to Afghan forces. Yet social and religious oppression continue to plague the country.

The rationale embedded in the goal of safeguarding national security can all too easily involve a country perpetrating the very acts that it would say it was defending its citizens from being subjected to. Winners write the history, while the labeling of motivations on the part of individuals who take up arms means that one person's oppressive terrorist is simultaneously someone else's "freedom fighter". Yet the propensity to use extreme oppression is embedded in the political apparatus of most countries. In April 2009, the U.S Department of Justice publicly released detailed memos describing the brutal interrogation techniques used by the Central Intelligence Agency (CIA) in the interrogation of senior Al Qaeda operatives between 2002 and 2005. Senior members of the Obama administration labeled 14 approved interrogation techniques, including waterboarding, as illegal torture. President Barack Obama was quoted as saying that the CIA torture represented "a dark and painful chapter in our history" and he pledged that the interrogation techniques would never be used again, however he did not want to prosecute those responsible (Mazzetti & Shane, 2009).

Aside from Syria and Afghanistan, other current high casualty conflicts include the Somali civil war, the Iraqi insurgency, the war in North-West Pakistan (an armed conflict between the Pakistan Armed Forces and armed religious groups, Central Asian militants including Al Qaeda, regional armed movements and elements of organized crime), the Mexican drug war, Sudanese nomadic conflicts, the war between Sudan and South Sudan and the Northern Mali conflict. The Libyan Transitional Council initially estimated that 30,000 people died in the recent Libyan civil war that saw the end of the regime of Muammar Gaddafi (Laub, 2011) who was shot and killed on October 20, 2011.

Democracy, despite the patchy protection its institutions generally afford citizens, is nevertheless the only system in which a country can change its ruler(s), or attempt to do so, without there being a very good chance that someone has to die first, and not infrequently the death toll can be very high (Ivory Coast, Yemen, Libya, Syria, Egypt, Tunisia, Bahrain, Burma, Iraq and Sudan are very recent examples). While democratic processes in Western democracies are often taken for granted, we cannot forget the social upheaval or years of relentless protest that preceded their official acceptance (e.g., that women were jailed, or even died, in pursuit of the right to vote).

Many might not be aware that the youngest British soldier to be killed in combat on the Western Front in World War I, John Condon, was aged just 14 (Spartacus Educational). By the end of the Battle of the Somme some 18,000 British "boy soldiers" had been killed or wounded (Middlebrook, 1971). The youngest British serviceman to be killed in World War II was Reginald Earshaw, killed when German planes attacked his ship off the east coast of Britain on July 6, 1941. He was aged 14 years and 152 days (BBC, 2010a). Yet the British use of child soldiers pales to almost insignificance compared with the Germans and Russians during World War II. The Germans drafted boys as young as 12 into military service. An entire SS Panzer Tank Division was manned by 16- and 17-year-old boys from Hitler Youth brigades (Eigen, 2009). The reality is that child soldiers have been the norm throughout history up until recent times. On September 16, 1863, Willie Johnston, 13 years old and just five feet tall, was awarded the Congressional Medal of Honor for his bravery during the Peninsula campaign in the American Civil War when he was aged just 12. He had enlisted in the Army at the age of 11 (Genealogy Forum). The Khmer Rouge in Cambodia made extensive use of child soldiers, including forcing them into the role of executioners, not infrequently of their own parents. An estimated 95,000 child soldiers were killed in the Iran-Iraq war (Jupp, 1988). In contemporary times, children have been pressured by organizations such as Al Qaeda or Hezbollah into becoming suicide bombers. In recent years it is estimated that child soldiers participated in three-quarters of the world's ongoing armed conflicts, numbering around a quarter of a million children (Singer, 2005). On the May 15, 2013, a report from the Secretary-General to the United Nations Security Council noted that as well as being used as soldiers, children in the ongoing Syrian civil war were being used as human shields, hostages and torture detainees (Children and Armed Conflict, 2013).

While the World Wars of the 20th century led to a heightened awareness about the devastation wrought by warfare and to the establishment of the United Nations, civil and ethnic wars remain. Typical of the 21th century thus far has been violence intruding upon civil life in a manner which exceeds the boundaries of rational thinking (e.g., political terror including suicide bombing and incidents of mass shooting) (Moghaddam, 2006). The puncturing of safety and predictability from violence that transcends expectation and rationality promotes its own breed of social oppression, where civil liberties are encroached upon in the name of protection. Technical opportunities for interconnectedness (e.g., via mobile phones and internet communications) have increased to a level unprecedented in history. Such that the populace is not only oppressed in their daily behavior by the threat of unforeseen mass violence, but also by governments and agencies designed to protect them. Thus, both threat and protection in such contexts facilitate oppression. Complex psychosocial factors that produce shame, disconnection and disenfranchishment seem to be linked to participation in violent behavior. Although political oppression cannot be solved by psychological means solely (Moghaddam, 2006), knowledge about individual origins of violent behavior, even in a single case, may be illustrative of a tendency which can be easily abused by any organization. Given their potential for interfering both with conflict resolution as well as for creating weak points to be abused in misleading individuals and masses, knowledge about maladaptive mental consequences of developmental as well as adult trauma seems to be crucial for creating a more peaceful world.

NOT SO DISTANT MEMORIES

Lloyd de Mause (2002, p. viii) observed that empathy for children was an uneven, late historical achievement and that "the world is now in a race between our slowly improving child rearing and our rapidly evolving destructive technology". In all societies, children and women are particularly vulnerable. As they began to have a voice they were historically focused on as unreliable witnesses to their own lives, suggestible, mendacious, seductive and untruthful. It is useful to remind ourselves of *a few* signal events that indicate to us just how recently the global community has begun to find a fledgling voice that adds substance to the words of John F. Kennedy (2013): "Freedom is indivisible, and when one man is enslaved, all are not free".

Acknowledgment of the rights of women has been a very recent achievement globally, and has required legislation to enforce. It was not until 1971 that Swiss women received full voting rights, a year before women in Bangladesh, 77 years after New Zealand women and 68 years after women in Australia. Female suffrage came to Liechtenstein in 1984, Bahrain in 2002 and Kuwait in 2005. In late September 2011, the Saudi Arabian king announced that women would be able to vote in local government elections and run for office starting in 2015. For 2,000 years women have played no voting role in the election of the head of state centered on Vatican City, a religious entity that enjoys observer status at the United Nations.

It is salutary to reflect that the Haitian slave revolution in 1791 established a free republic, yet slavery was not abolished until the mid-1860s in the USA and remained legal in Brazil until 1888. However, in 2007, in the largest anti-slavery raid in modern times in Brazil, over 1,000 slave laborers were freed from a sugar cane plantation (BBC, 2007a). As recently as 2008, 4,634 Brazilian slaves were rescued by government authorities from 255 different locations as part of an attempt to finally eradicate slavery. In 2012, Brazil's Labor Ministry announced that between 1995 and 2011 nearly 41,500 workers had been freed from slave-like conditions, including 2,271 during 2011. The Ministry admits that around 20,000 in Brazil still work in conditions tantamount to slavery (Freedom House, 2013).

In 2007, the North African country Mauritania for the third time officially abolished slavery, though 20% of the population (some 600,000 men, women and children) remain enslaved as bonded laborers (BBC, 2007b). In 2008, the Nepalese government legislated to free 20,000 forced laborers. According to the U.S. Department of State, between 10,000 and 15,000 women and girls from Nepal are trafficked to India and are sexually exploited every year, while 7,500 children are trafficked domestically for commercial sexual exploitation (Nepal Monitor, 2009). It is widely acknowledged that humans represent the third most trafficked "commodity" worldwide, after drugs and arms. It was reported in 2010 that Thailand and Brazil have the world's worst child sex trafficking records (Libertad Latino, 2011). Thailand's Health System Research Institute has reported that 40% of Thailand's prostitutes are children. It is approximated that around 10% of tourist dollars spent in Thailand goes on prostitutes. Up to 30 million of the world's population are estimated to exist in some form of slavery, the largest number in history but the lowest in terms of the percentage of the total population (Manav, 2011).

The United Nations Convention on the Rights of the Child is mankind's most widely accepted human rights treaty and it came into force in 1990. Only two countries in the world have not ratified it: Somalia (frequently described as a "failed state") and the USA, where political and religious conservatives have maintained a successful opposition that President Obama finds "embarrassing" (Freerepublic, 2013).

Although the mention of slavery tends to invoke images of Africans in chains, the construct of slavery in our global community is really a much broader one that can be applied to any oppressing circumstance where individuals are being exploited, abused, exposed to danger and discarded without meaningful and available access to protection, justice, information or the ability to stay in contact with loved ones. Some have had so little ability to access education, freedom of thought, freedom of movement or contact with the unoppressed that they might not fully appreciate how confined their prison really is. The child inducted at gunpoint into an African army; the adolescent girl from a poor village seeking a city job that finds herself via threats to her family forced into the sex trade; the individual from an oppressed minority who is in danger and without rights in his homeland; the sexually abused altar boy silenced by enduring shame and the power and credibility of his ongoing abuser; the incestuously abused woman subjected as an adult to unending decades of conditioning, abuse, shame and fear; the unpaid and brutalized laborer toiling as have thousands of his forebears to grow sugar cane; the very young women subjected to arranged marriages in the kingdoms of patriachal monarchs or within polygamous religious cults; and those oppressed by occupying, conquering or colonial powers—all represent facets of the global 21st-century slave.

Oppression, and the threat of oppression, underline mankind's need to devise and reform the processes by which society is organized. Niccolo Machiavelli (1469–1527) and Thomas Hobbes (1588–1679) were each demonized for attempting to portray models of human politics that reflected realistic portrayals of mankind as he/she is rather than as how we'd like to believe mankind is. We are all participant-observers of the human condition. It is worth repeating a few of their observations, starting with Machiavelli:

> Many have pictured republics and principalities which in fact have never been known or seen, because how one lives is so far distant from how one ought to live, that he who neglects what is done for what ought to be done, sooner effects his ruin than his preservation; for a man who wishes to act entirely up to his professions of virtue soon meets with what destroys him among so much that is evil (Machiavelli, 2007, p. 115).

> Men have less scruple in offending one who is beloved than one who is feared, for love is preserved by the link of obligation which, owing to the baseness of men, is broken at every opportunity for their advantage; but fear preserves you by a dread of punishment which never fails (Machiavelli, 2007, p. 124).

> There cannot be good laws where the state is not well armed (Machiavelli, 2007, p. 95).

Thomas Hobbes authored a congruent, if grim, realism. His most famous work, "Leviathan or The Matter, Forme and Power of a Common Wealth Ecclesiasticall and Civil" was written during the English civil war (1642–1651). Hobbes took positions that were in disagreement with Church teachings of his time and was accused among other things of being an atheist. In 1666, the House of Commons introduced a bill against atheism and profaneness and later that year it was ordered that the committee to which the bill was referred "Should be empowered to receive information touching such books as tend to atheism, blasphemy and profaneness . . . in particular . . . the book of Mr. Hobbes called the Leviathan" (British History Online). It is worth sampling the thinking that engendered such a reaction: "I put for the general inclination of all mankind, a perpetual and restless desire of power after power, that ceaseth only in death" (Hobbes, 1651; see rschindler); "The original of all great and lasting societies consisted not in the mutual good will men had toward each other, but in the mutual fear they had of each other" (Hobbes, 1651; see rschindler); "The obligation of subjects to the sovereign is understood to last as long, and no longer, than the power lasteth by which he is able to protect them" (Hobbes, 1651; see rschindler). In a generally similar vein, Abraham Lincoln (1809–1865) pithily observed, "A friend is one who has the same enemies as you have" (searchquotes.com).

To add a modern perspective, the human condition can be conceptualized as an enduring struggle between the dynamics of attachment and the dynamics of narcissism (Blatt, 2008). The attachment dynamic sees individuals bonded into family and tribal groups. It encompasses empathic connection, mutual support and brings with it a capacity to love and to grieve. The narcissistic dynamic is in many ways the opposite of attachment. Resources are exploited and individuals oppressed, personal priorities and personal gratifications are paramount. Narcissistic individuals are not encumbered by empathy and some such very talented and intelligent individuals can be very persuasive and attain prominent and powerful positions. At the extreme end of the narcissistic spectrum one encounters "malignant narcissism" or psychopathy in which any vestige of empathic connection is absent. Both the dynamics of attachment and the dynamics of narcissism are essential aspects of the human condition, but when the later engulfs the former the capacity for oppression looms.

OPPRESSION AND DISSOCIATIVE DISORDERS

An alternative paradigm with which to view dissociative disorders is to characterize them as a chronic human rights abuse syndrome of childhood. Here various forms of oppression operate, including oppression of the child by the abusive and potentially colluding non-abusive caretaker, and the multiple ways in which their lived experience is ignored or invalidated by social, political and medical systems. Research from every continent increasingly demonstrates the ubiquity of dissociative defences and the universality of the sorts of traumas that engender them (Sar, 2011).

Maintaining enduring silence is an essential feature of oppressive power. It is only when silence is overcome that resistance to oppression can be mustered (Prilleltensky, 2003). Removing silence heightens the power of the oppressed and destabilizes the power of oppressors. The internal blame of shame ("it's my fault") can be replaced with the external blame of humiliation ("it's the fault of another/others"), and rage and resistance may follow. Yet the desire to ignore, disavow and remain silent is a potent force within the human psyche. In the therapeutic setting, the challenge of attempting to explore descriptions of past trauma has highlighted that the syndromes that accompany complex trauma are likewise complex. In challenging the abuser's need for silence we must be able to tolerate ambiguity, avoid dichotomous thinking and refrain from making statements of apparent fact that go beyond verifiable data.

In our professional life we, the editors of this volume, have collectively spent many years dealing with incestuously abused individuals. Virtually all of them have previously been silenced by their abuser taking the stance that they need to be loyal to the "family"; that communications be treated secretly; that if they report anything to any outside authority they will get into trouble, won't be believed and could be arrested by police; or that they will be held responsible for breaking up the "family", an outcome that can only add to their shame and eviction from the grouping that has represented their primary attachments. Some are threatened with death if they speak to anyone about what secretly transpires within the family. Variations on this dynamic are identified in multiple other settings associated with ongoing oppression. General citizens, soldiers, policemen, politicians, professionals and others are repeatedly subjected to unsubtle pressures to adhere to the commands of powerful groups of individuals who can graphically outline the consequences, including disgrace, ongoing victimization, or worse, bestowed on any who breach unwritten codes and break the imposed silence to expose inconvenient truths.

Human rights abuses are only able to be investigated and documented where there is enough of an accessible police and justice system for this to be possible, and enough political awareness and resolve to recognize that *all* society generally benefits when such abuse and exploitation is publicly reported via a free press. Despite the fear and shame that so effectively silences the survivors of child abuse and maintains the silence of those who have crossed into adulthood without their abuse ever ending, the unprecedented ability to rapidly share digital information and graphic proof of abuse, allied with a seasoned international grouping of mental health professionals, human rights investigators, international groups of police targeting illegal internet-based child pornography rings, lawyers who no longer see prosecuting churches as off-limits, have established a bridgehead, despite the societal backlashes against accepting the seriousness and extent of child abuse or the self-serving rationalizations that the victims of oppression are somehow the architects of their own trauma.

It can be argued that the biggest challenges to the modern dissociative disorders field have come in the form of attempts to discredit or invalidate the collective scientific data underpinning the field by exploiting speculations that could not be, or have not been, satisfactorily proven. Part of the robust defense assembled in the face of individuals or organizations who for a variety of reasons want to conceptualize dissociative disorders as a social or iatrogenic construct, is the fact that dissociative individuals are identifiable in a wide range of cultures, including societies that have had little exposure to North American "contagions" (Yu et al., 2010). Moreover, dissociative processes are a core component of a number of so-called culture-bound syndromes or possession/trance states (see Hegeman, Chapter 6, this volume). Controversies associated with the dissociative disorders field play out differently in different societies. While divisions concerning so-called "recovered memory therapy" and alleged "Satanic Ritual Abuse" reached unprecedented heights in the USA, in other countries (e.g., Australia, Turkey, New Zealand) the professional polarization and controversy was more muted.

Consequences of childhood trauma and dissociative disorders, and their treatment, still remain avoided by mainstream health delivery systems, instigating a further mechanism of oppression for those suffering under the weight of their oppressive history. High levels of psychiatric comorbidity and limitations placed by managed care and restricted funding create oppressive therapeutic contexts for patients with a history of chronic traumatization. Suicidality and other types of self-destructive behavior require immediate clinical mamagement, however interventions limited to merely short-term treatment strategies stifle growth and resolution. "Revolving door" service delivery erodes hope.

The International Society for the Study of Trauma and Dissociation (ISSTD) for the first time in human history was responsible for assembling an enduring critical mass of individuals who were willing and able to examine the substance of what individuals need to dissociatively consign to other compartments within themselves in order to eke out, somehow, some semblance of attachment and growth in an otherwise emotionally barren and abusive childhood. For a significant minority, childhood abuse does not end, such that we find examples spread across the global community of individuals still being incestuously abused by their fathers into adulthood as well as being abused by others (see Middleton, Chapter 3, this volume).

Three decades after the ISSTD formed, its journal, the *Journal of Trauma and Dissociation (JTD)*, devoted in 2013 a special issue to exploring individual and societal oppression which incorporated global perspectives on dissociative disorders. This book has its origins in that collection. The chapters in this volume speak for themselves. But they also address a global commonality concerning populations of traumatized individuals, whether seeking asylum, therapy or acceptance after war or genocide or being physically and psychologically imprisoned in family settings. Such windows into human behavior paint an incomplete, but nevertheless very troubling, picture of a world in which the pursuit of power and the use of that power to sexually abuse and otherwise exploit can occur in many contexts and settings, but where the lack of empathy for victims and the associated lack of accountability for violating human rights goes to the core of the dynamics of the oppressor whether clothed in the garb of the preacher, the warrior, the politician, the citizen or the therapist.

The contributions incorporate a conclusion that the substance of cultural differences displayed in the syndromes of dissociative individuals has previously been overplayed (see Ross, Schroeder & Ness, Chapter 5, this volume). The chapters in this book demonstrate through a variety of examples that oppression is part of the human condition in democratic and undemocratic societies. And where oppression resides, dissociation is by necessity a constant companion.

REFERENCES

Aljazeera. (2012, December 13). Outrage over Argentina sex slavery acquittals. Retrieved from http://tinyurl.com/aseugz9

BBC. (2007a, July 3). 'Slave' labourers freed in Brazil. Retrieved from http://tinyurl.com/359yae

BBC. (2007b, August 9). Mauritanian MPs pass slavery law. Retrieved from http:// tiny.cc/sfhvfw

BBC. (2010a, February 5). Youngest World War II service casualty identified. Retrieved from http://tinyurl.com/yard44e

BBC. (2010b, September 3). Six men jailed for Portugal child sex abuse. Retrieved from http://tinyurl.com/2dzxupu

BBC. (2012, November 6). Wales child abuse: Theresa May launches inquiry. Retrieved from http://tinyurl.com/d5dbwfk

BishopAccountability.org. (2013, April 29). Countries with Bishops who have either abused or resigned because of complicity. Retrieved from http://tinyurl.com/ktpobc7

Black, I. (2013, June 14). Syria deaths near 100,000, says UN – and 6,000 are children. *The Guardian*. Retrieved from http://tinyurl.com/nb4dlk4

Blatt, S. J. (2008). *Polarities of experience: relatedness and self-definition in personality development, psychopathology, and the therapeutic process*. Washington, DC: American Psychological Association.

British History Online. House of Commons Journal Volume 8, 17 October 1666. Retrieved from http://tinyurl.com/oeaka3v

Bronowski, J. (2011). *The ascent of man*. Reading: BBC.

Brown, M. (1996, April 16) Police were slow to act on clergy sex assault claim. *Sydney Morning Herald*. Retrieved from http://tiny.cc/qqrosw

Bryant, N. (2009). *The Franklin scandal*. Walterville, OR: Trineday.

Card, C. (1996). Rape as a weapon of war. *Women and Violence*, *11: 4*, 5–18.

Cave, D. (2012, January 11). Mexico updates death toll in drug war to 47,515 but critics dispute the data. *The New York Times*. Retrieved from http://tinyurl.com/nu7daev

Chesser, S. G. (2012). Afghanistan casualties: Military forces and civilians. CRS Report for Congress. Retrieved from http://tinyurl.com/75vjcv7

Children and Armed Conflict. (2013). United Nations – Syrian Arab Republic. Retrieved from http://tinyurl.com/lvwfdwg

D'Antonio, M. (2013). *Mortal sins: Sex, crime, and the era of Catholic scandal*. New York: Thomas Dunne.

de Mause, L. (2002). *The emotional life of nations*. New York: Institute of Psychohistory.

De Sainte Croix. (2011, August 23). Brazil fights modern day slavery. *The Rio Times*. Retrieved from http://tinyurl.com/ket7so6

de Waal, F. (2000). *Chimpanzee politics* (Rev. ed.). Baltimore, MD: The Johns Hopkins University Press.

Eigen, L. D. (2009) Child soldiers are unfortunately nothing new. *Scriptamus*. Retrieved from http://tinyurl.com/qhwpsc4

Escobar, P. (2001). Masoud: From warrior to statesman. *Asia Times Online*. Retrieved from http://tinyurl.com/qhtxgrt

Evans-Pritchard, A. (2004, March 5). Judge tells of murder plots to block Dutroux investigation. *The Telegraph*. Retrieved from http://tinyurl.com/kcylxdt

Freedom House. (2013). Freedom in the world: Brazil. Retrieved from http://tinyurl.com/lbvekkb

Freerepublic (2013, January 6). UN Convention on the Rights of the Child would threaten the American family. Retrieved from www.freerepublic.com/focus/f-news/2162995/posts

Gargan, E. G. (2001, October 12). Taliban massacres outlined for UN. *Chicago Times*. Retrieved from http://tinyurl.com/kw6dyuq

Genealogy Forum. U.S. Civil war history & genealogy. Retrieved from http://tinyurl.com/lkfm963

GoreGrish.com (2011). Srebenica. Retrieved from http://tinyurl.com/lokz2hq

Halliday, J., Viner, K. & O'Carroll. (2012, October 9). Jimmy Savile linked with Haut de la Garenne children's home scandal. *The Guardian*. Retrieved from http://tinyurl.com/8n66syd

Herman, E. S. & Chomsky, N. (2002). *Manufacturing consent: The political economy of the mass media*. New York: Pantheon.

Hobbes, T. (ed, Shapiro, I.) (2010). *Leviathan or the matter, forme and power of a common-wealth ecclesiasticall and civil*. New Haven: Yale University Press.

Jupp, M. (1988, December 19). Letter to the editor: Child-soldier treaty has wide support. *The New York Times*. Retrieved from http://tinyurl.com/noj2pqp

Kennedy, J. F. (2013, January 6). John F. Kennedy; "Ich bin ein Berlier". Retrieved from The History Place; Great Speeches Collection website: www.historyplace.com/speeches/jfk-berliner.htm

Kidd, P. B. (2013). Mark Mala Valera: The Butcher of Wollongong. Retrieved from http://tiny.cc/92rosw

Jacobs, S. L. (2009). *Confronting genocide*. Plymouth: Lexington Books

Landers, A. (1992, September 13). The Masserman affair out in the open at last. *Chicago Tribune*. Retrieved from http://tinyurl.com/notz8cu

Laub, K. (2011, September 8). Libyan estimate: at least 30,000 died in the war. *The Guardian*. Retrieved from http://tinyurl.com/ctxor5p

Libertad Latina. (2011, March 14). The crisis of child sexual exploitation in Brazil. Retrieved from http://tiny.cc/f7gvfw

London 24 (2012, October 24) David Cameron reveals Jimmy Savile allegations to be investigated by Director of Public Prosecutions Keir Stamer. Retrieved from http://tiny.cc/27rosw

Machiavelli, N. (2007). *The prince*. London: Duncan Baird.

Manav, T. (2011, March 9). The challenges of counting a "hidden population". Retrieved from the CNN Freedom Project website: http://tiny.cc/59gvfw

Mazzetti, M. & Shane, S. (2009, April 16). Interrogation memos detail harsh tactics by the C.I.A. *The New York Times*. Retrieved from http://tiny.cc/tbhvfw

Middlebrook, M. (1971). *The first day on the Somme*. London: Allan Lane.

Middleton, W. (2005). Owning the past: claiming the present – perspectives on the treatment of dissociative patients. *Australasian Psychiatry, 13:1*, 40–49.

Moghaddam, F. M. (2006). *From the terrorists' point of view. What they experience and why they come to destroy.* Connecticut: Prager Security International.

Moghaddam, F. M. (2013). *The psychology of dictatorship.* Washington DC: American Psychological Association.

Moodley, K. (2013, March 13). We could have saved 300,000 lives in Rwanda. *CNBC*. Retrieved from www.cnbc.com/id/100546207

Myer, N. W. (2012). Enter the dragon: will China's deal of the century save Congo. *International Policy Digest*. Retrieved from http://tinyurl.com/qbcnnv2

Naidoo, J. C. & Rajab, D. M. (2005). The dynamic of oppression: a psycho-political analysis of the traumatic experiences of minority Asian Indians in apartheid South Africa. *Psychology and Developing Societies, 17*, 139–159.

Necrometric.com. Source list and detailed death tolls for man-made multicides throughout history. Retrieved from http://tinyurl.com/qj56s8k

Nepal Monitor. (2009, June 17). Human trafficking: Nepal official complicity serious: US report. Retrieved from http://tiny.cc/ddhvfw

New World Encyclopedia. Genocide. Retrieved from http://tinyurl.com/nj94vag

Noël, B & Watterson, K. (1992). *You must be dreaming.* New York: Poseidon.

Oliner, S. P. (2003). *Do unto others: extraordinary acts of ordinary people.* Boulder, CO: Westview.

Oliner, S. P. & Oliner, P. M. (1988). *The altruistic personality: rescuers of Jews in Nazi Europe.* New York: The Free Press.

Pace, E. (1994, November 15). Jules Masserman, 89, leader of psychiatric group, is dead. *The New York Times*. Retrieved from http://tinyurl.com/npr6f6a

People Pledge Union Information. Rwanda 1994. Retrieved from http://tinyurl.com/6qwqqk

Prilleltensky, I. (2003). Understanding, resisting, and overcoming oppression: Toward psychopolitical validity. *American Journal of Community Psychology, 31*, 195–201.

Prunier, G. (1995). *The Rwanda crisis: History of a genocide.* London: Hurst.

Rankin, B. (2013, January 11). 'There may be hundreds more': Jimmy Savile victims total "a mere drop in the ocean" and "could double". *Mirror*. Retrieved from http://tinyurl.com/kj2e8bm

Rawlins, A. (2013, January 11). Mexico's drug war. *Council on Foreign Relations*. Retrieved from http://tinyurl.com/3ftnsgd

Reuters. (2008, July 22). Karadzic lived as long-haired, new age doctor. Retrieved from http://tinyurl.com/lg5n7ss

rschindler. Thomas Hobbes, Leviathan (1651). Retrieved from www.rschindler.com/hobbes.htm

Sar, V. (2011). Epidemiology of dissociative disorders: An overview. *Epidemiology Research International, 2011*, Article ID 404538. doi:10.1155/2011/404538

searchquotes.com. Abraham Lincoln quotes. Retrieved from http://tinyurl.com/nvvgnh3

Sen, A. (2000). *Development as freedom.* New York: Anchor.

Singer, P. W. (2005). *Children at war.* Berkeley: University of California Press.

Spartacus Educational. Boy soldiers. Retrieved from http://tinyurl.com/mddy

systemicpeace.org. (2013). Global conflict trends: measuring systemic peace. Retrieved from http://tinyurl.com/7atwbev

Thompson, C. (2013, June 7). What's still to come in the Jerry Sandusky child sex abuse scandal. *Penn Live*. Retrieved from http://tinyurl.com/kot4ene

Todorovic, A. & de Quetteville, H. (2008, July 22). Radovan Karadzic: Medicine man captured by police on bus ride. *The Telegraph*. Retrieved from http://tinyurl.com/58qo56

Tyler, J. (2011, March 16). Massive Dutch-run child pornography ring revealed. *Radio Netherlands Worldwide*. Retrieved from http://tinyurl.com/k64v85m

United Human Rights Council. Genocide in Rwanda. Retrieved from http://tinyurl.com/3eeh7ha

United Nations Office on Drugs and Crime. (2007). Afghanistan opium survey: Executive summary. Retrieved from http://tinyurl.com/33jvca

White, M. (2011). *Atrocitology: Humanity's 100 deadliest achievements*. Melbourne: The Text Publishing Company.

Yu, J., Ross, C. A., Keyes, B., Li, Y., Dai, Y., Zhang, T., . . . Xiao, Z. (2010). Dissociative disorders among Chinese inpatients diagnosed with schizophrenia. *Journal of Trauma & Dissociation, 11*, 358–372.

Zakaria, F. (2004). When the UN fails, we all do. *Global Policy Forum*. Retrieved from http://tinyurl.com/m7y9fuc

Stimulus Deprivation and Overstimulation as Dissociogenic Agents in Postmodern Oppressive Societies

VEDAT SAR, MD and ERDINC OZTURK, PhD
Department of Psychiatry, Istanbul University, Istanbul, Turkey

Societal conditions associated with overstimulation or understimulation may precipitate and maintain oppression among individuals and communities by inducing dissociation. Distortion of reality and the flooding of everyday awareness with irrelevant information by mass media is a type of community-wide overstimulation. Alternatively, stimulus deprivation enables single-minded thinking to be narrowly preoccupied with rigid religious ideas, traditional rituals, and postmodern thought and behavior patterns. Provoked sex is utilized as a soothing tool for those who live in overstimulation and as an opportunity for transient enjoyment and rejuvenation for those who live in stimulus deprivation. Chronic exposure to disproportionate stimuli resurrects the trauma-based developmental detachment between the sociological and psychological selves of the individual at the cost of the latter. The enlarged sociological self of the individual is misused to induce a conforming identity transformation of individuals and entire communities that is a prerequisite to setting and maintaining an oppressive system. Constituting overstimulation itself, the enduring fear of chaos in a world akin to crisis enables deliberate acceptance of oppression to restore a sense of control. In fact, the expectancy of crisis triggers the trauma-related dissociative fears of individual internal chaos, which are misused, in turn, to aggravate fears of external chaos again. By facilitating the denial of internal fears rather than integrating them, psychological theories

---

The authors would like to thank Banu Ibaoglu Vaughn, MA, for her help in editing this manuscript. An earlier version of this article was presented at the 28th Annual Conference of the International Society for the Study of Trauma and Dissociation in Montreal in 2011.

and practices of the past century have failed in addressing the problem of individual and societal oppression.

Individual as well as societal roots of oppression have been a focus of interest for researchers and theoreticians from diverse disciplines. The experiences in Germany before and during World War II led sociologists to study the characteristics of the potentially authoritarian personality (Adorno, Frenkel-Brunswik, Levinson, & Sanford, 1950). A series of social psychology experiments demonstrated the astonishing willingness of the average individual to obey an authority figure who instructed them to perform acts that conflicted with their personal values (Milgram, 1963). Yet it remains unclear why an individual or a society allows itself to live under oppression, how oppression can be maintained, and why the affected subjects occasionally do not even develop awareness of it.

In this theoretical article, we propose that excessive, inconsistent, or diminished exposure to stimuli facilitates dissociation that is utilized by oppressive systems to evoke individual and societal submission. In the context of sociophysiology (Gardner, 1997), the working definition of stimulus here covers diverse types of input such as sensory perception, information, emotion, communication, attachment, knowledge, culture, religion, and art. Making the situation more complex is the fact that in postmodern societies, social stimuli are increasingly enriched by simulation and simulacra (Baudrillard, 1994). These are symbols and signs that replace conventional reality.

There are claims that contemporary societies facilitate dissociation (Gold, 2004; Schumaker, 2001). We hypothesize that this effect is achieved in individual and societal contexts through excessive stimulation and stimulus deprivation as observed in at least two ways: (a) flooding the community with irrelevant information delivered by mass media, which also distort reality; and (b) facilitating single-minded thinking by stimulus deprivation, as evidenced in rigid religious ideas, traditional rituals, and postmodern thought and behavior patterns. Provoked sex is utilized as a soothing tool or as an opportunity for transient enjoyment and rejuvenation. The disproportionate stimulation by societal means interferes with the individual's ability to achieve the integrative mode of consciousness (Winkelman, 2011) necessary to maintain a high level of awareness.

THE CENTURY OF THE SOCIOLOGICAL SELF

Compared to individuals in contemporary societies, the 19th-century individual was rather tradition directed (i.e., directed by personally assimilated sociocultural traditions) or inner directed (i.e., directed by individual desires and wishes). The development of urbanization, industrialization, mass media, public relations, marketing, digital computers, electronic communication devices, the Internet, and more recently social media has created a new type of individual who is prone to being controlled from outside (Battegay, 1987). This shift toward other-directedness (Riesman, 1950) took on a new dimension in the era of globalism, when communities were forced to undergo rapid changes in lifestyle, law, ethics, traditions, and social rituals without being prepared.

In an earlier paper on the theory of the functional dissociation of the self, we introduced the concept of the sociological self as an interface between society and the individual (Sar & Ozturk, 2007). In fact, as an individual mental process, it is more than an interface. The sociological self represents (as does the psychological self) a pattern of thinking, experiencing, and behavior that can utilize and interact with every mental capacity (e.g., emotions, alter personalities, the trauma-self) in its own way. The properties of the sociological and psychological selves are universal (see Table 1). The specific task of the sociological self is to save the psychological self from the destructive influences of others and to buffer psychological trauma. In contrast to the more unitary psychological self, if overloaded, the sociological self can be fragmented. The psychological self delivers observations and estimations about subjective experiences. It maintains the capacity of pure love, an intention toward maturity, a sense of individual uniqueness and self-orientedness. However, in contrast to the sociological self, once detached, the psychological self has limited authority on the actions of the individual. Healthy interpersonal relationships are based on a harmonious development and coupling of the sociological and psychological selves. However,

TABLE 1 Properties of the Sociological and Psychological Selves

Sociological self	Psychological self
Modeling, imitation, copying	Creativity
Eclecticism	Authenticity
Dogmatism	Possibilities
Polarization	Synthesis
Negotiation	Choice
Reversibility	Constancy
Competition	Self-expression
Single-focus awareness	Multi-focus awareness
Cruelty	Compassion
Affiliation	Contact
Fusionary relationships	Boundaries
Metaphors, metonyms, symbols	Signs
Fantasies	Facts
Heroes and heroines	Icons
Religion	Spirituality

Notes: Adapted from Sar & Ozturk (2007).

developmental traumatization leads to detachment between the two selves. Subsequent enlargement and fragmentation of the sociological self restricts the further development of the psychological self and keeps it frozen.

Both excessiveness and scarcity of stimuli threaten the psychological self and cause the sociological self to be hypertrophied. An optimal average stimulus level supports the psychological self and its harmonious relationship with the sociological self. These effects are based on distinct properties of the two selves in relation to adaptation (e.g., perception of reality, synthesis, association, decision making). Whereas the sociological self benefits from its properties in processing the disproportionate stimulation, the properties of the psychological self need a protected space to operate. Developmental detachment between the two selves may be exacerbated by disintegrating experiences in adult life, such as cumulative traumatization, a single disruptive traumatic experience, deep disappointment, and exposure to disproportionate stimuli. The latter may happen after a drastic change in average stimulus level due to factors such as migration, psychiatric disorder, imprisonment, torture, compulsory life changes, or simply the exercise of choice.

In order to nurture the capacity of endurance or, alternatively, to induce overadjustment in the new generation, societies and families may enhance the development of the sociological self among their offspring, which may be misused by others and by the overall society to induce and maintain oppression. What is tragic is that a detached and enlarged sociological self may turn out to be a malevolent and nonempathic force not only for the individual but also for the family and society. People with an enlarged sociological self may learn how to become skillful with it for their own gain (e.g., by finding a special niche for their occupational and social capacities somewhere within contemporary society). Thus, the sociological self provides the basis for social alters that can collude with others' in group relationships (deMause, 2002). We propose that the extreme dominance by the sociological self enables a socially dangerous and destructive style that characterizes the reversible person of our time (Sar & Ozturk, 2007). Rather than constituting an adaptive dialogical self (Blackman, 2005), reversibility is an ultraformalist obsessive position of the sociological self associated with an increased tendency to be directed by others. This is a consequence of being exposed to disintegrating experiences in adult life while striving for successful flexible adjustment to the oppressive environment. Although the reversible person may appear to be a strong opponent on the surface, he or she may become a covert (or overt) ally of the power.

It is ironic that political fates of contemporary democratic societies rely largely on swing voters who behave as saturation-dependent consumers asking for immediate service rather than as proactive citizens with long-term rational plans and commitments for the future of their society and the world. Misused in countries with limited resources to aggravate the sense of dependency among disadvantaged populations, in social welfare states and mass democracies this condition has pushed communities and leaders into a collision of mutual manipulation. Although the leaders have allegedly been responding to the desires and wishes of their voters (Curtis, 2002), in fact they have been addressing the voters' detached, enlarged, and fragmented sociological selves. In this era, psychology has infiltrated every domain of life (i.e., from marketing to politics) as a legitimate tool facilitating the sociological selves of individuals rather than nurturing integrative processes.

EVOLUTIONARY ROOTS OF OBEDIENCE AND DISOBEDIENCE

Before moving toward further elaboration of the subtle psychological ways of setting and maintaining individual and societal oppression, an examination of the biological roots of obedience and disobedience (i.e., acceptance of or uprising against authority) is indicated.

Under conditions of threat, self-preservation rather than self-regulation becomes the predominant mode of existence for individuals and societies (Ford, 2009), which is common in dissociative states. According to the BASK (behavior, affect, sensation, knowledge) model of dissociation, evolutionary action systems operate in a relatively autonomous fashion in those conditions (Braun, 1988). However, not only fight and flight but also the more passive responses such as freezing and submission serve as a defense in all species, facilitating obedience to the perpetrator's claims with the intention of survival (Nijenhuis, Spinhoven, Vanderlinden, Van Dyck, & Van der Hart, 1998). In addition, dissociation leads to a constriction of consciousness (Meares, 1999). Thus, higher order and complex communications are rendered relatively inaccessible during a dissociative state, yet the person remains relatively sensitive to simpler, lower order instructions. Such a condition may make the subject ready to fulfill instructions administered as simple commands.

In traumatic entrapment situations, appeasement becomes also a potentially relevant strategy leading to pacification, conciliation, and submission (Cantor & Price, 2007). What is interesting is that it appears to be primarily relevant only to one's own and mostly social (mammalian) species. The paradoxical development of reciprocal positive feelings between hostages and their captors is known as Stockholm syndrome (Auerbach, Kiesler, Strentz, Schmidt, & Serio, 1994; Ochberg, 1978). This phenomenon enhances captives' coping with traumatic experiences. From an evolutionary perspective, this is described as reverted escape (Chance, as cited in Cantor & Price, 2007). After being attacked, monkeys and apes tend to return to the attacker for comfort and safety rather than turning to another member of their group (Cantor & Price, 2007). Paradoxically, a dissociative crisis may also facilitate disobedience by eliciting active responses such as fight and flight, the disruption of enduring attitudes, and associations leading to the discovery of positive possibilities one was not aware of. However, this is less likely for individuals under oppression.

Individuals who have been subjected to periods of prolonged and intense coercive persuasion (brainwashing) may experience dissociation (American Psychiatric Association, 1994). Stimulus deprivation serves as a preparatory phase before the enforced transformation of identity during this process. In the first phase of brainwashing, the intermittent delivery of stimuli in a variable ratio reinforcement schedule targeting basic somatic needs (i.e., sleep, appetite, defecation) and degrading procedures is utilized to create an obedient and suggestible state. The second phase of brainwashing is based on the delivery of excessive stimuli covering a narrow set of information to establish single-minded thinking. This corresponds to the detachment of the sociological self from the psychological self, the freezing of the latter, and the utilization of the former to achieve conforming and enduring changes in identity as the aim of the third and final stage. Thus, we propose an additional defense utilized by individuals and societies exposed to oppression that seems to be specific to humankind: transformation of identity.

MODULATION OF DISPROPORTIONATE STIMULI

Freud (1920/1975) saw the central nervous system as protected by a shield (Reizschutz), a stimulus barrier defending from excessive stimulation. In trauma, the barrier is suddenly and violently breached, overwhelming the nervous system with an influx of stimuli it can not bind or handle. From a physiological perspective, chronic overstimulation may lead to habituation or exhaustion. In contrast, denervation and other forms of stimulus deprivation cause an increase in the magnitude of subsequent responses, a phenomenon commonly referred to as denervation supersensitivity. However, stimulus deprivation may weaken the individual's orientation to reality because the person is not buffered against the predominance of internal stimuli. These response patterns may constitute physiological prototypes of diminished or increased reaction tendencies to internal and external triggers seen in post-traumatic and dissociative conditions. It is ironic that one may come across incidents of psychotherapy characterized by a combination of stimulus deprivation and overstimulation. Deprivation by an ever-listening therapist (while the patient is flooded by internal stimuli) or overstimulation by persistent speculative interpretations (while the patient is deprived of reality-based stimuli) is countertherapeutic for trauma-related disorders in particular.

Recent neurobiological research has documented the fact that traumatic stimuli trigger two types of reaction: one is primarily avoidant and the other predominantly intrusive and hyperaroused (Lanius et al., 2010). The former constitutes emotional overmodulation, which is related to excessive corticolimbic inhibition. This can lead to subjective disengagement from the emotional content of the traumatic memory. In contrast, the under-modulation type of response leads to a subjective reliving of the traumatic events. As demonstrated by intrusions and avoidance of traumatic mental content being two components of posttraumatic stress disorder, both types of response may co-occur. Each of these three options constitutes a threat to the integrity of mental functioning and represents dissociation. We propose that although disproportionate stimulation interferes with the mental capacity of developing links between thoughts, emotions, and behaviors, stimulus modulation is essential for maintaining homeostasis and healthy adaptation.

Besides childhood neglect, cultural and social conditions that continue into adulthood, such as poverty, restrictions due to traditions and conservativism, political control on mass media, and oppression of creativity, may contribute to stimulus deprivation. Excessive stimulation may be a consequence of either intrusive or overprotective caretaking and/or spoiling a child. As observed in dysfunctional communication patterns of families (Ozturk & Sar, 2006), a combination of overstimulation and understimulation is the most prevalent condition. As a rather direct contribution by the society, floods of information delivered by mass media and other sources, exposure to age-inappropriate information, and interpersonal boundary violations may lead to stimulus overload. This is also embedded in contemporary popular culture affecting both children and adults: vampire stories, fantasy role playing, computer games, drug abuse, underground music and literature, fragmented art products, information overload from the Internet and mass media, and provoked consumerism by advertisements.

In fact, simulating individual freedom, the consumerism-bound permissiveness of contemporary societies leads to overstimulation. Unlimited consumption is made possible by the delivery of substances removed of their essence (such as decaffeinated coffee, diet products, safe sex) that guarantee incomplete satisfaction (Zizek, 2007). Constituting itself as a double-bind, this postmodern hypocrisy aggravates stimulus dependency due to permanent abstinence, including that of interpersonal relationships. Like stimulus deprivation, chronic overstimulation also causes craving for stimuli or even dependency on them that becomes visible when the subject enters into abstinence due to spontaneous life changes.

We assume that sex serves as a soothing tool (i.e., an intermittent period of limited stimulation) for chronically overstimulated individuals and as a transient enjoyment and rejuvenation for those who live with stimulus deprivation. Thus, sex itself may become an object of dependency. Sex is also utilized as a domain of cultural double-binds. In some non-Western cultures, social life may be restricted for women by quasi-religious or conservative injunctions, whereas in the same community, sex is provoked in diverse ways, including in the restrictions themselves. Thus, making sex taboo in daily discourse does not change its role as a hidden agenda in double lives as a stronger urge for sexual experience. Foucault (1976/1998) challenged the idea that sexuality had been repressed in Western societies since the 17th century. To the contrary, he claimed that sexuality gained an unnecessary predominance in the daily discourses of Western societies, potentially hiding the repression of something else.

HEROES AND HEROINES AS SHARED RESCUERS

An appropriate average stimulus level leads to the nonbiased perception of both oneself and others. Disproportionate stimulation and subsequent dissociation facilitate a negative perception of both oneself and others (Sar, Islam, & Ozturk, 2010). To compensate for this painful experience of impaired sociopsychological mutuality, one enters into fusionary relationships with potential rescuers in the form of heroes or heroines. These are individuals, organizations, or ideas perceived as dominant others (Arieti & Bemporad, 1980) despite their average features. The latter point makes them easy to identify with; hence, their common attractiveness in the community. Heroes and heroines differ from icons of true quality in their subjectively attributed values. Both heroes and icons circulate among individuals, groups, and society and assist in the transformation of identities in every age group. Unlike the icons with their universal and timeless positive qualities that are usually adopted by relatively integrated individuals, heroes and heroines may be positive or negative and represent the spirit of the era only. Icons nurture the psychological self, whereas heroes and heroines serve the enlargement of the sociological self. Including negative heroes, the latter become overt or covert leaders one is prone to follow and submit to.

In stimulus deprivation, fusionary relationships with heroes have a rather positive orientation with feelings of love and admiration. This restores impaired self-esteem. Here, the subject has no intention of replacing the hero. This relationship has a rather self-protective function. Thus, it only minimally causes personal boundary problems. However, in the case of excessive stimulation, the subject enters into an ambivalent relationship with, and remains under the control of, the hero. This leads to blurred personal boundaries. This time, the heroes with whom one is fused contribute to the denial of low self-esteem rather than restore it. These heroes may be substituted by any dominant other, such as religion, ideology, passionate love, or even fashionable trademarks. They may be exchanged by each other partially or totally. Not infrequently, they may be substituted by stimulating or sedating illicit substance(s) that boost dissociative fragmentation and generate a downward spiral of dependency. In postmodern overstimulated societies beset by simulacra, imaginary heroes and heroines may emerge. In preserved communities where real relationships and touchable heroes or heroines prevail (such as the popular girl of the neighborhood or the old wise man of the village) there is no need for imaginary versions of them.

We propose that the alter personalities of people with dissociative identity disorder (DID) modulate disproportionate stimulation of the abusive caretaker by triangulation (i.e., they are involved as a third element). According to the perspective of game theory, the triangle is the smallest stable relationship system that tolerates more tension than a dyad (Bowen, 1978). If the tension is too high for one triangle to contain, it spreads to a series of interlocking triangles (i.e., the emergence of additional alter personalities). Following the properties of the fragmented sociological self (see Table 1), alter personalities are prone to take role(s) in the classic drama triangle (Karpman, 1968)—that is, not only as rescuer(s) but also as abuser(s) and victims inside. This self-perpetuating internal ghetto is resistant to change until effective therapeutic intervention is available (Frankel & O'Hearn, 1996). As dissociative patients are both fearful and preoccupied in their relationships (Sar et al., 2010), a decision to engage in psychological change requires for them almost a guarantee or certainty of the potential effectiveness of the intervention. Such perception can only be generated through the delivery of exact signs by the therapist that prove that he or she is capable of helping.

IDENTITY DIFFUSION AND FRAGMENTATION OF IDENTITY

In a screening study on a college sample in Turkey, 1 in 10 students fit the diagnostic criteria for Diagnostic and Statistical Manual of Mental Disorders, Fourth Edition (DSM–IV) borderline personality disorder (Sar, Akyuz, Kugu, Ozturk, & Ertem-Vehid, 2006). Higher than expected for a nonclinical and high-functioning population, this rate possibly reflected states of identity diffusion (i.e., characterized by detachment between the sociological and psychological selves) rather than a severe and lifelong personality disorder. Nevertheless, 3 in 4 subjects with the alleged personality disorder had a concurrent DSM–IV dissociative disorder including DID. A multivariate analysis revealed two tracks: one characterized by borderline symptomatology and reports of childhood abuse and the other characterized by childhood emotional neglect and overt dissociative experiences alongside elevated minimization scores in trauma reports (i.e., possible denial of childhood abuse). We hypothesize that the former track is associated with overstimulation and the latter with understimulation. What is interesting is that a comparison of borderline phenomena in Turkish and Dutch patients with DID also yielded two different components (Sar, Yargic, & Tutkun, 1996). The Turkish patients displayed intense anger or an inability to control anger, chronic feelings of emptiness and boredom, efforts to avoid abandonment, and intense but unstable relationships more frequently than the Dutch patients. The latter group was characterized by frequent mood swings, physically self-damaging acts, identity confusion, and impulsive and unpredictable behavior. With more than three decades of globalism, one might expect that these differences in the 1990s may now have disappeared.

Dissociation may assist an individual or a community to survive in a world of conflicting messages (Krüger, Sokudela, Motlana, Mataboge, & Dikobe, 2007). It may therefore be an appropriate tool in such conditions for maintaining a balanced, coherent self-in-society (i.e., an individual connected to other people). However, this is only possible by an intervening personal psychological process that filters information. In addition to the first filter, which consists of brain resources dealing with externally originated sensory information, a second dissociative filter screens sensory, emotional, and thought-related information so that only a manageable selection of information occupies the person's consciousness. However, such balance may be challenged by internal and external threats and stimuli that would lead transiently to a dissociative crisis.

One's behavior in a dissociative crisis shows the type of his or her potential response (i.e., obedience or disobedience) when faced with further oppression. We propose that this potential response type depends on the lifelong average stimulus level to which one has been exposed. In clinical conditions, the severity of dissociative symptoms is correlated with the strength of the intention for disobedience to an oppressive environment (e.g., to an abusive family). A sensorimotor (conversion) symptom is rather an incomplete response to forced submission. Alternatively, struggle for control (i.e., competition) between alter personalities demonstrates the desire for disobedience to oppression (Ozturk, 2009b). This type of reaction may take the form of an acute transient dissociative psychosis well known to clinicians exposed to oppressed people living in helpless conditions (Sar & Ozturk, 2009). A persistent sensorimotor (conversion) symptom or a dissociative psychosis may be the last attempt at escape (i.e., seeking help) from total annihilation (i.e., suicide) during an impasse that may remain covered by the predominant symptomatology. Endemic suicides by a brutal method such as self-burning among oppressed women raised in conditions of stimulus deprivation (Rezaie, Khazaie, Soleimani, & Schwebel, 2011) correspond to treating oneself as an object (Ozturk, 2009a). Such experiences may be utilized in the recruitment of suicide bombers by terrorist organizations. In contrast, the honor suicide of resisting individuals may be considered a defiant stand against the conforming identity transformation (i.e., soul death) imposed by the oppressive system.

SOCIETAL OPPRESSION AND TRANSFORMATION OF IDENTITIES

Oppression in society starts slowly and develops gradually. It has early signs. Before overt oppression, there is usually an initial overstimulated period when individuals feel relatively free and unlimited, as if they had busted from their fetters. The historical Weimar era in Germany has been pointed out as an example of flourishing freedoms, followed by growth panic and oppression (deMause, 2002). An increased socioeconomic mobility is permitted in this period, for instance by incited migration from countryside to towns and liberal tax policies that allow material speculation. Individuals affected by this transition easily enter into deviant lifestyles they are not psychologically equipped to deal with.

Communities in such an excited or manic period seek leaders who can supposedly regulate the expanding social life. This position is usually filled by a hero who becomes the authoritarian leader of the later oppression phase. Representing a social disruption, a subgroup (i.e., those with reversible personality in particular) in the community actively enters into an alliance with the oppressive system and, as opinion leaders, misleads others (e.g., letting the public perceiving an average person as a hero). Alternative options are submission, disobedience, or negotiation and denial. The latter mean replacing the reality with utopian scenarios. What the community receives over time is an overregulation by the authoritarian leader, which triggers the next stage of revolt followed by a renewed search for regulation.

Oppressive systems shape individuals, institutions, and organizations by obsessive and utopian measures. Absurd types of orders for organizing daily life replace rational ones. These absurd orders are difficult or even impossible to meet. For instance, the introduction of allegedly better standards in medical, tax, education, or judicial services may create confusion as these regulations are in conflict with existing rules (e.g., legal, constitutional) of the system. They may be presented as reforms aimed at alleged democratization, adjustment to international standards, or a more clean society. The standards are amended frequently to test the resilience of the community and to induce obedience by fatigue. These measures induce obsessive apprehensions and fears, leading to panic and inappropriate decision making among affected individuals who know that they are closely tracked by the authorities in an era of high-tech or e-governance. Dissociative elements may also enter the scene that point toward the desire for defiance during the early period of oppression. However, when the authoritarian leader consolidates power, this engenders a shift from an obsessive to a depressive condition in the community, further enhancing the leader's control. The subsequent period of dissociation leads to collapse and submission or, less likely, to an uprising.

Oppression covers all aspects of human existence in such a society (i.e., from spiritual to somatic), because oppressive systems tend to nurture uniformity that may to an extent reflect the degree of stimulus deprivation. They impose a single, distorted, or overplayed reality and resist a rather broad and integrated perception of multiple aspects of it (Schumaker, 1995). This aims at aligning individuals on a narrow and uniform perception of reality that may take on a utopian fashion in its most extreme form. The systematic distortion of reality by mass media may accompany this. Reality shows, soap operas, and contests that broadcast allegedly entertaining content demonstrate and legalize the degradation of humans for any reason (e.g., money, competition, fear). The authoritarian leader also joins this campaign in demeaning his or her fellow citizens.

A reinterpreted version of religion that is adapted to the needs of the system replaces true spirituality (Metzinger, 2010). This is utilized by the system as a source of authority that delivers decisions and rules about what is permitted and what is not. The government may even pursue biopolitics, which regulates populations through biopower, that is, the practice of modern states to regulate their subjects through "an explosion of numerous and diverse techniques for achieving the subjugations of bodies and the control of populations" (Foucault, 1976/1998, p. 140). For example, flooding the daily agenda of the society with themes such as abortion control, a hyperfocus on obesity and weight loss, the cessation of smoking, pestilences (e.g., bird flu), religious standards of dressing (e.g., the shape of women's headscarves), alleged reevaluation of emotionally laden historical events, and purification by operations supposedly uncovering dirty relationships keeps a population distracted from understanding larger world issues. Last but not least, the utilization of conspiracy, terror, and war to control the masses is not limited to modern times, and similarities in style are flagrant throughout history, as explored in a recent fictional account (Eco, 2010).

One either fights against or ignores oppression or transforms his or her self-identity in order to submit. Subjects who refuse to transform themselves, or those who do so radically, are particularly at risk of being oppressed. As conformers, the latter lose any base to resist and may subsequently become victims to be publicly sacrificed (e.g., scapegoated) by the authority as evidence of its power. Oppression creates feelings of defeat that further interfere with the ability of the individual to master the conflict. Fighting against oppression assists personal evolution. Individuals who can neither fight against oppression nor transform themselves fall into depression, a final stage that represents no possibility of revolt.

CONCLUSIONS

The world is, again, in crisis. Nobody knows how this crisis will unfold; how, when, and by whom it will be controlled; or whether the world is akin to a chaos (i.e., the collapse of social order leading to violence, war, poverty, and mental debility). With their enlarged sociological selves, politicians and even authoritarian leaders are ready to sell themselves as protectors or rescuers to frightened individuals and masses (Curtis, 2004). As a new modality, prolonged crisis and the threat of chaos have the potential to serve to control individuals and masses by oppressive systems now and in the future.

In expectancy of restoring a sense of control, people become prone to deliberately submitting to oppressive leaders or systems when threatened by a potential chaos. In fact, the threat of external chaos triggers dissociative fears of internal (i.e., individual) chaos and is itself also enhanced by the latter. Promotion of the sociological self among individuals in the community facilitates this collision and prevents societies from solving the dissociative process that leads to the crises. In fact, the threat of prolonged crisis itself constitutes overstimulation nurturing dissociation (i.e., it disturbs a sense of control and lets the psychological self freeze).

With their biased approach, the psychological theories and practices of the past century were not able to develop any insight into this impasse. Instead, they only assisted their intellectual consumers in denying the fears of individual internal chaos and obtaining temporary relief by legalizing fantasies as substitute realities, and so did societal overstimulation through preventing people from perceiving realities in an integrated manner (i.e., making associations between stimuli) by inducing interruptions of consciousness and exhaustion. Consequently, although people were persuaded about the possibility of external chaos as the primary threat, they have not been able to develop the courage necessary to overcome it. Nurturing this courage remains an expectancy from theories and practices of the, hopefully, upcoming century of the psychological self. Solving this challenge requires an integrated consciousness (i.e., not getting lost in fantasy while trying to convert a utopia to reality).

REFERENCES

Adorno, T. W., Frenkel-Brunswik, E., Levinson, D. J., & Sanford, R. N. (1950). *The authoritarian personality*. New York, NY: Norton.

American Psychiatric Association. (1994). *Diagnostic and statistical manual of mental disorders* (4th ed.). Washington, DC: Author.

Arieti, S., & Bemporad, J. R. (1980). The psychological organization of depression. *American Journal of Psychiatry*, *137*, 1360–1365.

Auerbach, S. M., Kiesler, D. J., Strentz, T., Schmidt, J. A., & Serio, C. D. (1994). Interpersonal impacts and adjustment to the stress of simulated captivity: An empirical test of the Stockholm syndrome. *Journal of Social and Clinical Psychology*, *13*(2), 207–221.

Battegay, R. (1987). Narzisstische Störungen im Lichte der modernen Psychoanalyse [Narcissistic disorders in the light of modern psychoanalysis]. *Schweizer Archiv für Neurologie und Psychiatrie*, *138*, 45–59.

Baudrillard, J. (1994). *Simulacra and simulation*. Ann Arbor: University of Michigan Press.

Blackman, L. (2005). The dialogical self, flexibility and the cultural production of psychopathology. *Theory & Psychology*, *15*(2), 183–206.

Bowen, M. (1978). *Family therapy in clinical practice*. Northvale NJ: Jason Aronson.

Braun, B. G. (1988). The BASK (behavior, affect, sensation, knowledge) model of dissociation. *Dissociation, 1*, 4–23.

Cantor, C., & Price, J. (2007). Traumatic entrapment, appeasement and complex post-traumatic stress disorder: Evolutionary perspectives of hostage reactions, domestic abuse and the Stockholm syndrome. *Australian and New Zealand Journal of Psychiatry, 41*, 377–384.

Curtis, A. (2002). *The century of the self* [Television documentary film]. London, England: BBC Four.

Curtis, A. (2004). *The power of nightmares. The rise of the politics of fear* [Television documentary film]. London, England: BBC Two.

deMause, L. (2002). *The emotional life of nations*. New York, NY: Institute of Psychohistory.

Eco, U. (2010). *Il cimitero di Praga [The Prague cemetery]*. Milan, Italy: Bompiani.

Ford, J. (2009). Dissociation in complex posttraumatic stress disorder or disorders of extreme stress not otherwise specified. In P. F. Dell & J. A. O'Neil (Eds.), *Dissociation and dissociative disorders:* DSM-V *and beyond* (pp. 471–483). New York, NY: Routledge.

Foucault, M. (1998). *The history of sexuality: Vol. 1. The will to knowledge*. London, England: Penguin. (Original work published 1976)

Frankel, A. S., & O'Hearn, T. C. (1996). Similarities in responses to extreme and unremitting stress: Cultures of communities under siege. *Psychotherapy: Theory, Research, Practice, Training, 33*, 485–502.

Freud, S. (1975). Jenseits des Lustprinzips [Beyond the pleasure principle]. In *Studienausgabe Bd. III, Psychologie des Unbewussten [Study edition Vol. III, The psychology of the unconscious]* (pp. 213–272). Frankfurt am Main, Germany: S. Fischer Verlag. (Original work published 1920)

Gardner, R. (1997). Sociophysiology as the basic science of psychiatry. *Theoretical Medicine, 18*, 335–356.

Gold, S. N. (2004). Fight club: A depiction of contemporary society as dissociogenic. *Journal of Trauma & Dissociation, 5*(2), 13–34.

Karpman, S. B. (1968). Fairy tales and script drama analysis. *Transactional Analysis Bulletin, 7*(26), 39–43.

Krüger, C., Sokudela, B. F., Motlana, L. M., Mataboge, C. K., & Dikobe, A. M. (2007). Dissociation: A preliminary contextual model. *South African Journal of Psychiatry, 13*(1), 13–21.

Lanius, R. A., Vermetten, E., Loewenstein, R. J., Brand, B., Schmahl, C., Bremner, J. D., & Spiegel, D. (2010). Emotion modulation in PTSD: Clinical and neurobiological evidence for a dissociative subtype. *American Journal of Psychiatry, 167*, 640–647.

Meares, R. (1999). The contribution of Hughlings Jackson to an understanding of dissociation. *American Journal of Psychiatry, 156*, 1850–1855.

Metzinger, T. (2010, November). *Spiritualitaet und intellektuelle Redlichkeit* [Spirituality and intellectual honesty]. Plenary address held in "Meditation and Science," Interdisciplinary Conference for the Study of Meditation and Consciousness, Berlin, Germany.

Milgram, S. (1963). Behavioral study of obedience. *Journal of Abnormal and Social Psychology, 67*, 371–378.

Nijenhuis, E. R. S., Spinhoven, P., Vanderlinden, J., Van Dyck, R., & Van der Hart, O. (1998). Somatoform dissociative symptoms as related to animal defensive reactions to predatory threat and injury. *Journal of Abnormal Psychology, 107*, 63–73.

Ochberg, F. (1978). The victim of terrorism: Psychiatric considerations. *Studies in Conflict and Terrorism, 1*(2), 147–168.

Ozturk, E. (2009a). Dissosiyatif kimlik bozukluğunun psikoterapisi [Psychotherapy of dissociative identity disorder]. *Psike, 2*, 75–83.

Ozturk, E. (2009b). Dövüs Kulübü: Cifte yasamlar, cifte kendilikler [Fight club: Double lives, double selves]. *Psike, 2*, 39–49.

Ozturk, E., & Sar, V. (2006). "Apparently normal" family: A contemporary agent of transgenerational trauma and dissociation. *Journal of Trauma Practice, 4*(3–4), 287–303.

Rezaie, L., Khazaie, H., Soleimani, A., & Schwebel, D. C. (2011). Is self-immolation a distinct method for suicide? A comparison of Iranian patients attempting suicide by self-immolation and by poisoning. *Burns, 37*, 159–163.

Riesman, D. (1950). *The lonely crowd*. New Haven, CT: Yale University Press.

Sar, V., Akyuz, G., Kugu, N., Ozturk, E., & Ertem-Vehid, H. (2006). Axis I dissociative disorder comorbidity in borderline personality disorder and reports of childhood trauma. *Journal of Clinical Psychiatry, 67*, 1583–1590.

Sar, V., Islam, S., & Ozturk, E. (2010, October). *Childhood trauma, attachment styles, alexithymia and suicidality in dissociative disorders: A comparison with major depression*. Paper presented at the 27th Annual Conference of the International Society for the Study of Trauma and Dissociation, Atlanta, GA.

Sar, V., & Ozturk, E. (2007). Functional dissociation of the self: A sociocognitive approach to trauma and dissociation. *Journal of Trauma & Dissociation, 8*(4), 69–89.

Sar, V., & Ozturk, E. (2009). Psychotic presentations of dissociative identity disorder. In P. F. Dell & J. A. O'Neil (Eds.), *Dissociation and dissociative disorders:* DSM-V *and beyond* (pp. 535–545). New York, NY: Routledge Press.

Sar, V., Yargic, L. I., & Tutkun, H. (1996). Structured interview data on 35 cases of dissociative identity disorder in Turkey. *American Journal of Psychiatry, 153*, 1329–1333.

Schumaker, J. F. (1995). *The corruption of reality: A unified theory of religion, hypnosis, and psychopathology*. Amherst, NY: Prometheus Books.

Schumaker, J. F. (2001). *The age of insanity: Modernity and mental health*. Westport, CT: Praeger.

Winkelman, M. (2011). A paradigm for understanding altered consciousness: The integrative mode of consciousness. In E. Cardeña & M. Winkelman (Eds.), *Altering consciousness: Multidisciplinary perspectives* (Vol. 1, pp. 23–41.) Santa Barbara, CA: Praeger.

Zizek, S. (2007). From objet a to subtraction. *Lacanian Ink, 30*, 131–141.

The Role of Abusive States of Being in Interrogation

FRANK W. PUTNAM, MD
Department of Psychiatry, University of North Carolina at Chapel Hill, Chapel Hill, North Carolina, USA

Interrogation, the questioning of persons detained by police, military, or intelligence organizations, is designed to extract information that a subject may resist disclosing. Interrogation techniques are frequently predicated on inducing mental states of despair, dread, dependency, and debility that weaken an individual's resistance. Descriptions of techniques from 2 Central Intelligence Agency training manuals are illustrated by examples from interviews of and writings by Murat Kurnaz, who was held at Guantánamo Bay Detention Camp for 5 years. Interrogation techniques are designed to create a destabilizing sense of shock; undermine an individual's grasp on reality; and provoke internal psychological division, self-conflict, and confusion. The long-term effects of interrogation often include posttraumatic stress disorder as well as states of anxiety, depression, and depersonalization.

The ultimate goal of an interrogation is the extraction of information that is of value to the interrogator. Interrogation is traditionally conceptualized as the questioning of crime suspects, prisoners of war, defectors, refugees, illegal immigrants, spies, agents of foreign powers, or others considered enemies of the state. In some instances, the interrogatee (individual being interrogated) is willfully resistant and may seek to mislead the interrogator. Given the importance of obtaining true information, military, police, and governmental intelligence organizations have developed psychological and

---

I would like to thank Lisa Connelly, MA, for her help in editing this manuscript.

physiological approaches to extract information, which they hope is accurate, from interrogatees.

This article examines some of the psychological approaches to interrogation from the perspective of state theory (Putnam, 1997). In brief, state theory holds that the induction of specific, discrete states of consciousness (e.g., a panic attack, depression, trance, fear, narcosis, excruciating pain) alters an individual's thinking, judgment, and even moral values, undercutting their integrity of the self and thus diminishing resistance. A number of interrogation techniques, especially coercive methods, are directed toward creating states of debility, dependency, and dread that undermine an interrogatee's capacity for resistance.

The source material is drawn from counterintelligence interrogation training manuals used by the Central Intelligence Agency (CIA). The manuals were released under a Freedom of Information Act request after the *Baltimore Sun* threatened to sue the CIA. An official press release accompanying the declassification of the manuals dismissed the contents, stating that only "two dozen short passages . . . contained material that either was not or could be interpreted not to be consistent with U.S. policy" (Office of the Assistant Secretary of Defense/Public Affairs Office, 1992). The *Baltimore Sun* published a four-part series (June 11–18, 1995) highlighting the role of the 1983 manual in the training of the infamous Honduran Battalion 3–16 death squad known for kidnapping, torture, and murder during the 1980s.

A number of versions are available on the Internet. The material quoted here comes from either the *KUBARK Counterintelligence Interrogation* manual dated July 1963 or a set of lecture notes that compose the *Human Resource Exploitation Training Manual* (hereafter, the HRE manual) dated 1983. My copy of the HRE manual quotes the KUBARK manual verbatim on many points. It also includes multiple crossed-out sections and handwritten revisions and additions.

At least 1,000 copies of these manuals were used in the counterintelligence training of Latin American military personnel by United States Southern Command (USSOUTHCOM) and at the School of the Americas from 1989 to 1991 (Department of Defense, 1992). It is likely that other foreign and U.S. military personnel received interrogation training based on versions of these manuals. An internal investigation by an Assistant to the Secretary of Defense for Intelligence Oversight (Werner E. Michel) found that the manuals "contained objectionable material, [and] were compiled without the required doctrinal controls" (Department of Defense, 1992, p. 1).

The manuals have a strong Cold War orientation and often refer to communists. Although they explicitly eschew torture, the infliction of pain, and inhumane treatment, the manuals describe their use in order to familiarize students with these techniques. At several points, the manuals expressly note that information extracted under torture is likely to be "unreliable" and that "the routine use of torture lowers the moral caliber of the organization that uses it and corrupts those that rely on it as the quick and easy way out" (CIA, 1983a, p. A2, Item C). The HRE manual originally read, "While we do not stress the use of coercive techniques, we do want to make you aware of them and the proper way to use them" (CIA, 1983a, p. A2, Item D). This sentence was subsequently revised to read, "While we deplore the use of coercive techniques, we do want to make you aware of them so that you may avoid them" (CIA, 1983a, p. A2, Item D).

The manuals are outdated (1963, 1983a, 1983b) and therefore not necessarily representative of current interrogation practices used by the CIA. In particular, justifications for specific approaches are based on outdated psychoanalytic theories prevalent during the 1950s and 1960s. The 1983 manual is typewritten with handwritten additions and contains fragmentary sentences and incomplete quotations, suggesting revisions without a thorough proofing. Nor do the manuals comment on the use of sexual abuse or the humiliation and degradation that characterized the interrogations at the Abu Ghraib prison in Iraq. Scientific research cited for sensory deprivation, hypnosis, and narcosis also dates to the same decades. However, recent accounts by Guantánamo internees of their interrogations and experiences in U.S. detention centers indicate that most of the coercive techniques described in the manuals continue to be practiced today.

Murat Kurnaz, a Turkish citizen born in Germany, was arrested in Peshawar, Pakistan, in December 2001, where he had gone to learn more about Islam following his marriage to a devout Muslim woman. He was transferred to U.S. custody (reportedly for a bounty of $3,000) and initially held at Kandahar prison in Afghanistan. He was subsequently transferred to Guantánamo and classified as an "enemy combatant." He was held at Guantánamo from February 2002 until August 2006, even though U.S. and German intelligence had determined by the end of 2002 that he was not involved in terrorist activities. He was eventually released after the German chancellor appealed to President George W. Bush. Kurnaz wrote a book about his experience, *Five Years of My Life: An Innocent Man in Guantánamo,* and was interviewed by multiple major U.S. and international news organizations. He alleges that he was tortured and that he witnessed the killing of several fellow detainees. Examples are drawn from Kurnaz's writing and interviews to illustrate the application of interrogation techniques described in the manuals.

BASIC THEMES

Both manuals divide interrogation techniques into two basic types: noncoercive and coercive. They both emphasize that the fit between the technique chosen and the interrogatee's personality is critical. If the wrong technique(s)—relative to the subject's personal weaknesses—is chosen and the subject successfully resists, it is likely that subsequent techniques will also fail because the interrogatee's capacity for resistance is now reinforced.

The manuals stress the need for "questioners" to be qualified in terms of training, experience, and familiarity with the interrogatee's language and culture and to have a "psychological understanding of the subject" (CIA, 1983b, p. L4, Section IV, Item I). An interrogation plan is developed that evaluates the fit between the techniques and the subject's weaknesses. The HRE manual requires that the plan take into account whether solitary confinement, sensory deprivation, threats, or other coercive techniques are also used, as they will influence the choice of technique.

Non-Coercive Techniques

The HRE manual states the following:

> All non-coercive "questioning" [quotation marks and punctuation in this and subsequent quotations are in the original] techniques are based on the principle of generating pressure inside the subject without the application of outside force. This is accomplished by manipulating him psychologically until his resistance is sapped and his urge to yield is fortified. (CIA, 1983b, Section K1, Item B)

The interrogator seeks to "disrupt radically the familiar emotional and psychological associations of the subject" (CIA, 1983b, Section K1, Item C).

> Once this disruption is achieved, the subject's resistance is seriously impaired. He experiences a kind of psychological shock, which may only last briefly. But during which he is far more open to suggestion and far likelier to comply, than he was before he experienced the shock. (CIA, 1983b, Section K1, Item D)

A variety of non-coercive techniques are detailed in both manuals, with the HRE manual copying KUBARK verbatim in most instances. The techniques are given descriptive names such as "going next door," "nobody loves you," "we know everything," "news from home," "the witness," and "Ivan is a dope." Many use a team approach, usually with a good cop/bad cop slant. The HRE manual reads as follows:

> The number of variations in techniques is limited only by the experience and imagination of the "Questioner." The success and skill of an experienced "questioner" lie 'in his ability to match the techniques selected to

> the personality of the subject and his rapid exploitation at the moment of shock. (CIA, 1983b, Section K1, Item G)

A technique called "nonsense questioning" is quoted here in its entirety to provide an example of non-coercive approaches to interrogation:

> *Nonsense Questioning*
>
> Two or more "questioners" ask the subject questions which seem straightforward but are illogical and have no pattern. Any attempted response by the subject is interrupted by additional unrelated questioning. In this strange atmosphere the subject finds that the pattern of thought which he has learned to consider normal is replaced by an eerie meaninglessness.
>
> At first he may refuse to take the questioning seriously. But as the process continues day after day, it becomes mentally intolerable and he begins to try to make sense out of the situation. Certain types of very orderly and logical subjects begin to doubt their sanity and in their attempts to clarify the confusion make significant admissions and betray valuable information. (CIA, 1983b, Section K13, Item L)

A major contention of the evidence used against Murat Kurnaz was that he had been closely associated with Selcuk Bilgin, who had become a suicide bomber. Despite his continued protestations that they had only been friends for a short period because of common interests in sports and raising dogs, Kurnaz was unceasingly interrogated about their relationship:

> The interrogations continued always with the same questions. I told my story over and over—my name, my family, why I was in Pakistan. Nothing I said satisfied them. I realized that my interrogators were not interested in the truth. (Kurnaz, 2010, p. 2)

Ultimately it was established that Bilgin, the alleged suicide bomber, was alive and well.

Coercive Techniques

The theory of coercion is focused on methods for inducing a regressed state in the interrogatee. The HRE manual states the following:

> The purpose of all coercive techniques is to induce psychological regression in the subject by bringing a superior outside force to bear on his will to resist. Regression is basically a loss of autonomy, a reversion to

> an earlier behavioral level. As the subject regresses, his learned personality traits fall away in reverse chronological order. He begins to lose the capacity to carry out the highest creative activities, to deal with complex situations, to cope with stressful interpersonal relationships, or to cope with repeated frustrations. (CIA, 1983b, p. K1, Section L1, Item A)

Penciled in below this paragraph is "The use of most coercive techniques is improper and violates . . . [indecipherable word]" (CIA, 1983b, p. K1, Section L1, Item A).

The manuals describe three basic elements common to coercive techniques: debility (physical weakness), dependency, and dread (CIA, 1983b, pp. K1–K2, Items L-3–L-5). The principal coercive techniques are arrest, detention, the deprivation of sensory stimuli, threats and fear, debility, pain, heightened suggestibility and hypnosis, and drugs (CIA, 1963, p. 103). These are used in various combinations to create a state of regression in interrogatees. "The usual effect of coercion is regression. The interrogatee's mature defenses crumble as he becomes more childlike" (CIA, 1963, p. 103).

It is noted that debility techniques date back centuries and include prolonged restraint; prolonged exertion; extreme heat, cold, or moisture; and deprivation of food and sleep. Random disruption of normal cycles of sleep, eating, and hygiene is identified as an especially potent technique for destroying a subject's capacity to resist. A handwritten notation to the HRE manual adds, "However, if successful—it causes serious psychological damage and therefore is a form of torture" (CIA, 1983b, p. K2, Item L3).

In his writing and in interviews with established news organizations, Kurnaz describes electroshocks, the forcing of his head under water and then hitting him in the stomach to make him inhale (essentially a form of waterboarding), being hung by his hands in chains for days, food and sleep deprivation (he lost 80 pounds), and prolonged exposure to freezing cold or extreme heat. He reports being repeatedly beaten, seeing detainees killed in front of him, being shackled to the floor in a fetal position for days, being blasted with pepper spray and injected with psychoactive drugs, and being sexually molested by three female interrogators.

Dependency involves creating a situation in which the interrogatee becomes dependent on the interrogator for all of his or her basic needs. The HRE manual cautions that the creation of "dread," defined as intense fear and anxiety usually created by threats, can be counterproductive in that if the interrogator is forced to actually carry out a threat it may come as a relief for the subject. Or, "If the debility-dependency-dread state is unduly prolonged, the subject may sink into a defensive apathy from which it is hard to arouse him" (CIA, 1983b, p. K3, Item L5).

In coercive techniques, the moment of arrest plays a critical role. It should be timed for when the subject least expects it, ideally in the early hours of the morning when mental and physical capacity for resistance is at a low ebb. The subject is then detained and completely cut off from his or her contacts and resources. The manuals note the following:

> A person's sense of identity depends upon a continuity in his surroundings, habits, appearance; actions, relations with others, etc. Detention permits the "questioner" to cut through these links and throw the subject back upon his own unaided internal resources. Detention should be planned to enhance the subject's feelings of being cut off from anything known and reassuring. (CIA, 1983b, Item L9, B)

The manuals favor solitary confinement as a form of detention, observing that it "acts on most persons as a powerful stress" (CIA, 1983b, p. K6, Section L10, Item C). Results of experiments by Dr. John Lilly at the National Institute of Mental Health are cited as evidence that sensory deprivation rapidly breaks down an individual's will by "depriving the subject's mind of contact with an outer world and thus forcing it in upon itself" (CIA, 1963, p. 91).

> The more completely the place of confinement eliminates sensory stimuli, the more rapidly and deeply will the interrogatee be affected. Results produced only after weeks or months of imprisonment in an ordinary cell can be duplicated in hours or days in a cell which has no light (or weak artificial light which never varies), which is sound-proofed, in which odors are eliminated, etc. An environment still more subject to control, such as a water-tank or iron lung, is even more effective. (CIA, 1963, p. 91)

Murat Kurnaz describes being punished with solitary confinement for an act of kindness:

> Despite all of this, I looked for ways to feel human. I have always loved animals. I started hiding a piece of bread from my meals and feeding the iguanas that came to the fence. When officials discovered this, I was punished with 30 days in isolation and darkness. (Kurnaz, 2010, p. 2)

Threats are most effective when delivered in a cold and calculated manner, but they must also contain an escape route for the interrogatee. The escape route often is in the form of an acceptable rationalization that the interrogatee can use to justify to himself or herself compliance with the interrogator's demands. The escape route repeatedly offered to Murat Kurnaz was to sign a confession that he was a terrorist. Even in the final minutes before he was released to German authorities, he was asked to sign a confession to being a terrorist.

The effects of the actual infliction of physical pain are viewed as unpredictable and highly dependent on the subject's attitude and previous experiences with pain. More potent is the creation of a situation in which the individual self-inflicts pain and therefore must struggle against himself or herself.

> It has been plausibly suggested, that, whereas pain inflicted on a person from outside himself may actually focus or intensify his will to resist, his resistance is likelier to be sapped by pain which he seems to inflict upon himself. "In the simple torture situation the contest is one between the individual and his tormentor (. . . and he can frequently endure). When the individual is told to stand at attention for long periods, an intervening factor is introduced. The immediate source of pain is not the interrogator but the victim himself. The motivational strength of the individual is likely to exhaust itself in this internal encounter. . . . As long as the subject remains standing, he is attributing to his captor the power to do something worse to him, but there is actually no showdown of the ability of the interrogator to do so. (CIA, 1963, p. 94)

Hypnosis and drugs are included under coercive techniques, although the manuals treat them as more suggestive or deceptive than probative. Martin Orne's theories about the nature of hypnosis are quoted extensively in the KUBARK manual. In essence, the manuals hold that a resistant subject cannot be forced to divulge information under hypnosis, but in a trance state he or she can be manipulated into believing that it is okay to reveal information.

> Once an interrogatee is in a hypnotic trance, his understanding of reality becomes subject to manipulation. For example, A KUBARK interrogator could tell a suspect double agent in a trance that the KGB is conducting the questioning, and thus invert the whole frame of reference. In other words, Orne is probably right in holding that most recalcitrant subjects will continue effective resistance as long as the frame of reference is undisturbed. But once the subject is tricked into believing that he is talking to friend rather than foe, or that divulging the truth is the best way to serve his own purposes, his resistance will be replaced by cooperation. The value of hypnotic trance is not that it permits the interrogator to impose his will but rather that it can be used to convince the interrogatee that there is no valid reason not to be forthcoming. (CIA, 1963, p. 96)

The use of drugs during interrogations is also regarded more as a suggestive technique than as a pharmacological device for extracting factual information. In fact, both manuals indicate that placebos may be more effective than actual medications. "Just as the threat of pain may more effectively induce compliance than its infliction, so an interrogatee's mistaken belief that he has been drugged may make him a more useful interrogation subject than he would be under narcosis" (CIA, 1963, p. 98).

> The subject's primary source of resistance to confession or divulgence may be pride, patriotism, personal loyalty to superiors, or fear of retribution if he is returned to their hands. Under such circumstances his natural desire to escape from stress by complying with the interrogator's wishes may become decisive if he is provided an acceptable rationalization for compliance. "I was drugged" is one of the best excuses. (CIA, 1963, p. 99)

STATES OF BEING

The notion of a state of mind, state of consciousness, or state of being is so ubiquitous in discussions of psychological processes—by both professionals and the general public—that it passes virtually unnoticed. For example, there are many instances of the use of this concept of "state" in the *Diagnostic and Statistical Manual of Mental Disorders* (e.g., depressed state, anxious state, psychotic state), but nowhere in that bible of psychiatric diagnoses is "state" defined. Collectively people think of a person's state of mind as a discrete but transient mental process that both is marked by and influences mood, thinking, and behavior.

There is, however, a scientifically robust—although widely dispersed—scientific literature on the nature of discrete states of consciousness, including studies of infant behavioral states, hypnotic states, sleep states, vegetative states, psychotic states, meditative states, psychedelic drug-induced states, possession states, and creative states, among others. These scientific literatures are remarkably congruent in their findings that states of being—although defined differently by various disciplines—are discrete, transient psychological and physiological configurations that serve to organize a person's cognition, physiology, behavior, and sense of self or identity (Putnam, 1994).

Many aspects of cognition in particular show state-dependent features. Studies looking at learning and the recall of information in subjects experiencing a variety of powerful mental states (e.g., manic depression, panic attacks, hypnosis, drug or alcohol intoxication) find that memory and associations can be state dependent, particularly for certain types of information (Szostak, Lister, Eckardt, & Weingartner, 1994). Common experience demonstrates that many individuals while in an extreme mental state (e.g., rage, deep depression, intoxication, blind panic) have impaired judgment, fail to make use of what they know, or deviate from their usual moral values.

It should be apparent from the preceding quotations that an overriding theme in the theory and practice of interrogation is the imposition of mental states that lower or eliminate interrogatees' resistance to revealing information. This is done by completely disrupting interrogatees' worlds, separating them from the people, possessions, and routines that defined their prior existence and substituting a stressful new environment, controlled by the interrogator, that strips them of their usual resources, breaks down their psychological defenses, and undermines their sense of identity. In this new reality, interrogatees are no longer the same people they were before their arrest.

Coercive techniques add physical and physiological stressors together with painful and overwhelming mental states such as fear, helplessness, hopelessness, and dread. Deprivation and random availability of sleep and food prevent the interrogatee from reestablishing stabilizing biological rhythms and developing predictable routines to anchor his or her existence. Punishments in the form of self-inflicted torment are imposed in an effort to turn the individual against himself or herself. The demands of his body for the cessation of pain, relief from restraint, or rest from exertion are set against the interrogatee's will to resist.

Stripped of resources, isolated from social support, deprived of sensory stimulation, in pain or under physical duress, subject to unpredictable food and sleep, and filled with dread, most individuals will not be in a normal state of mind. Although time limits are not explicitly specified, examples mention periods of days, weeks, and even months, testifying to relentless application over long periods. With sufficient time, the beliefs, values, habits, and ideologies that defined the individual are wiped away or relegated to another time and place and thus lose their power over current thought, motivation, beliefs, and values. The individual's very identity may be divided and the parts placed in self-conflict, depriving him or her of a unified sense of self to undergird his or her resistance. The aim is to create a childlike state of dependency and submission to the paternal authority of the interrogator.

THE LONG-TERM EFFECTS OF INTERROGATIONS

In this article examples were included to provide a tangible reality to what is otherwise a dry theoretical discussion of a disturbing subject. Murat Kurnaz was chosen as an example because his story was current, it had been widely distributed on the Internet, and he had been interviewed by major news organizations. Presumably his story was carefully vetted (within in the limits of the records available) because of the serious nature of his allegations of torture. Independent studies of the effects of coercive and non-coercive interrogations are difficult to conduct for many reasons. Interrogations are conducted in secret, and verification of the details by neutral observers is rarely available. Surveys of former interrogatees provide a major source of information, but factual substantiation is difficult. Isolating the unique effects of specific interrogation methods from other non-interrogation experiences, deprivations, and trauma is virtually impossible. Most authorities consider coercive interrogation methods to be a form of torture, and many studies of torture victims include a large percentage of former interrogatees. Many interrogatees report that they would say or do almost anything to make coercive techniques stop (Costanzo, Gerrity, & Lykes, 2007).

Murat Kurnaz describes his current situation as "trying to put my terrible memories behind me" (Kurnaz, 2010, p. 3). The day he was freed he learned that his wife had divorced him and his grandfather and favorite uncle had died. He has since remarried and has a baby daughter. He suffers from frequent headaches and nightmares. He is distrustful of people and the media, in part because he was identified in the German press as a dangerous Islamist. He says that he did not initially seek publicity and only told his story after journalist Andreas Förster interviewed him following an investigative report on the news website Truthout.

Research with victims finds that torture often produces long-term effects on psychological, social, familial, and economic functioning (Costanzo et al., 2007). Many torture survivors meet diagnostic criteria for posttraumatic stress disorder. In addition, they frequently have significant depression, anxiety, emotional instability, and social withdrawal. They complain of confusion, disorientation, problems with memory, and difficulty concentrating. They have severe sleep problems, frequent nightmares, and sexual dysfunction. Profound post-torture changes in victims' personalities have been described and were instrumental in the inclusion in the International Classification of Diseases–10 of a diagnosis of enduring personality change after catastrophic experience (World Health Organization, 1992).

Many of the symptoms and long-term sequelae experienced by torture victims also can be understood from a state perspective. Some symptoms are in the form of pathological states (e.g., hyperarousal, depression, anxiety, depersonalization, nightmares, flashbacks, and abreactions). Other symptoms reflect disruptions in the biological mechanisms and rhythms modulating state (e.g., abnormal sleep patterns, excessive startle responses, explosive anger, and emotional instability).

Although most of the states evoked by the application of coercive and non-coercive techniques are not dissociative per se, they are sufficiently different from the interrogatee's normal states of being that they disrupt the individual's sense of identity and access to prior core beliefs, memories, and values. In this sense, they force the individual to become a different person from who he or she was—and therefore more vulnerable.

Finally, a brief comment about the role of academics in the development of interrogation techniques. Research by Martin Orne, who received government funding to research "the nature of special states of consciousness and trance states," (Ross, 2006, p. 43) is prominently quoted in the manuals. John Lilly's work at the National Institute of Mental Health on the psychological effects of sensory deprivation is also cited. Other leaders in the fields of psychiatry and psychology at that time, such as Louis J. (Jolly) West, MD, were instrumental in identifying the power of the debility–dependence–dread state to sap an interrogatee's resistance (Farber, Harlow, & West, 1966). Academics cannot prevent military and police agencies from adapting public domain research findings in interrogation. Academics can and should refuse to participate in research directed primarily at developing new approaches to coercive interrogation. Both the American Psychological Association and the American Psychiatric Association have policies prohibiting members from engaging in coercive interrogations and/or torture (Costanzo et al., 2007).

REFERENCES

Central Intelligence Agency. (1963, July). *KUBARK counterintelligence interrogation, Part II* (pp. 61–112). Retrieved from http://tiny.cc/862ls

Central Intelligence Agency. (1983a). *Human resource exploitation training manual, Part I* (pp. 1–67). Retrieved from http://tiny.cc/38ktn

Central Intelligence Agency. (1983b). *Human resource exploitation training manual, Part II* (pp. 68–124). Retrieved from http://tiny.cc/umf1y

Costanzo, M., Gerrity, E., & Lykes, M. B. (2007). Psychologists and the use of torture in interrogations. *Analyses of Social Issues and Public Policy, 7*, 7–20.

Department of Defense. (1992, March 10). *Memorandum for the Secretary of Defense, improper material in Spanish-language intelligence training manuals, Sec Def Cont Nr. X58571*. Retrieved from http://tiny.cc/qsk35

Farber, I. E., Harlow, H. F., & West, L. J. (1966). Brainwashing, conditioning and DDD (debility, dependency, and dread). In R. Ulrich, T. Stachnik, & J. Marbry (Eds.), *Control of human behavior* (pp. 322–330). Glenview, IL: Scott, Foresman.

Kurnaz, M. (2010). Notes from a Guantanamo survivor. *The New York Times*, 1/8/2010. Retrieved from http://www.nytimes.com/2012/01/08/opinion/sunday/notes-from-a-guantanamo-survivor.html

Office of the Assistant Secretary of Defense/Public Affairs Office. (1992, August 27). *Fact sheet concerning training materials inconsistent with U.S. Policy*. Retrieved from http://www.gwu.edu/~nsarchiv/nsa/archive/news/dodmans.htm

Putnam, F. W. (1994). The switch process in multiple personality disorder and other state-change disorders. In R. M. Klein & B. K. Doane (Eds.), *Psychological concepts and dissociative disorders* (pp. 283–304). Hillsdale, NJ: Erlbaum.

Putnam, F. W. (1997). *Dissociation in children and adolescents: A developmental perspective*. New York, NY: Guilford Press.

Ross, C. A. (2006). *The C.I.A. doctors. Human rights violations by American psychiatrists*. Richardson, TX: Manitou Communications.

Szostak, C., Lister, R., Eckardt, M., & Weingartner, H. (1994). Dissociative effects of mood on memory. In R. M. Klein & B. K. Doane (Eds.), *Psychological concepts and dissociative disorders* (pp. 187–206). Hillsdale, NJ: Erlbaum.

World Health Organization. (1992). *The ICD-10 classification of mental and behavioural disorders: Clinical descriptions and diagnostic and guidelines*. Geneva, Switzerland: Author.

Parent–Child Incest that Extends into Adulthood: A Survey of International Press Reports, 2007–2012

WARWICK MIDDLETON, MBBS, FRANZCP, MD
The Cannan Institute, La Trobe University, University of Queensland, University of New England, University of Canterbury

Although the subject of ongoing incestuous abuse during adulthood has never been addressed in a systematic way by the professional literature, accounts of such cases have been appearing for many years. The Josef Fritzl case added a new impetus to reporting such abuses in the popular press. This study presents 51 such cases from 25 countries that appeared in English language press accounts over six years commencing January 2007. These cases are discussed in the light of minimal coverage of such issues in the professional literature. The results of this study suggest that cases of enduring incest are not rare and typically incorporate decades of sexual abuse, frequently result in pregnancies, and commonly incorporate ongoing violence and death threats.

In May 2008, an Argentinian, Eleuterio Sorio, was jailed for 16 years, having kept his young daughter a sexual prisoner while fathering two children with her. When she became pregnant with the first child in 1993 at age 13, her mother left their abode in Buenos Aires with her five other children. On the occasions Sorio's daughter fled the home, she was forced to return by her father threatening her children, often at gunpoint. Maria Leuzzi, representing a local service for rape victims reflected on a reality that cases like Eleuterio Sorio's are not uncommon, saying, "Here we have many Josef Fritzls" (*Metro*, 2008). Josef Fritzl achieved global notoriety in 2008 when it was discovered that he had imprisoned his already sexually and physically abused teenage daughter, Elisabeth, in a locked cellar beneath his family home for 24 years. He produced seven incestuously fathered children, one of whom died as a baby, with Fritzl incinerating the body in a furnace. If ongoing incestuous abuse can go on indefinitely in the house of an outwardly friendly man like Josef Fritzl (Marsh & Pancevski, 2009) who appeared to a neighbor to have a "perfect family unit", then there must be many other cases.

Adult incestuous abuse is not a modern phenomenon. There were nineteenth-century cases of chronic incestuous abuse that appear to be, if it were possible, more extreme

---

This paper represents an update and extension of a previously published paper, Middleton, W. (2013). Parent–child incest that extends into adulthood: A survey of international press reports, 2007–2011, *Journal of Trauma and Dissociation*, 14: 184–197.

even than those of Joseph Fritzl. Sacco (2009) reports the case of Joel W. Perkins, a Connecticut man tried in 1871. He confessed that for ten years he had repeatedly raped every one of his six daughters. The jury convicted him of murdering three of the six babies that resulted. In another case, a "well-to-do" Indiana farmer was convicted in 1869 for the rape of all six of his daughters and at least one granddaughter.

Although I could find no published series examining ongoing incest during adulthood, a number of individuals such as Marilyn Van Derbur and Sue Silverman have written autobiographical accounts describing incestuous abuse extending beyond their eighteenth birthday, and refugees from polygamous cults (such as Carolyn Jessop) or freed long-term child kidnap victims (e.g., Elizabeth Smart) that bring a focus to other variations on long-term incest-like abuse occurring in "family" settings.

Some individuals without children of their own to abuse long term literally steal someone else's. Included in this grouping is Michael Devlin who abducted an 11-year-old boy, Shawn Hornbeck, in 2002, to be followed by the kidnapping of another boy, 13-year-old William Benjamin "Ben" Ownby in 2007 (*Mail Online*, 2007). Jaycee Dugard, 11 at the time, was abducted near her home by Phillip and Nancy Garrido in 1991 and remained missing for 18 years during which time she bore Garrido (a paroled sex offender) two daughters (Leff & Thompson, 2011). In May 2013, Ariel Castro of Cleveland was charged in relationship with the abduction in August 2002 of Michelle Knight, then 20, the abduction in April 2003 of Amanda Berry, then 16, and the abduction in April 2004 of Gina DeJesus, then aged 14. Castro lived in an unremarkable middle-class street where he would have visits from his brothers and fellow musicians, Pedro and Onil. Amanda Berry emerged from her decade's imprisonment accompanied by her six-year-old daughter. Castro's paternity was confirmed by DNA testing. Police removed ropes and chains from his house. Authorities charged Castro with multiple counts of rape and stated that the women were subjected to death threats, repeated beatings and multiple forced miscarriages. In a 2004 manifesto discovered by police, Castro alluded to his own sexual abuse (Trotta & Gray, 2013). A neighbor, Juan Perez, who had known Ariel Castro for years said of him: "He was a fun guy. I mean, parents trusted him. He talked to the parents. He was just a regular guy on the street. He put on that great mask that everyone thought he was a good guy" (Quigley, 2013).

THE PROFESSIONAL LITERATURE

The earliest psychoanalytic case (aside from Freud's Dora) that was published and for which the case notes survive was that of a highly dissociative 22-year-old woman (Rachel C) who was entwined in multigenerational ongoing incestuous abuse, and who over time was observed to have marked amnesias, fugue states, hallucinations and "splits" in her personality. Her analyst, Louville E. Eugene Emerson, saw her for the first time in January 1912. Just prior to Rachel entering treatment with Emerson, her father had offered to pay her for having sex with him. The father continued to solicit Rachel between sessions with her therapist. Rebuffed by her on one occasion, her father insinuated that she and her analyst were sexual partners. Emerson, early in the treatment, concluded that Rachel's father was a "sadist", a man who routinely teased and tormented his daughter while conducting liaisons with a string of secret lovers, one of whom he brought home expecting Rachel to serve her dinner. Rachel reported that her father first digitally penetrated her when she was seven and from that time she and her brother had frequent incestuous relations. By the time she was 13 or 14, Rachel's father was having intercourse with her. Several times her mother walked in on them. No protection was offered; instead she accused Rachel, blaming her for all of what had happened as well as accusing her of incest with her brother. In a theme familiar to anyone in the twenty-first-century trauma field, Rachel oscillated between rage at her parents and self-hate. The latter manifested itself at times by cutting, including a two-inch gash to her left breast (Lunbeck & Simon, 2003).

In the same year that Emerson was embarking on the treatment of Rachel C, a 12-year-old Erich Fromm was confronted with the suicide of an attractive young woman who was a friend of his family:

> Maybe she was twenty-five years of age; she was beautiful, attractive and in addition a painter, the first painter I ever knew. I remember having heard that she had been engaged but after some time had broken the engagement; I remember that she was almost invariably in the company of her widowed father. As I remember him, he was an old, uninteresting, and rather unattractive-looking man, or so I thought (maybe my judgment was somewhat biased by jealousy). Then one day I heard the shocking news: her father had died, and immediately afterwards she had killed herself and left a will which stipulated that she wanted to be buried together with her father (Fromm, 1962, p. 4).

A shaken Fromm was left to grapple with the question, "How is it possible that a beautiful young woman should be so in love with her father, that she prefers to be buried with him to being alive to the pleasures of life and of painting?" (1962, p. 4).

Enrico Morselli's patient Elena, described by Ellenberger (1970, p. 138) as "perhaps the most remarkable case of multiple personality ever published", was admitted as a 25-year-old to Morselli's clinic in Milan. This followed a stay of several weeks with her father at Lake Maggiore, for which initially she had no recall.

> Gradually, Elena recovered her forgotten memories at the cost of terrifying emotional abreactions. She remembered having been the victim of her father's incestuous attacks (the reality of which was confirmed from other sources). Most horrifying for her was the memory of his attempts to put his tongue in her mouth (p. 139).

Morselli published the case in 1930.

The genesis of dissociative identity disorder (DID) lies with chronic inescapable trauma in childhood, in that to avoid being overwhelmed or to minimize the affective response to traumas which often involve incest, the child dissociates. Overt sexual abuse of daughters by fathers commonly ceases before or during early adolescence due to social/sexual awareness, the intervention of a relative, escape from the home, discovery of abuse by a mother who is willing to act, fears on the part of an incestuous father about pregnancy and the child evolving some boundaries based on her experiences with friends and non-abusive relatives. However, many fathers exert psychological control and household dominance in a manner akin to Josef Fritzl, such that the now adult child remains in a destructive attachment to someone who controls them through conditioning and the manipulation of shame and fear.

There has been a longstanding interest in the mechanisms whereby a conditioned propensity to abuse is transmitted across the generations with dissociation providing a mechanism that in some ways assists the survival of the individual but at the same time allows such abuse to remain hidden. Braun (1985) presented data on 18 patients with DID. Some evidence of dissociative phenomena was reported and/or observed in the family histories of all 16 female and 2 male DID cases (age range: 19–50). In regard to one of the patients, data was presented, based on corroborative history and direct clinical observations showing probable DID in four successive generations – in two grandfathers, one grandmother, both parents, the patient, the patient's brother and sister and the sister's daughter. Though not discussed, data was presented showing that eight of the 18 patients continued to live with their family of origin after age 18 and that a further five had some sort of fluctuating living arrangement, with only five having permanently left.

Highly quoted studies of incest fail to make specific reference to ongoing incest during adulthood. For example, no such case is described in Herman's 1981 text, *Father-Daughter Incest* or in the 2000 updated edition, nor was such a case described in Russell's 1986 ground-breaking work on the epidemiology of child sexual abuse, *The Sexual Trauma: Incest in the Lives of Girls and Women*. This type of ongoing abuse was also not discussed in *Incest-Related Syndromes of Adult Psychopathology* (Kluft, 1990).

Courtois (1988) mentioned the problem and briefly described such an individual, a young woman who presented with the words *HELP ME* carved on her arm. She described the woman's family as "solidly upper middle-class and appearing to be well-functioning to the outside community" (p. xiv).

The issue of the chronically incestuously abused adult patients is not particularly addressed in the first substantive texts on the diagnosis and treatment of multiple personality disorder (DID) appearing in 1989 (Putnam, 1989; Ross, 1989). Putnam stated:

> I am struck by the quality of extreme sadism that is frequently reported by most [DID] victims. Bondage situations, the insertion of a variety of instruments into vagina, mouth, and anus; and various forms of physical and sexual torture are common reports. Many multiples have told me of being sexually abused by groups of people, of being forced into prostitution by family members, or of being offered as a sexual enticement to their mother's boyfriends (p. 296).

Putnam though only makes brief reference to the fact that "actual abuse of adult MPD patients by family members does occur and can touch off devastating crises" (p. 296). Such matters are absent or barely touched on in the great majority of subsequent texts on either dissociation or incest, though case examples periodically appear. Courtois (2010) is an exception stating that she has "now worked with a number of clients whose abuse continued into their adult years and whose abusers, mostly fathers, largely considered their daughters their property to do with as they pleased" (p. 32). She stated that the prevalence of such cases is unknown though observed: "If the incest goes undiscovered or attempts at disclosure or intervention are ineffective, the incest begun in the child's toddler years may well continue into adolescence and sometimes even into adulthood" (pp. 115–116).

Periodically, ongoing incest during adulthood surfaces in the professional literature as a seemingly incidental element in the discussion of another topic. For example,

Kinsler (1995) describes of his emotional reactions to the apparent suicide by overdose of a female patient of his, a mental health worker with DID. Though details of her history are not focused on, her abusers included her father. Kinsler rings her parents.

> Marcie's father, the one who kept sending her revealing little black dresses even into her forties, doesn't even choose to come to the phone . . . Marcie felt that her mother hated her because of the real closeness between them. Daughter as dangerous rival to mother, object of narcissistic extension to Dad (pp. 102–103).

We are not told whether Marcie's father continued to abuse her during adulthood, but the description tends to imply this.

In a departure from previous editions, the *Guidelines for Treating Dissociative Identity Disorder in Adults, Third Revision* (International Society for the Study of Trauma and Dissociation, 2011) explicitly acknowledges that long-term incestuous abuse frequently merges with some form of organized abuse, that some patients with DID are still being incestuously abused at the time of presentation and that for others a sudden deterioration in their ability to function may signal the renewed involvement of a prior abuser.

A recent case study of an individual named as "Grace" by Salter (2013) starts with a reflection that incest which progresses into adulthood is relatively frequent, yet nevertheless poorly understood:

> In light of the frequency of reports of prolonged incestuous abuse in mental health settings, the lack of information in the research literature about the contexts in which it is possible for the sexual abuse of a girl to continue undetected into adulthood is concerning (p. 149).

In Grace's case the incest continued up to the time of her finding a husband but the entwined attachment to her parents saw the marriage fail, while the impact of the ongoing incest had seen her expelled from school and missing out on educational opportunities. Salter quotes the 50-plus-year-old Grace:

> My dad never wanted me to move away. I was never allowed to have boyfriends, or any male friends at all. Even up until I was 25. I was never allowed to have anyone over at the house, even for tea, nothing like that (p. 152).

Salter observes that the themes of power and captivity that characterize the sort of prolonged abuse cases epitomized by Josef Fritzl's treatment of his daughter Elisabeth "were also present in Grace's story, albeit in more mundane and everyday forms" (p. 161).

> In the claustrophobic confines of the family compound, Grace's father set into operation a web of perpetually invalidating relations that left Grace lonely, miserable, and disconnected from her own thoughts and feelings. This pattern of invalidation and coercion would ultimately outlive Grace's time on the farm and follow her throughout her adult life, as her parents employed financial and emotional strategies to ensure that she remained nearby and compliant. Importantly, the subordinate subject position crafted for Grace within her father's regime of abuse also persisted long after his capacity to directly control her had diminished. She

> continued to act as her parents' 'waitress' to the time of the interview. She suggested that acting otherwise would endanger her inheritance, but she acknowledged that she was also doing so in the pursuit of a deeply held wish for the validation and support that her parents promised, but never provided (p. 161).

In light of the scant systematic study of ongoing incestuous abuse during adulthood, this chapter is focused on drawing together key themes from the international press, in which such cases have in recent years been covered with unprecedented frequency.

BACKGROUND INTERNATIONAL PRESS COVERAGE

The journalist Alexanda Artley published a number of articles and a 1993 book that detailed the life of Tommy Thompson and his principal victims: his wife and two daughters. The saga of extreme abuse started with Thompson's marriage in 1951 and concluded with his family shooting him in front of his TV in 1988. Thompson beat his wife almost daily. He unambiguously conveyed his intentions to sexually abuse his then 10- or 11-year-old daughter: "Ye know I have sex with your mam, June? Well, now I want it with you as well" (Artley, 1993, p. 167). When she tried to reason with him, her father, who was wielding an axe at the time, with rising anger put his face very close to hers, saying,

> Whatever I tell you to do, you do it, whether you like it or not. And if anybody gets to know anything at all about what's going on in this house, it doesn't matter who or what position they're in, I'll shoot the lot of ye (p. 168).

Emphasizing ownership he insisted his daughters wear wedding rings and he forced them and his wife to wear identical cheap red jackets. When the sisters finally mustered the courage to shoot their father with his gun, police found a freshly painted house and an almost clinical neatness to the room containing Tommy's body, shot twice in the chest for certainty.

Rose West was only the fourth woman to stand trial as a serial killer in the United Kingdom. Her conviction for killing ten women or girls was only partially eclipsed by her equally sadistic husband who had committed suicide before trial, having been spectacularly arrested along with Rose in February 1994: a prelude to the full police excavation centered on what the press described as the "house of horrors" in Cromwell St, Glouster. Fred West was raised in a rural village by an illiterate sexually abusing father who introduced him to bestiality at age eight and by a mother who seduced him at the age of 12. Fred would boast that his father had slept with his sisters, while he himself had impregnated at least one of them who was aged 13 at the time, leading to charges. His sister refused to name Fred and the case was dismissed. As a child, Rosemary was sexually abused by her sadistic father and her paternal grandfather and in the boundary-less home environment she grew up in, she was regularly sexually involved with younger siblings. Even while Rosemary West was living with Fred, her father would visit to sleep with her, with Fred's knowledge. Fred was to claim that his murdered daughter, Heather, was actually fathered by Rose's father, Bill Letts (Woodrow, 2011).

In August 2003, a 51-year-old man received a 15-year sentence in the Swindon Crown Court (England). His then 31-year-old daughter had experienced two decades of sexual assaults from her father from age eight and had given birth to the first of six children to her father at age 19. Despite the alarming number of children (three of whom had genetic disorders and disabilities), neither her mother or other relatives pressed the issue of the identity of the father (BBC, 2003).

Such cases did not ignite a confluence of societal awareness. However, following worldwide reporting on Josef Fritzl, press reports emerged featuring a "Columbian Fritzl" (*Mail Online*, 2009), an "Australian Fritzl" (Rintoul, 2009), an "Italian Fritzl" (Pisa, 2009), a "German Fritzl" (*Sky News*, 2011), among others. The frequency of press coverage of such stories peaked in 2009, the year of Fritzl's widely reported trial. The six years beginning January 2007 was chosen as the data examination window for this study because it reflected a period that was likely to be particularly informative as it incorporated the year prior to the Fritzl phenomena and then charted the proliferation of such press accounts, to be followed by some waning as hypothetically such reports became less novel.

METHODS

The popular fascination with Josef Fritzl provided an unprecedented opportunity to source multiple press reports of cases of broadly similar incestuous abuse, many involving fathers every bit as controlling. Extensive English language Google searches using a substantial variety of relevant key words (e.g., *incest, adult, sex slave, monster*) for the six-year period from January 2007, were conducted retrospectively beginning in 2008 and prospectively through until the end of 2012. The object was to identify online press reports that broadly conformed to a description of *ongoing incestuous abuse during adulthood and/or multigenerational sexual abuse, and/or incestuous abuse involving imprisonment or death*. The most productive manner of wording Google searches was to link the name *Fritzl* with the different countries of the world (e.g., *American Fritzl, Polish Fritzl*). All cross-references to related articles were followed up, and repeated checks for updates were made.

In order to produce a press-derived preliminary profile of the common characteristics associated with ongoing incestuous abuse during adulthood, I documented features reported with at least two fathers and discuss them in the following section. In nearly all instances reported, phenomena occurred much more frequently than twice, the only exception being suicide/attempted suicide of incestuously fathered offspring (occurring in respect of the "Sheffield Gaffer" and Armando Gomez).

RESULTS

In this section, the spectrum of cases identified during the years in question is described and a profile of common characteristics derived from reports of severe long-term abuse compiled. Press reports relating to 51 cases that broadly conformed to the italicized descriptor above were identified. Cases came from 25 countries and are outlined in Table 1 (extensive references are available on request). Although most news stories generally followed the essential core features of the Fritzl case, in which a daughter or daughters were kept as virtual or actual prisoners of their father (referred to below as a "Fritzl-like" pattern), some variations require explanation. The brevity of some reports made it difficult to be certain that sexual abuse extended beyond the eighteenth birthday. This was the case with Goel Ratzon, arrested in 2010 on charges of enslavement, rape and incest, who was reported to have fathered a minimum of 37 children (and probably many more) having had sex with multiple "wives" and various daughters (Lappin, 2010), and with the tyrannical gun-toting Jeffrey York, arrested in Ohio in 2010 having kept his wife and seven children captive for many years (Harwood, 2010). Similar issues pertained to the man from Ljubljana, Slovenia, who allegedly fathered a child to his 15-year-old daughter but against whom there had been previous allegations of sexual abuse involving a daughter, then aged 17 (B92.NET, 2009).

Six cases of adult incest did not conform to a Fritzl-like pattern, with four involving a variation on an adult child re-contacting a biological parent after many years (in one case being a man contacting his biological mother). For example, in 2009 Mackenzie Phillips, actress and daughter of singer John Phillips, disclosed that her father had been incestuously involved with her from her late teens until she became pregnant at age 30 and had a termination (Phillips, 2009). In December 2010, Columbia Professor David Epstein was arrested for having a three-year sexual relationship with his then 24-year-old daughter (*Mail Online*, 2010a). A couple of other cases in this genre associated with self-promotion and a questionable story were not included.

A particularly prominent story involving alleged organized multigenerational incest, imprisonment, incest pregnancies, forced bestiality and killings, centered on six members of the Mohler family from Missouri who were arrested in November 2009. Burrell Mohler, Sr., his brother, and Mohler's four sons were accused of gross sexual abuse in multiple forms towards Burrell Mohler, Jr.'s daughters (Netter, 2009).

An analysis of the 51 identified international cases reveals at least 29 that were associated with living incestuously fathered children, and of these, only three were not characterized by threats and violence. (It was not clear from the limited information whether *Bronislaw K.* from Poland had also fathered the "granddaughter" he developed a sexual interest in – see *New Poland Express*, 2012 – though an article in Polish confirmed the existence of at least one incestuously fathered child, a seven-year-old son – see *Fakt.pl*, 2012 – and his trial report confirmed that he had raped his granddaughter – see *Gazeta Wbuska* 2012.) Twenty-five of the remaining 26 cases were associated with elements of extreme threats, violence or imprisonment. Bearing in mind the brevity of information in some reports, at least eight involved the use of firearms. The sort of violence experienced by daughters was frequently extreme; Juana Elvira Gomez described being beaten for "any reason" by her father who always had a loaded gun and who would attack her with a rod or a machete. She bore ten children to her father, including her first born, a son, who committed suicide at 16 when he found out his paternity (*thestar.com*, 2010). There was insufficient information available to clarify how much violence occurred in the Slovenian case.

The average duration of incestuous abuse associated with these 25 cases was between 19 and 20 years. (This duration is probably conservative, given that published durations of sexual abuse of daughters could be imprecise, for example, the duration of sexual abuse perpetrated by the Bradford man on his stepdaughter and daughter, in published accounts, has to be a minimum of 11 years but could be substantially higher, see *Huffington Post*, 2012.)

Many such cases related to daughters held in sexual slavery for decades, with at times large numbers of pregnancies resulting (e.g., Arcebio Alvarez, Armando Lucero, Jose Agostina Pereira, Armando Gomez, the "Sheffield Gaffer", Detlef Spies). An extreme response to news of Fritzl's crime occurred with a Russian incest victim, Olga Androva, who at age 26 had endured ten years of abuse from her stepfather and had three children by him. After watching coverage of Fritzl's daughter giving evidence of her extreme abuse, Olga took her abuser's rifle and shot him through the head (*The London News*, 2009). Another of the incestuous abusers, Jose Agostina Pereira, was decapitated in a prison riot in 2011.

The longest period of reported incestuous abuse in any of the 51 cases involved the 80-year-old Austrian, Gottfried Wagner, who allegedly sexually abused his two daughters for over 41 years (*Herald Sun, 2011*). A 72-year-old Croatian was arrested in May 2011, accused of raping his 46-year-old daughter over a 35-year period (*Croatian Times*, 2011), and Adolf Bergbauer was arrested in March 2011, accused of raping his daughter for 34 years (*Huffington Post*, 2011). Perhaps the deadliest abuser was Mexican Jorge Iniestra Salas, arrested in September 2011. He was accused of imprisoning and abusing two teenage stepdaughters, the progeny of his social worker girlfriend, over a seven-year period and fathering five children by them. He allegedly beat one of them to death and smothered the three-month-old baby they had together (Boyle, 2011).

In many press accounts there are references to the families and members of the local community being aware of the ongoing abuse but not effectively intervening (e.g., in the Gouardo, Spies and Shamblin cases). Raymond Gourdao did not hide being the father of his stepdaughter's six children, indeed he even openly boasted about it, and it was common knowledge among the 396 inhabitants (including the mayor) of the French village of Coulommes. A neighbor described Gouardo as a "violent man" who abused his family "all day long", adding, "Nobody wanted to know" (Millot, 2007).

TABLE 1: Incestuous Abuse During Adulthood and/or Multigenerational Sexual Abuse, Imprisonment, or Deaths: International Press Reports, 2007–2012

John McMillan, Scotland 2007, two incestuously fathered children, three daughters abused, one for 16 years

Raymond Gouardo, France 2007, 28 years of abuse, six incestuously fathered children

John Deaves, Australia 2008, seven-year incestuous relationship, two incestuously fathered children

Josef Fritzl, Austria 2008, 31 years of abuse, seven incestuously fathered children

Mr Y and Ms A, New Zealand 2008, incestuous relationship, both convicted

Eleuterio Soria, Argentina 2008, two incestuously fathered children

Maltese man, Malta, 2008, 11 siblings, extreme abuse, two killed, one committed suicide

Krzysztof Bartoszuk, Poland 2008, two incestuously fathered children – forced adoptions

Sheffield case, UK 2008, 30 years of abuse, 19 pregnancies, nine incestuously fathered children

Kishore Chava, Mumbai, India 2009, incestuously abused two daughters, nine years of abuse

Armando Lucero, Argentina 2009, 27 years of abuse, seven incestuously fathered children

"Anish Sharma", Chandigarh, India 2009, eight years of abuse

Beth Carpenter's father, Scotland 2009, two incestuously fathered children, three sisters abused

Nikolay Kirkov, Russia 2009, three incestuously fathered children

TABLE 1: continued

Lindolfo Thibes, Los Angeles, USA 2009, 20 years of abuse, three incestuously fathered children

Irish couple, Donegal, Ireland 2009, raped by parents, mother gave birth to son's child(?)

Chelmsford case, UK 2009, 33 years of abuse, two incestuously fathered children

John Phillips, USA 2009, ten-year incestuous relationship with daughter, one pregnancy

Moe, Victoria case, Australia 2009, 30 years of abuse, four incestuously fathered children

Melbourne Doctor case, Australia 2009, four-year incestuous relationship, one incestuously fathered child

Daniel Rinehart, USA 2009, 14 years of abuse, four incestuously fathered children (three died)

"Heinz", South Africa 2009, raped 18-year-old imprisoned daughter up to three times per day for two months

Mohler family, USA 2009, six alleged perpetrators (father, uncles, grandfather), multiple child victims

Arcebio Alvarez, Columbia 2009, 11 children to daughter, eight surviving, (14 pregnancies)

Michele Mongelli, Italy 2009, 25 years, forced abortion, son, Giuseppi abusing own four daughters

"Irish Fritzl", Ireland 2009, imprisoned, repeatedly raped, five incestuously fathered children

Ljubljana man, Slovenia 2009, one incestuously fathered child, three daughters abused

Jose Agostina Pereira, Brazil 2010, eight incestuously fathered children to two daughters, abused two of the children

Goel Ratzon, Israel 2010, 37-plus children to wives and daughters

Malaysian man, Malaysia 2010, wife and two daughters fled household, 28-year sentence

Melbourne man 1, Australia 2010, nine years of abuse, one intellectually disabled daughter abused/prostituted

Melbourne man 2, Australia 2010, 14 years of abuse, two daughters abused

Kirkland mother, USA 2010, 18-month sexual relationship with adult son aged

Jeffrey York, USA 2010, wife and seven children held captive for up to 15 years, rape/imprisonment

Detlef Spies, Germany 2010, eight incestuously fathered children, prostituting daughter and stepdaughter

Aswad Aleyinde, USA 2010, six incestuously fathered children, five abused daughters

Armando Gomez, Argentina 2010, 30 years of abuse, ten incestuously fathered children (one committed suicide)

Former radio announcer, Mbabane, Swaziland 2010, several years of abusing daughter from age 14

David Epstein, USA 2010, three-year incestuous relationship with 24-year-old daughter

Josef Sablatura, Czech Republic 2011, 22 years of abuse, two incestuously fathered children

TABLE 1: continued

Man from Zadar, Croatia 2011, 35 years of abusing mentally disabled daughter
Harry Larsen and Tine Jensen, Denmark 2011, ten children abused, including 21-year-old daughter
Gottfried Wagner, St Peter am Hart, Austria 2011, 41 years of abuse, two daughters abused
Jorge Iniestra, Mexico 2011, five incestuously fathered children, two daughters abused, two murders
Adolf Bergbauer, Germany 2011, 34 years of abuse, three incestuously fathered children, two died
Man from Jutland, Denmark 2012, 16 years of abuse, nine children abused (including seven of his own)
Bradford man, UK 2012, three incestuously fathered children to daughter and step-daughter
Bronislaw K., Poland 2012, one incestuously fathered child, abused daughter for 30-plus years, raped granddaughter
Seweto man, South Africa 2012, three incestuously fathered children
Charles Shamblin Jr., USA 2012, three incestuously fathered children, 13 years of abuse
Father and daughter from Dunedin, New Zealand 2012, one incestuously fathered child

Analysis of common characteristics of the broader grouping of incestuous fathers and associated family dynamics represented by individuals such as Michele Mongelli, Detlef Spies, Arcebio Alvarez, the Sheffield "Gaffer" and Josef Fritzl produces a profile that frequently but not exclusively includes:

- Subjecting a daughter to thousands of acts of sexual abuse, usually extending over decades
- Father seemingly deliberately having an ongoing number of children
- Father's active avoidance of contraceptives
- Father outwardly appearing as a good neighbor/citizen
- Death threats to daughter and/or daughter's children to ensure compliance
- Forcing daughter to deny the abuse to any enquiring authorities
- Extending sexual abuse to daughter's siblings and offspring
- Forcing children to perform sexual acts on each other
- Keeping the incestuously abused daughter in the family home long term
- Years of concern by child safety authorities without definitive intervention
- Father threatening daughter with loaded guns/knives/axes, and so on
- Father perpetuating acts of severe physical violence
- Psychological domination of daughter by father
- Daughter(s) having a very isolated existence at best, and being a prisoner at worst
- Fathers never spontaneously calling a halt to the abuse or admitting guilt
- Father telling daughter that it was his right to have sex with her
- Daughter used as a sex slave with whom to enact sexual or sadistic fantasies

- Daughter left for periods with father or abandoned to him entirely
- Daughter being forced to reenact scenes from hardcore pornography
- Incestuous pregnancies resulting in stillbirths, deaths or congenital illnesses
- Suicide/attempted suicide of offspring of incestuous abuser
- Use of "home schooling" to limit daughter's contact with the outside world
- Limited or no formal education provided for incestuously fathered children
- Father sexually abusing daughter in front of her children
- Father frequently changing address to thwart authorities
- Father threatening or warning off potential boyfriends
- Father not registering births of incestuously fathered children
- Father abusing alcohol
- Mother abandoning daughter, remaining silent or defending husband
- Mother claiming to be unaware of incestuous abuse spanning decades
- Mother beaten and threatened in similar fashion to daughter
- Assaults by father to produce termination of a pregnancy
- Despite DNA-proven paternity, father forcing daughter to testify in court
- High infant mortality of incestuously fathered children
- Large numbers of incestuously fathered progeny
- The sexually abused daughter(s) never having the opportunity to marry
- Evidence of children's enduring attachment to parental perpetrators
- Initial extreme reluctance for victims to cooperate with police investigations
- Local community aware of abuse but not intervening
- Once arrested, father blaming daughter/other family members

The selected representative international cases described below, and their dynamics, have much in common with the majority of cases.

The Sheffield "Gaffer" (United Kingdom)

In November 2008, it was reported that a self-employed businessman from Sheffield had been sentenced to life in prison after admitting raping his two daughters over a 30-year period. He made them pregnant 19 times; nine children being born, seven of whom remained alive. Police had been notified of the ongoing abuse more than 20 years before the "Gaffer" was arrested. Official action was endlessly forestalled by the man repeatedly changing address, such that his daughters never remained in one place long enough to confide in friends. When he made the eldest pregnant at 14 he beat her in the abdomen in a crude attempt to make her lose the baby. When she subsequently gave birth and the authorities did not catch on, he realized that there was money to be made from government child support benefits. He threatened to kill both daughters as well as their children if they ever spoke out. So disturbing was the home environment that his son attempted to commit suicide at the age of only seven. On March 10, 2010, a Serious Case Review documented a catalogue of failures by 28 agencies and more than 100 care workers (Sims, 2008: Greenhill, 2010).

Arcebio Alvarez (Columbia)

In March 2009, Arcebio Alvarez, 53, appeared in court on charges of incestuously abusing Alba Nidia Alvarez, a 35-year-old woman who claimed to be his daughter.

Arcebio Alvarez claimed that he was innocent, saying Alba was not his biological daughter: "I adopted her. We agreed to have a romantic relationship because we really loved each other. But she was not my own child" (*Mail Online*, 2009). Alba described how from the age of nine she was raped repeatedly and had become pregnant on 14 occasions, giving birth 11 times during 24 years of incestuous abuse. Her first child arrived when she was 13 (*Mail Online*, 2009). DNA testing proved Arcebio to be her biological father and the biological father of seven of her eight children. Rather than finding protection in her family, Alba experienced an uncle trying to abuse her in similar fashion to her father. When as a teenager Alba developed a romantic attachment to a 17-year-old neighborhood boy, her father turned up at the boyfriend's house with a gun in his hand forcing Alba to end the relationship. According to Alba, her father did not just rape her, but had designs on her daughters also (*Semana*, 2009).

Man from Moe (Australia)

In 2009, a Victorian man was charged by police having raped his daughter, then in her 40s, almost daily for 30 years while keeping her a virtual prisoner and fathering her four children. He discouraged her from making any friends. All her children were born with health issues in major Melbourne hospitals, with one dying with severe developmental problems shortly after birth. The rapes began in the 1970s when the daughter was 11 and continued until 2007, two years after the woman had first approached police having been encouraged by a neighbor. Fearful at that time, she refused to press charges. None of the woman's children's birth certificates recorded the name of the father, and he, like Tommy Thompson, used the threat of violence to ensure compliance and silence. The family was known to authorities for more than 30 years. DNA tests established paternity. In December 2009, the father pleaded guilty to 13 counts (five of incest, five of rape, two of indecently assaulting a girl under the age of 16, and one of assault) (Rintoul, 2009). The woman's mother claimed no awareness of any abuse despite living with her daughter, husband and grandchildren until 2005.

Detlef Spies (Germany)

Spies, a 48-year-old West German lorry driver, was arrested in August 2010 and charged with 350 counts of sexual abuse and grievous sexual assaults on minors. He was accused of forcing his then 27-year-old stepdaughter, Natascha, to give birth to eight of his children, as well as sexually abusing his daughter, Jasmin, and his stepson. The offences occurred over 23 years, dating from 1987 when he began sexually abusing his four-year-old twin stepchildren. Spies was also convicted for prostituting Natascha and his biological daughter 35 times with two men. Natasha's brother said "everyone" knew about the abuse and Spies' alcoholism. At one stage there were no less than 15 children living in Spies' house. Natascha's brother observed that no one had the courage to go to the police and that authorities had made many basic mistakes with previous investigations – such as questioning the children while Spies was present. Gabriele Schulte, who delivered three of Natascha's babies, was seemingly reassured by the veneer of normalcy exhibited by Spies. "He was always polite and you could have a good conversation with him" (*Sky News*, 2011; Bates, 2011). In passing sentence, Judge Winfried Hetger observed, "Jasmine today is completely torn apart. She told the court that she still loves her father" (thejournal.ie, 2011).

Harry Larsen and Tina Jensen (Denmark)

In June 2011, Harry Larsen and his wife Tina Jensen from Brondeslev became the first couple in over 30 years to be convicted of child neglect in Denmark. Larsen's crimes included regularly raping his 21-year-old eldest daughter, imprisoning her in a room without heating or electricity, forcing her to engage in sexual acts with her stepbrother and threatening to kill his sons. Both parents blamed each other for the majority of the abuse. Larsen testified that his wife would force the older ones of the ten children to beat the younger ones. Living in squalid conditions, the family moved frequently to try and avoid the suspicions of local authorities, though two councils, Lolland and Skanderborg, had previously been alerted about possible abuses within the family without initiating any investigation (*Ice News*, 2011). In December 2011, on appeal, Larsen's indefinite sentence was reduced to a fixed 11-year term, despite being found guilty of an additional charge, that of forcing his eldest daughter to engage in a sexual act with a horse. Jensen's four-year sentence was not changed by the court despite being found guilty of the charge of forcing her eldest daughter to dig her own grave. Two of Jensen's children attended her hearing and were reported as joking with and hugging their mother (*The Copenhagen Post*, 2011).

Charles Shamblin Jr. (United States of America)

Shamblin, then 56 years old, from Pratt, West Virginia, was sentenced to prison in July 2012 having allegedly sexually abused his daughter from when she was aged seven until she was 20, fathering three children in the process. The first birth occurred when his daughter was just 14 years old, with paternity testing in 2012 confirming him to be the father of all three. Shamblin's daughter-in-law commented: "The community up there looked the other way. . . . They knew what was going on. They've seen the bruises, they've seen the marks on the children and on their mother and they looked the other direction." The daughter-in-law said that the incest had been reported to police 20 years before Shamblin's conviction but his daughter refused to cooperate and DNA testing was not available. "She completely denied it. The state, the prosecuting attorney and the deputy said that they couldn't do nothing" (Thompson, 2012).

Although there is a demonstrated propensity for incestuous abusers to produce children, there are examples of individuals suffering extreme abuse over long periods without births. A prominent example is "Laura", the daughter of Michele Mongelli, a 64-year-old Italian scrap metal worker with eight sons and two daughters, who was arrested for allegedly sexually abusing his 34-year-old daughter over 25 years and for encouraging his then 41-year-old son, Giuseppi, to follow his example. Giuseppi was accused of sexually abusing not only his sister, but also his four young daughters, aged six to 20. It was alleged by investigators that Michele had been raping Laura since she was nine and had held her as a sex slave.

The prosecutor described Laura, according to a family rule, as being "reserved" for her father. Laura had complained to authorities as a 19-year-old about the abuse, but her complaint had been judged unreliable on the grounds that she was "disturbed".

Laura stated: "My father didn't just rape me but my sister also. Her eldest child was fathered by our father. . . . My brother raped me first and then my father and the same thing happened to my younger sister" (Pisa, 2009). Laura revealed how she was forced by her father to have an abortion.

After Laura contacted police in October 2008, they planted listening devices in the family home and car. In one transcript, Giuseppi's eight-year-old daughter is heard saying, "Dad, get your hands off me. You are a bastard, stop it" (Pisa, 2009). Another bugging device in the house picked up the girl being told, "Get to bed, if you're asleep you won't feel a f***ing thing" (*Ninemsn*, 2009).

On April 4, 2009, a recording, claimed to be that of Michele Mongelli, was played in court. The voice was heard to say, "Come on, you are mine – get up." This was followed by muffled words and the sounds of sex. Mongelli denied the voice was his but the Turin judge was not persuaded (Pisa, 2009).

In January 2012, a 55-year-old Danish man, referred to in the media as "Denmark's Fritzl", was charged with the sexual abuse of nine children, of whom seven were his own. Over a 16-year period in the northern and eastern regions of Jutland the man allegedly abused his son from age four, often sealing his mouth with tape and binding his hands. He was accused of abusing another son, then aged 17, between the ages of six and 11, with that son, and three of his brothers, forced to rape their younger sister. From age five, she was in turn repeatedly sexually abused by her father. On one occasion he allegedly bound her legs before suspending her on hooks and sexually assaulting her. Child welfare officers suspected the man was a possible abuser as early as 2005 but took no action for five years. Following on as it did from the Larsen-Jensen case, Denmark's social minister, Karen Hækkerup, called for a review of how such investigations were handled, stating, "These types of cases are just coming out of the woodwork right now" (*The Copenhagen Post*, 2012).

DISCUSSION

Despite it being mentioned in the form of anecdotal references or in the occasional case study, and despite it representing a clinical dilemma wherever it is referred to, there has been little attempt to assemble cases of ongoing incest during adulthood for meaningful comparative study in the scientific literature. This is puzzling as such individuals may experience more instances of severe, chronic trauma, and hence possibly experience more dissociation than even typical patients diagnosed with dissociative disorders.

In analyzing the 33 studies that examined the prevalence of major dissociative disorders in various settings, Dell (2009) cited the median percentages of patients with diagnosable DID in nonclinical populations as 1.1%. Individuals who have experienced severe and prolonged incest into adulthood may well have a severe dissociative disorder as a result of, and as a way to cope with, this degree of traumatization. Artley (1993) alludes to this:

> June [Thompson] kept her eyes tightly shut and tried to send her mind elsewhere – floating up to the ceiling or close to the window – to pretend that his fiercely concentrating face, the small heap of still warm clothing neatly folded beside her on the bed and the motion of his body might belong somewhere else, with no real connection to her (p. 185).

Clinically one does not generally see individuals experiencing long-term incestuous abuse extending into the adult years where they don't fulfill full diagnostic criteria for DID.

In reporting on a series of 62 patients with DID, Middleton and Butler (1998) found that 13% reported the continuation of incestuous/physical abuse beyond the time of presentation (as an adult of 18 or over). If the percentage of individuals with DID in the general population is even close to the median percentage (1.1%) quoted by Dell (2009), and, congruent with my ongoing clinical experience, approximately 13% of patients with DID experience the continuation of incestuous/physical abuse beyond the time of presentation and as an adult, it is apparent, as demonstrated by burgeoning press reports, that incest continuing into adulthood is far from rare. Such victims carry high suicide risk (and, one expects, high risk of being murdered or dying accidentally), suggesting many are never encountered clinically because they are already dead. Kluft (1995) described six patients known to him with DID who had completed suicide. He stated that four of the six had been abused as adults and that two patients, and intermittently a third, remained enmeshed with their abusers. Four of the six had many alleged abusers. One patient had a history of numerous severe suicide attempts and was markedly prone to dishonesty and boundary-less behaviors.

Press articles understandably focus on the sensational. They generally do not rely on testimony of actual incest victims and do not publish contemporary photographic portraits of victims (though in this regard, Juana Elvira Gomez, Alicja Bartoszuk, Anne Marie Wilson, Ashley Rinehart and Alba Nidia Alvarez are exceptions). Although press accounts are helpful in spontaneously including facts about issues of perceived popular interest and in documenting commonality about many things, they do not establish the general presence or absence of other relevant phenomena (e.g., although it is known that Aswad Ayinde, a self-professed prophet, held extreme and idiosyncratic religious beliefs and deliberately impregnated his daughters to create a "pure bloodline" (Rogers, 2013), we know little about any particular religious beliefs on the part of nearly all the other fathers). While we know that some of the fathers such as Krysztof Bartoszuk, the "Sheffield Gaffer", Detlef Spies and Bronislaw K. were heavy drinkers, we cannot be sure just how generalized such behavior was. Similarly, although a number of fathers such as Raymond Gouardo, Josef Fritzl, Detlef Spies and Armando Lucero had a prior history of criminal activity before being arrested in connection to incest-related offences, in most cases we are unsure of their status in respect to this issue, though the Chelmsford man who sexually abused his daughter for 33 years had no prior convictions.

Generally speaking, the more children that lived in the households of these incestuous abusers, the more sexual abuse victims there were, with some abusers fathering large numbers of progeny; for example, Alwad Ayinde fathered six children arising out of sexual abuse of his five daughters, three of whom he impregnated (Rogers, 2013) – in total he fathered 18 children, nine to his wife, three to two other women and six to his daughters (*Mail Online*, 2010b). Armando Lucero, in addition to the seven children he fathered with his daughter was reported as having had 15 other children (Simpson 2009). Meanwhile Josef Fritzl fathered 14 children, seven to his wife and seven with his daughter, Elisabeth (Marsh & Pancevski, 2009).

While undoubtedly some of the abusive fathers lived in fairly squalid circumstances (e.g., Harry Larsen, Charles Shamblin, Jeffrey York, Jose Agostina Pereira), others lived in dwellings that would not have looked in any ways remarkable within their community (e.g., Josef Fritzl, Gottfried Wagner, Michele Mongelli, Bronislaw K., Armando Lucero, and the man from Moe). While repeatedly there were descriptions of local communities being seemingly generally aware of the ongoing abuse (sometimes extending over decades) without effectively intervening, and of child welfare agencies and police being very slow to take definitive action, there were also press reports of long-term friends/neighbors of some abusers who were shocked at the revelations when they finally came (e.g., in the cases of Josef Fritzl, John McMillan and Bronislaw K.), just as there was shock expressed by neighbors when the quiet but friendly bus driver and local musician, Ariel Castro, was arrested in relation to keeping three kidnapped women in his unremarkable looking house for periods of up to over a decade (Quigley, 2013). John McMillan's daughter, Anne Marie Wilson, sexually abused by her father for 16 years and made pregnant six times, lived with constant death threats to her and her mother. She described her father as a "control freak" who never let her out of his sight, but outwardly she said, "We were a normal family and my father had many friends and a good social life. No one suspected anything" (Silvester, 2008).

Some fathers went through the motions of concealing their ongoing incest from their wives (e.g., Josef Fritzl, Detlef Spies, John McMillan and Beth Carpenter's father), while with others the incest was conducted quite openly – e.g., Daniel Rinehart, Raymond Gouardo, Krzysztof Bartoszuk and Aswad Aleyinde. Even where there was some concealment in the family home, journalists writing about mothers who claimed not to know about decades of incest occurring in the family home and producing multiple pregnancies found such denials hard to accept.

Short press reports tend to focus on the central players and thus the sexual abuse that victims experience at the hands of others associated with their incestuous father don't get a lot of comment (e.g., in the case of Arcebio Alvarez's daughter, there is peripheral mention of an abusive uncle, but no detail, *Semana*, 2009). Alicja Bartoszuk describes her axe-wielding father, assisted by two other men and her uncle, terrorizing her boyfriend, abducting her and then locking her in her grandmother's house (*Croatian Times*, 2010). In the case of Lindolfo Thibes, sentenced to 109 years in prison, although contemporary press reporting doesn't mention it, a Court of Appeal's summary states, "On two occasions, the victim had sex with other men in order for appellant to watch" (P. v. Thibes, 2010). In a few cases, organized abuse is prominently reported (e.g., Detlef Spies regularly prostituting his daughter and stepdaughter), and with the multigenerational aspects of reported abuse in the Mongelli and Mohler families. However, unless novel in themselves, the trend suggested by the cases mentioned here is that the wider abuse networks associated with the father usually go unreported in short press accounts.

General conclusions about the nature of attachment to perpetrators, the abuse history of parents, sexual conditioning, the extent of dissociative phenomena, the spectrum of self-harming and reenactment behaviors, suicidality and the deficits of selfhood in individuals subjected to ongoing incestuous abuse during adulthood have awaited the assembly of a representative series of such individuals, the subject of a recent study which closely examines the abuse experiences and phenomenology of ten such women (Middleton 2013). There has been to a fair degree a decoupling of the incest and dissociation literatures such that it is possible to find texts on dissociative disorders that have little coverage of the dynamics of incest, as well as texts on incest that barely mention dissociation. The complexities of the group highlighted here provide compelling reasons for an integrated focus.

CONCLUSIONS

"These guys live amongst us, they hide in plain sight."
John Walsh (Rafferty, 2013)

Assembled press accounts of ongoing incestuous abuse during adulthood provide convincing evidence of the existence of an internationally represented class of extremely oppressive abusers and a larger group of highly traumatized victims existing within the complex trauma spectrum and about which clinical data to date has principally been anecdotal. Highlighted by press accounts is the reality that extreme incestuous abuse can occur for decades under the very eyes of the broader community, including child protection services. While one particular case, that of Josef Fritzl, resulted in popular fascination with his locked underground dungeon, it was in its basic dynamics fairly similar to many other examples reviewed here, where fear; lack of maternal protection; attachment to incestuously produced offspring; lack of viable safe alternatives; limited education; and an extremely controlling, dangerous, entitled and violent father, were frequently highlighted in press reports.

REFERENCES

Artley, A. (1993). *Murder in the heart*. Hamish Hamilton: London.

B92.NET. (2009, January 30). Slovenia in shock after discovery of its own 'Fritzl' case. Retrieved from http://tiny.cc/dvow4

Bates, T. (2011, February 15). 'German Fritzl' admits fathering 7 children with stepdaughter. *AolNews*. Retrieved from http://tinyurl.com/mdfujwt

BBC. (2003, August 19). Incest father of six jailed. Retrieved from http://tiny.cc/ebwhn

Boyle, L. (2011, September 9). First pictures of 'Mexico's Fritzl' and the horrifying dungeon where 'he abused teenage girls and fathered five children'. *Mail Online*. Retrieved from http://tiny.cc/tuvfw

Braun, B. G. (1985). The transgenerational incidence of dissociation and multiple personality disorder: A preliminary report. In R.P. Kluft (Ed.), *Childhood Antecedents of Multiple Personality* (pp. 127–150). Washington DC: American Psychiatric Press.

Courtois, C. A. (1988). *Healing the incest wound*. New York: Norton.

Courtois, C. A. (2010). *Healing the incest wound – 2nd Edition*. New York: Norton.

Croatian Times. (2010, February 5). Daughter welcomes jail for Polish Fritzl. Retrieved from http://tinyurl.com/m42r27x

Croatian Times. (2011, May 23). Croatian Fritzl arrested after raping his daughter for 35 years. Retrieved from http://tiny.cc/gn368

Dell, P. F. (2009). The long struggle to diagnose multiple personality disorder (mpd): Partial mpd. In P.F. Dell & J.A. O'Neill (Eds.), *Dissociation and the Dissociative Disorders: DSM-V and Beyond* (pp. 403–428). New York: Routledge.

Ellenberger, H. (1970). *The discovery of the unconscious: The history and evolution of dynamic psychiatry*. New York: Basic Books.

Fakt.pl. (2012, March 30). Polski Fritzl! 30 lat gwałcił córkę, a później. Retrieved from http://tinyurl.com/l4knd2d

Fromm E. (1962). *Beyond the chains of illusion: My encounter with Marx and Freud*. New York: Simon & Schuster.

Gazeta Wbuska. (2012, April 2). "Polski Fritzl" terroryzował rodzinę. To już koniec horroru. Retrieved from http://tinyurl.com/lv8st38

Greenhill, S. (2010, March 11). Childhoods stolen by the British Fritzl. *Mail Online*. Retrieved from http://tiny.cc/25aqy

Harwood, J. (2010, September 7). Jeffrey York may have held his wife and seven children captive for as long as 15 years. *The First Post*. Retrieved from http://tiny.cc/ystgd

Herald Sun. (2011, August 26). Austrian horror house worse than Fritzl's. Retrieved from http://tiny.cc/01aym

Herman, J. L. (1981). *Father—daughter incest*. Cambridge, MA: Harvard University Press.

Herman, J. L. (2000). *Father—daughter incest, with a new afterword*. Cambridge, MA: Harvard University Press.

Huffington Post. (2011, December 12). 'German Fritzl' Adolf Bergbauer who had sex with daughter 500 times is cleared of rape. Retrieved from http://tiny.cc/ydlwz

Huffington Post. (2012, March 2). Man who raped daughter jailed for 19 years. Retrieved from http://tinyurl.com/m3chugs

Ice News. (2011, June 29). Denmark incest and abuse parents jailed. Retrieved from http://tinyurl.com/mk2plhl

International Society for the Study of Trauma and Dissociation. (2011). Guidelines for treating dissociative identity disorder in adults, 3rd revision. *Journal of Trauma & Dissociation*, *12*(2), 115–187.

Jessop, M. (2011, February 9). Convicted child molester beheaded by fellow inmates in Brazilian prison riot. *The Blaze*. Retrieved from http://tinyurl.com/ms8npbb

Kinsler, P. J. (1995) A story for Marcie. *Dissociation*, 8(2), 100–103.

Kluft, R. P. (1990). *Incest-related syndromes of adult psychopathology*. Washington DC: American Psychiatric Press.

Kluft, R. P. (1995). Six completed suicides in dissociative identity disorder patients: Clinical observations. *Dissociation*, 8(2), 104–111.

Lappin, Y. (2010, February 11). Alleged Tel Aviv cult leader described as charismatic, yet domineering. *J. Weekly Com*. Retrieved from http://tiny.cc/m2twn

Leff, L. & Thompson, D. (2011, June 3). Jaycee Dugard case: Shocking new details released. *Huffington Post*. Retrieved from http://tinyurl.com/p828wfm

Lunbeck, E. & Simon, B. (2003). *Family romance, family secrets: Case notes from an American psychoanalysis, 1912*. New Haven: Yale University Press.

Mail Online. (2007, October 11). Paedophile used boy he held captive for four years to lure second child. Retrieved from http://tinyurl.com/pq3kxdp

Mail Online. (2009, 29 March 2009) Columbian 'Fritzl' accused of fathering ELEVEN children with his daughter during a 25-year rape ordeal. Retrieved from http://tinyurl.com/mhmgzsd

Mail Online. (2010a, December 10). Ivy League professor charged with incest after 'three-year sexual relationship with his daughter'. Retrieved from http://tiny.cc/sx6n0

Mail Online. (2010b, March 13). Fugees video director 'had six children with own daughters to preserve his own bloodline and survive Doomsday'. Retrieved from http://tinyurl.com/csrn3yt

Marsh, S. & Pancevski, B. (2009). *I'm no monster: The horrifying true story of Josef Fritzl*. New York: Berkley.

Metro. (2008, May 22). Father kept daughter as sex slave. Retrieved from http://tiny.cc/pbrqt

Middleton, W. (2013). Ongoing incestuous abuse during adulthood. *Journal of Trauma and Dissociation*, *14*: 251–272.

Middleton, W. & Butler, J. (1998). Dissociative identity disorder: An Australian series. *Australian and New Zealand Journal of Psychiatry*, *32*, 794–804.

Millot, O. (2007, May 9). Only the heart of darkness. *Libération*. Retrieved from http://tinyurl.com/nxl2m3p

Netter, S. (2009, November 22). Missouri sex abuse case gets even more grotesque. *abc News*. Retrieved from http://tiny.cc/x1rf2

New Poland Express. (2012, May 18). Polish Fritzl suicide attempt. Retrieved from http://tinyurl.com/kvjpp62

Ninemsn. (2009, March 28). 'Italy's Fritzl' taught son to rape: Police. Retrieved from http://tiny.cc/igfzf

P. v. Thibes. (2010). Court of Appeal of the State of California, filed 3/2/10 P.v. Thibes CA2/2. Retrieved from http://tinyurl.com/m9n27q7

Phillips, M. (2009). *High on arrival*. New York: Simon Spotlight Entertainment.

Pisa, N. (2009, April 3). 'Italian Fritzl' sex slave trial underway. *Sky News*. Retrieved from http://tiny.cc/a4rjc

Putnam, F. W. (1989). *Diagnosis and treatment of multiple personality disorder*. New York: Guilford.

Quigley, R. (2013, May 7). Revealed: Kidnap suspect's daughter jailed for 25 years for attempted murder of her 11-month-old baby. *Mail Online*. Retrieved from http://tinyurl.com/c3gxqpd

Rafferty, A. (2013, May 7). Jaycee Dugard family felt 'same joy' when Cleveland woman rescued. *NBC News*. Retrieved from http://tinyurl.com/p2o4pfh

Rintoul, S. (2009, September 18). Dad controlled freed 'incest victim'. *The Australian*. Retrieved from http://tiny.cc/cto6a

Rogers, J. D. (2013, March 1). Fugees' 'Killing Me Softly' music video director on trial for raping and impregnating his daughters. *Madame Noire*. Retrieved from http://tinyurl.com/cfzem46

Ross, C. A. (1989). *Multiple personality disorder: Diagnosis, clinical features and treatment*. New York: Wiley.

Sacco, L. (2009). *Unspeakable: Father-daughter incest in American history*. Baltimore: Johns Hopkins University Press.

Salter, M. (2013, February 17). Grace's story: Prolonged incestuous abuse from childhood into adulthood. *Violence Against Women, 19*: 146–165. Published online. Retrieved from http://vaw.sagepub.com/content/19/2/146

Semana. (2009, April 29). The daughter of the Colombian monster. Retrieved from http://tinyurl.com/lk7ofzn

Silvester, N. (2008, May 11). Pregnant six times by my dad; exclusive Scots sex slave victim breaks silence after dungeon horror. *Sunday Mail* (Glasgow Scotland). Retrieved from The Free Library http://tinyurl.com/m7rh5b7

Simpson, A. (2009, May 11). Argentina's Fritzl: Monster of Mendoza accused of fathering seven children by daughter. *The Telegraph*. Retrieved from http://tinyurl.com/kut8jac

Sims, P. (2008, December 20). Our ordeal at hands of 'British Fritzl': Son breaks silence to tell of abuse and rapes. *Mail Online*. Retrieved from http://tinyurl.com/ctxsst

Sky News. (2011, February 23). Wife of 'German Fritzl" refuses to testify. Retrieved from http://tiny.cc/ne6o2

The Copenhagen Post. (2011, December 16). Child sex abuser gets reduced sentence.. Retrieved from http://tinyurl.com/7rp4rqu

The Copenhagen Post. (2012, January 20). Sex abuse cases to be reviewed. Retrieved from http://tinyurl.com/7vkfgg9

thejournal.ie. (2011, March 22). German father convicted of 162 abuse counts. Retrieved from http://tinyurl.com/mus2ema

The London News. (2009, August 4). Life for Russian sex slave who killed stepdad after watching Fritzl's TV trial. Retrieved from http://tiny.cc/6d0nd

thestar.com. (2010, November 26). Argentine woman says father abused her for 30 years; had 10 kids with her. Retrieved from http://tinyurl.com/n3cvos7

Thompson, P. (2012, July 22). Man jailed for incest after fathering daughter's three children when she was just FOURTEEN. *Mail Online*. Retrieved from http://tinyurl.com/dy2a4q9

Trotta, D. & Gray, K. (2013, May 10). Longest-held Cleveland captive now out of hospital, in seclusion. *Reuters*. Retrieved from http://tinyurl.com/cvw7fcz

Woodrow, J. C. (2011). *Rose West: the making of a monster*. London: Hodder & Stoughton.

Ongoing Incestuous Abuse During Adulthood

WARWICK MIDDLETON, MBBS, FRANZCP, MD
The Cannan Institute, Brisbane, Queensland, Australia; La Trobe University, Melbourne, Victoria, Australia; University of Queensland, Brisbane, Queensland, Australia; and University of New England, Armidale, New South Wales, Australia

Individual cases of adult incestuous abuse have surfaced repeatedly in the lay and professional literature of the past 1.5 centuries without it occasioning systematic investigation, such as the reporting of a case series of individuals subjected to such extreme abuse. Yet substantial numbers of patients with dissociative identity disorder at the time of presentation report incestuous abuse continuing into the adult years, and for many the abuse is ongoing. Data relating to a series of 10 such incestuously abused women are presented. These patients were sexually abused from a very early age (typically from before age 3), with the manipulation of their sexual response a key component in conditioning an enduring sexualized attachment. Shame and fear were also used to ensure compliance and silence. The women, when able to speak of it, describe the induction by their paternal abuser of orgasm at an early age, typically around the age of 6. The women have high indices of self-harm and suicidality and are prone to placing themselves in dangerous reenactment scenarios. The average duration of incestuous abuse for this group of women was 31 years, and the average estimate of total episodes of sexual abuse was 3,320. Most women do not feel that they own their body and experience being "fused" to their father. Their mother was reported as an active

---

A version of this article was given as a plenary presentation at the 6th World Congress for Psychotherapy on August 27, 2011, in Sydney, Australia.

participant in the sexual abuse or as having done nothing to protect their daughter despite seeing obvious evidence of incest. The fathers, despite a propensity to use or threaten violence, were generally outwardly productively employed, financially comfortable, and stably married and half had close church involvement. However, suicide and murder occurred within the 1st- or 2nd-degree relatives of these women at a high frequency. All 10 had been sexually abused by various groupings of individuals connected to their fathers.

Well more than a quarter of a century ago, Goodwin (1985) observed that childhood sexual abuse was "the category of abuse with the longest and most fascinating history of disbelief" (p. 5), while Summit (1989) observed that psychiatrists have tended to be "reluctant followers" rather than leaders in advancing concerns about child abuse. Goodwin (1993) noted that the rediscovery of child abuse had been "reluctant and halting, meeting resistance at every step" (p. 90). Salter (2003) made the point that "sexual predators are stunningly effective at gaining control over their victims" (p. xi) and that very few ever spend time in prison because "they simply take on the lifestyle and manner of genuinely nice people, and it is understandable, if tragic, that we can't tell the difference" (p. 139). Bryant (2009), in his 7-year investigation of the Franklin scandal, meticulously documented the ability of powerful networks of perpetrators to subvert the political, law enforcement, and justice systems and even to silence the press. Groth (1979) described his conclusions after spending more than 8 hr assessing a multiple murderer: "At his best, Eric impressed us as personable, likable, and friendly. He was able to express affect which ranged from warm humor to painful hurt freely, openly, and appropriately" (p. 46). Groth's research findings were that despite the personable persona of many perpetrators, some 5% of all rapes were sadistic in nature. Salter described in some detail the innate human tendency to view the world through rose-colored glasses (i.e., as we would like it to be rather than as it really is). As early as 1984 Kluft reported diagnosing dissociative identity disorder (DID) in one or both parents in 40% of his cohort of childhood DID cases, while Braun (1985) reported on a personal series of 18 patients with DID in which some evidence of dissociative phenomena was observed and/or reported in the families of all 16 female and 2 male cases.

A concern with the multigenerational aspects of dissociative disorders as well as with the sadism experienced by many with DID has been present from early on in the modern dissociative disorders field, yet there has been a clear reluctance, despite references to such cases existing, to examine what actually happens in the lives of individuals for whom incestuous (frequently sadistic) abuse never ceases. At one level this could represent a resistance to relinquishing the rose-colored glasses and accommodating one's worldview to the reality of the last frontier of extreme ongoing abuse (i.e., abuse that essentially never ends), and at another level it could represent a self-preserving caution on the part of a field traumatized by previous attempts to define areas of extreme abuse with respect to ritual abuse, mind control, and related entities. Kluft (1994) referred to a finding that the average individual with DID had been sexually abused over a 10-year period and then conceptualized the challenges associated with treating such individuals by invoking what he termed "the mathematics of misery": "If a victim of father-daughter incest is violated twice a week, 50 weeks a year, for 10 years, then approximately 1,000 incestuous violations have occurred" (p. 124). Clearly such a victim has a whole different order of magnitude of psychological issues compared with an individual whose principal trauma has been limited to, say, one episode of rape (yet this in itself can have serious psychological consequences). But what if one were to extend Kluft's mathematical model past the 30-year mark, and what if the frequency of sexual abuse generally occurred at about the same frequency as it did in the first 10 years? An analysis of this world is what forms the basis of the present study.

HISTORICAL ACCOUNTS

Sacco (2009) identified more than 500 reports of father–daughter incest referenced in more than 900 newspaper articles across the United States, particularly between 1817 and 1899. One concerned Joel W. Perkins, tried in 1871 in Connecticut. Jenkins confessed that for 10 years he had repeatedly raped all six of his daughters. He was convicted by jury of murdering three of the six babies that resulted. In 1869 a well-to-do Indiana farmer was convicted of having raped all six of his daughters and at least one granddaughter. The eldest daughter testified that the incest had continued for so long that she had no idea whether her children were the offspring of her husband or her father. "Yet what the newspaperman considered most surprising was 'that the old man . . . has for years been a member of the church, and has always been upright and honorable'" (p. 33).

By 1906 Prince had published the first monograph dealing in detail with what today would be called DID; however, the study of dissociative disorders was effectively buried by psychoanalysis (which gave a central importance to Oedipal fantasy and beliefs in hysterical mendacity) and by the broadening of Kraepelin's construct of dementia praecox to the schizophrenia of Bleuler (Middleton, Dorahy, & Moskowitz, 2008).

Occasionally a publication would surface dealing with actual abuse and the dissociation of the victim. As referenced elsewhere (Middleton, 2013), the earliest psychoanalytic case (aside from Freud's Dora) that was published and for which case notes survive was Rachel C, treated by Louville E. Eugene Emerson over the period 1912–1915 (Lunbeck & Simon, 2003). It is significant that such an early psychoanalytic case should revolve around the dynamics of the incestuous family structure, ongoing incest during adulthood, and a highly dissociative patient who over time was observed to have had fugue states, marked amnesias, "hallucinations," and "splits" in her personality. Rachel oscillated between self-hate for initiating sex (expressed at one juncture by inflicting a 2-inch gash to her left breast) and rage at her parents.

Morselli's case of "Elena," published in 1930, represents another account of incestuous abuse occurring during adulthood (Ellenberger, 1970). Elena was admitted under Morselli's care in 1925 and gradually recovered her

> forgotten memories at the cost of terrifying emotional abreactions. She remembered having been the victim of her father's incestuous attacks (the reality of which was confirmed from other sources). . . . Her flight into a French personality was thus an attempt to repress the memory of her father's "tongue" and for his incestuous attacks in general. (p. 139)

CONTEMPORARY ACCOUNTS IN THE PROFESSIONAL LITERATURE

Very little was published in the psychoanalytic literature about actual incest/sexual abuse until the 1990s, by which time it had long been apparent that incest, far from being rare, as was claimed in leading texts up to around 1980, was endemic. The popular press had been awash for many years in numerous reports of severe incestuous abuse before psychoanalysis was able to belatedly recognize that no one had ever been cured of an "oedipal fantasy" (Simon, 1992). A unique and much neglected paper by Yates published in 1982 detailed the effects of being prematurely eroticized as a young child. Yates described such children as maintaining high levels of sexual arousal and of being orgasmic as preschoolers.

Yates (1982) made the point that "the incestuous union may be the only available source of nurturance in an emotionally barren family" (p. 482). She observed,

> In my experience, many incestuous children are uncommonly erotic. They are easily aroused, highly motivated and readily orgasmic. The degree of eroticization seems closely related to the intensity and duration of the incestuous union. The original mode (e.g., heterosexual or homosexual, oral-genital, extra-genital) remains highly cathected. These observations are consistent with the observation that sexual responsiveness is learned behavior. (p. 482)

As severe incestuous abuse (and associated childhood traumas) and the genesis of dissociative disorders, trauma spectrum disorders, complex posttraumatic stress disorder, and so on, became more robustly linked together, the phenomena of reported satanic ritual abuse and lack of historical accuracy for some recovered memories of childhood trauma became lightning rods for a growing backlash that particularly targeted the dissociative disorders field. The field adopted a new defensiveness as it navigated these turbulent waters, becoming doubly circumspect about uncorroborated reports concerning various forms of ritual abuse.

In 1990, under the editorship of Richard Kluft, the multi-author text *Incest-Related Syndromes of Adult Psychopathology* was published. One major adult incest-related syndrome that did not feature in this text was . . . incest. Herman's 1981 text had likewise not mentioned ongoing incestuous during adulthood, nor was it covered in the second edition of her book or by Russell (1986) in her large-scale community study of childhood sexual abuse and incest. Yet adult incestuous abuse has surfaced repeatedly in the lay and professional literatures of the past century and a half without it engendering any systematic investigation or the reporting of a series of individuals subjected to such extreme abuse. There had been a brief reference to the case of a young woman subjected to ongoing incestuous abuse by her "solidly upper middle-class" parents in Courtois's (1988, p. xiv) text on incest, whereas Putnam, in his 1989 text on multiple personality disorder, made a brief reference to the phenomenon, noting that "actual abuse of adult [multiple personality disorder] patients by family members does occur and can touch off devastating crises" (p. 296).

The fact that such patients were not rare in the dissociative disorders field, and that they pose particular challenges, was demonstrated in a 1995 paper by Kluft in which he analyzed the cases of six patients with DID who were well known to him and who had committed suicide. Four were abused during adulthood, and two individuals, and intermittently a third, remained enmeshed with their abusers. Four had many alleged abusers. Nearly a decade earlier Kluft (1986) had tangentially touched on the problems of ongoing abuse in the adult multiple personality disorder patient, observing that "when patients' current external life circumstances are difficult and/or patients remain enmeshed with their abusers, their treatment becomes singularly difficult because they rarely can tolerate the discontinuing of their dividedness and dissociative defenses" (p. 55).

The most comprehensive multi-author dissociation text of its day was edited by Michelson and Ray (1996), but it only briefly touches on incest. When in 1997 the International Society for the Study of Dissociation released guidelines for treating DID (International Society for the Study of Dissociation, 2000), there was no reference to the treatment needs of adult patients still subject to ongoing incestuous abuse. The largest compendium of chapters on dissociation and dissociative disorders ever published is the text edited by Dell and O'Neill (2009). The issue of ongoing incestuous abuse during adulthood does not directly appear, though Kluft (2009) provides a case study in which the potential for additional abuse at the hands of a past abuser is canvassed. Clearly Kluft has a very acute awareness that his patient with DID remains at substantial risk of reabuse, despite the passage of many years. Courtois (2010) stated that she has "now worked with a number of clients whose abuse continued into their adult years and whose abusers, mostly fathers, largely considered their daughters their property to do with as they pleased" (p. 32). She stated that the prevalence of such cases is unknown.

The most recently revised DID treatment guidelines (International Society for the Study of Trauma and Dissociation, 2011) explicitly acknowledge that long-term incestuous abuse commonly merges with organized abuse, that some individuals with DID are still being incestuously abused at the time of presentation, and that for others a sudden deterioration in their ability to function may signify the renewed involvement of a prior incestuous abuser. Yet relying on the scientific literature, it would be easy to assume, even today, that ongoing incest during adulthood is something that happens rarely. What initially challenged this belief is the lay literature.

CONTEMPORARY ACCOUNTS IN THE LAY LITERATURE

Periodically, extreme cases incorporating ongoing incestuous and/or multigenerational abuse surfaced in the lay press over the years, including the case of Tommy Thompson, who was finally killed in 1988 by his two adult daughters, who had suffered lifelong abuse (Artley, 1993). Another case was that of a 51-year-old father sentenced to 15 years imprisonment in the Swindon Crown Court in August 2003. His then 31-year-old daughter had experienced two decades of his sexual assaults from age 8 and had given birth to the first of six children to him by age 19. Despite the alarming number of children (three of whom had genetic disorders and disabilities), none in the family pressed the issue of the identity of the father (BBC, 2003).

The Josef Fritzl case reached global consciousness in 2008 and more than any other factor seemed to ignite worldwide reporting in the lay press of cases of incestuous abuse extending into adulthood (Middleton, 2013). Fritzl had sexually abused his daughter Elisabeth for a total of 31 years, 24 years of which involved her being held captive in a locked cellar, where she gave birth to seven children, one of whom died 3 days after birth (Marsh & Pancevski, 2009). She was subjected to an estimated total of 3,000 sexual assaults by Fritzl (The Telegraph, 2010).

Subsequent to the Fritzl case many broadly similar cases were reported. A study analyzing such press reports (Middleton, 2013) identified 44 cases from 24 countries reported in the English language over 5 years from January 2007 and accessible via Internet searches. At least 24 of these cases were associated with living incestuously fathered children, and of these, only 2 were cases that were not characterized by long-term threat and violence. Of those cases involving violence and the birth of incestuously fathered children, the average duration of incestuous abuse was approximately 20 years. In at least eight cases, including that of Fritzl, the abusive father was reported as using guns to ensure compliance. Two of the abusers, Fritzl and Jorge Iniestra Salas, were charged with murder, and at least two of the abusers were themselves murdered (Nagpal, 2009; The Blaze, 2011).

Many such fathers, Fritzl included, often looked unremarkable to the outside world, living comfortably in a family environment and gainfully employed. Yet at home they were enormously entitled, psychologically dominating, and controlling in the extreme, forcing their daughters to deny abuse to any that might inquire and frequently reinforcing such commands with weapons, death threats, and beatings. So confident were they in their abusive practices that abuse would occur in front of wives or their daughter's children. Courtois (2010) cited a notorious case in the District of Columbia involving "a man who had engaged in incest with all of his own children into their adult years in addition to all of his foster children" and who "was named the foster father of the year in his community" (p. 152). Something approaching a Messianic complex was attributed to a couple of fathers, Aswad Ayinde (Mail Online, 2010) and Goel Ratzon (Frenkel, 2010). Some fathers, such as Michele Mongelli (Pisa, 2009) or Burrell Mohler, Sr., allegedly would facilitate a son or sons actively entering into the transgenerational abuse pattern of the family. Their daughters were isolated at best and in the more extreme cases were kept as actual prisoners at home. Many of the fathers actively wanted their daughter to have children with them. Arcebio Alvarez from Columbia made his daughter pregnant 14 times, resulting in 11 births and 8 surviving children (Mail Online, 2009).

None of the fathers who had continued the incestuous abuse from childhood ever spontaneously desisted, and the longest period of incestuous abuse that surfaced in press reports was in regard to the 80-year-old Austrian Gottfried Wagner, who allegedly sexually abused his two daughters over a 41-year period (Herald Sun, 2011). Such fathers frequently treated their daughters as sex slaves, forcing them to reenact scenes from hardcore pornography, something that many such men were fixated on. They would claim it was their right as a father to have sexual access to their daughter long term, yet even when exposed, and despite DNA evidence establishing paternity, they would frequently mount a prolonged court defense, trying somehow to rationalize the abuse as a consensual or love relationship. Usually the daughters led very isolated lives. Potential boyfriends were warned off. Some fathers involved others in the abuse of their daughter via prostitution (e.g., Detlef Spies; The Link, 2011) or via the involvement of other family members (e.g., Michele Mongelli, Pisa, 2009; or allegedly Burrell Mohler, Sr., Netter, 2009).

Child safety authorities and police repeatedly demonstrated extreme tardiness in taking any definitive action (e.g., in respect to the Sheffield "Gaffer" a Serious Case Review in March 2010 spelled out a catalogue of failures by 28 agencies and more than 100 care workers that stretched back many years; Greenhill, 2010). Mothers offered no more protection, either abandoning their daughter(s) to the father, becoming a co-abuser, remaining silent, or defending their husband. Even in households moderately to heavily populated with incestuously fathered children, such as those of Detlef Spies, Josef Fritzl, Amando Lucero (Pertossi, 2009), Raymond Gouardo (IOL News, 2008), or Beth Carpenter's father, marriages were nevertheless very enduring.

Although the lay press rarely prints a sophisticated analysis of the psychological effects these so-called monsters have on their victims, some windows periodically emerge. Jaycee Lee Dugard, then an 11-year-old, was kidnapped by Phillip and Nancy Garrido on June 10, 1991, from a school bus stop, having been immobilized by a stun gun. Taken to Antioch on the outskirts of San Francisco, she was locked in a soundproofed room erected in the Garridos' backyard. There she was repeatedly sexually assaulted by Phillip Garrido, a paroled rapist. Her spontaneous description of how she coped was typical of the dissociative responses of so many who have had to endure inescapable ongoing trauma: "There was a switch. I had to shut off. [I] just went someplace else . . ." Jaycee put it simply: "You just do what you have to do to survive." Jaycee described Nancy as being in some ways just as manipulative as her husband (Sawyer, 2011). An early report (Gardner & Bowden, 2009) described Jaycee as expressing guilt about bonding with her abuser, even though the alternative could well have been death.

With respect to Tommy Thompson's daughter June, Artley (1993) recounted how during sexual abuse

> June kept her eyes tightly shut and tried to send her mind elsewhere—floating up to the ceiling or close to the window—to pretend that his fiercely concentrating face, the small heap of still warm clothing neatly folded beside her on the bed and the motion of his body might belong somewhere else, with no real connection to her. (p. 185)

BACKGROUND TO THE PRESENT STUDY

Analyzing 33 studies that examined the prevalence of major dissociative disorders in various settings, Dell (2009) cited the median percentages of patients with diagnosable DID in nonclinical populations as 1.1.

In reporting on a series of 62 patients seen in Brisbane, each of whom fulfilled diagnostic criteria for DID, Middleton and Butler (1998) included the finding that 13% of this group reported the continuation of incestuous/physical abuse beyond the time of presentation (as an adult; i.e., beyond their 18th birthday). Subsequent clinical experience is congruent with the observation that the percentage of patients with DID who have experienced ongoing incestuous abuse (usually involving a father) during the adult years is as least as high as was reported in 1998.

Clinically speaking one does not generally see dissociative individuals with a history of long-term incestuous abuse extending into the adult years who do not fulfill full diagnostic criteria for DID. Such individuals are at particularly high risk for suicide, and, in order to be still alive (and not chronically psychotic), they will have needed to dissociate to the extent that such a diagnosis defines.

METHODOLOGY

In order to better document the particular personal characteristics, family dynamics, and phenomenology associated with ongoing incestuous abuse during adulthood I selected a personal sample of 10 women who had been exposed to such a phenomenon. Ten seemed to be a sufficiently high number for common trends and representative issues to become apparent. These individuals were identified in late 2009 when the extent of clinical contact resulted in enough data for meaningfully examination. Clinical data were collected and tabulated over an extended period, with all data collection being informed by the lay and professional literatures and by ongoing clinical experience.

It transpired that I was actively treating 10 such individuals when this study was contemplated. Aside from these 10 there has been substantial contact with a larger number of others in the spectrum of adult incestuous abuse seen either before data began being tabulated in late 2009 or subsequently.

RESULTS

Family Structures and Demographics

As of early 2011 the women ranged in age from 26 to 57, with an average age of 41. First contact with these individuals spanned 1993 to 2009. Three were married, four were divorced or separated, and the other three had never married. Half were occupied by work or full-time study. Four were working, or had previously worked, as some sort of health professional. At least six of the women had had children. In the case of one, an incestuously fathered child had been given up for adoption when she herself was a young adolescent schoolgirl. I saw a photo taken of her in the company of her mother as a heavily pregnant 14- to 15-year-old. She stated, "Mum and Dad stuck together and called me a 'slut.' I recall them saying, 'We're going to say it's your 14-year-old boyfriend and that you sleep around.'" With half, at one stage or other I had some form of direct personal contact with one or both of the parents.

None of the 10 had parents who were not married at the time of their birth. Only one set of these parents ever divorced. Even then they seemingly remained on friendly terms. Three of the patients had lost their fathers and two of these had also lost their mothers. None was an only child, and they came from official sibships that averaged out at just under four. Membership of sibships, however, could be complicated, with one patient fully aware that a young man who was officially her cousin was in reality a half-brother, having arisen out of a sexual union between her father and his sister-in-law. Another was aware that a child born to a younger sister, at the time attributed to a nonexistent boyfriend, was in fact fathered by her own father. At least 4 out of the 10 women were aware of the existence of incestuously fathered children to relatives that were no more distantly related than an aunt or uncle. One reported her father siring children with five different women.

Characteristics of the Abuse

Although all 10 had been abused sexually by their fathers and by multiple others, the majority (80%) had also experienced sexual abuse by one or more of their grandparents. A total of 60% reported being sexually abused by an uncle and 40% by a sibling. The average age at which sexual abuse was reported as starting was 2.7 years, progressing to full intercourse at 3.8 years. The mean duration of incestuous abuse was 31 years (the same period experienced by Josef Fritzl's daughter Elisabeth). The average number of sexual abuse episodes was 3,320 (a figure close to the estimated number of abuse episodes that Elisabeth Fritzl was subjected to). The average age of this group of women, 41, was close to the age of Elisabeth Fritzl at the time of her release from captivity. A total of 70% experienced some variation of multigenerational/extended family sexual abuse. For example, one reported being sexually abused by both grandfathers, by her father, by her mother, and by both brothers (one in tandem with her then-husband on occasion), and this brother continued the abuse up to contemporary times until curtailed by a court order (only for her then to be sexually abused by a treating doctor). She also had had sexual contact with her only sister in the context of their abuse by their father. Another reported being abused by her grandfather, father, mother, and brother.

Two reported long-term sexual abuse at the hands of three generations of their fathers' families (i.e., a grandfather, father, and brother), whereas a third reported extensive sexual abuse involving her father and to a lesser degree her mother, as well as earlier sexual abuse by a maternal uncle and, on one occasion, her maternal grandfather.

With no patient was her sexual abuse limited to only her father, and aside from other family members sexual abuse for at least 80% also occurred in some variant of child prostitution. Some fathers forced their daughter to provide sexual favors for work- or church-related groups of men.

All reported their mother witnessing their sexual abuse by their father, and 90% reported seeing their father sexually abuse other children. Moreover, 70% of the mothers were reported as also being directly involved in some aspect of sexual abuse on occasion, and in 30% of cases this extended to directing the father to have sex with the daughter. One described her mother inciting the abuse by saying, "Do it to her more Mikey! Break her!" Another described her father sexually abusing her in the kitchen while her mother did chores at the sink. At night she would hear her mother encouraging her husband to go to her bedroom and have sex with her, a prelude to their own sexual encounter. Finally, 90% were aware that at least one other sibling was also subjected to incestuous abuse.

No mother reported the abuse to any child protection authority. When someone else did make a notification, all mothers ultimately supported their husband/ex-husband. In two cases, when allegations of the father's sexual abuse of his daughter had prominently surfaced, the mothers had considered for a short time leaving their husband but within a couple of weeks or so had shifted in their declared position and were back with the father, where they remained.

With half the group pregnancy was first experienced at an age of 17 or younger, with the earliest pregnancy being at around age 12, and 70%–80% had experienced one or more terminations (of incest pregnancies) and a generally similar number had experienced miscarriages. The probability that one or more of their children was incestuously fathered was an issue for at least 60%. Around 80% had been through the abortion of one or more incest-related pregnancies. A similar percentage reported that their father wanted them to have a child.

As with many examples in the international press nearly all (90%) received death threats from their father or threats that they would go to hell, and 70% at one time or other had experienced their father and/or grandfather encouraging suicide. A concerted attempt by their father to kill them was reported by 30%. In addition, 70% described on occasion being tied up or otherwise constrained during episodes of abuse, and many had experienced extreme violence, whereas 80% experienced being locked in rooms or kennels as a child. The proportion who had experienced physical abuse injuries of sufficient magnitude to warrant surgery or who carried internal genital injuries occasioned by abuse was 70%. A total of 80% of the fathers were witnessed being cruel to animals. No less than 90% reported the use of dogs in their sexual abuse. In all cases the father and/or brother were involved in taking pornographic pictures of the daughter. Almost the first act of one of these women on her father's death was to burn his photo collection. One carried extreme scarring to one leg caused, she said, by her father attacking her with an activated edge trimmer. Another stated, "I had a double-barreled shotgun held at my head. I heard them say, 'She's too cute to kill.'"

Four had experienced the murder and/or suicide of a close relative or friend, and indeed one had sustained multiple such losses. One had had a grandmother murdered by her partner; another's grandfather, uncovered as an incestuous abuser, killed himself. Another individual's paternal uncle had committed suicide.

These women were brought up in dangerous environments, with 80% experiencing abusers using guns to threaten or intimidate, the use of guns incorporated into the sex act, or their abusers threatening to shoot them. One reported bullets being regularly fired in her vicinity, another's grandfather ultimately committed suicide with the same gun used to threaten her and her cousin, a third experienced her father discharging a gun beside her head, and a fourth carried a scar attributed to a deliberate wound occasioned by an air rifle.

Several described guns being inserted vaginally. The extremes of violence and threat that were woven into one woman's life at the hands of her father, an associate of her father, and others in her extended family or social network might stretch comprehension, but for the fact that so much of it was corroborated by newspaper articles. One sibling was murdered by her husband, who then committed suicide. The same man who kept a handgun had also severely abused her in multiple ways, including deeply scalding her in a bath as a child. An uncle committed suicide. Two cousins separately committed suicide. A very close friend was shot in front of her, and she took an active role in tackling the armed killer. Another close friend was murdered by an ex-partner and father of her children, who, apart from killing her, tried to cut out her heart. Both killers at the time of this writing remained in jail. The stepdaughter of one of her primary abusers was in jail for murdering her partner. Another close friend died tragically in a motor vehicle accident. Both her father and his deeply criminal and armed younger abuse partner had tried at various times to induce her to suicide. She described her father throwing her off a balcony onto the roof of a building below. On another occasion, attacked by a sibling, she crashed through a second-floor glass window onto the ground below. She was midway through surgical repairs to grievous vaginal injuries inflicted on her decades ago. Multiple others on the periphery of her life had died of overdoses or been murdered.

The Families

Outwardly, the fathers of these women seemed unremarkable. All were, or had been, gainfully employed. Their financial circumstances ranged from modest to extremely wealthy. At least half had been, or were, closely involved with a church. One died as a lifetime member of a fundamentalist religion that espoused the principle of women playing a subservient role to men. Another tried to establish a second career as a Pentecostal preacher.

Of the women, 90% knew their father had had a dysfunctional upbringing, and three stated that he had himself been incestuously abused. Three had witnessed a grandfather having sex with their father. Each of these women, based on her observations of him switching, was certain, or believed it likely, that her father also had DID. A fourth woman held a similar belief. Only two felt confident that their father did not have a condition akin to DID.

In addition, 60% knew or believed that their mother had herself been sexually abused; 20% believed that their mother herself had a major dissociative disorder, whereas a further 30% suspected it.

As with Detlef Spies and the Sheffield "Gaffer," more than half the fathers had a history of heavy drinking. Clearly, the fathers, once married, executed dominance over their households. In 90% of cases the father would walk around the house naked or nearly naked. One lived in a house, a converted hall, with few internal walls, and he would have sex with his wife at various places in the dwelling in front of his children, who likewise were kept naked. Another would repeatedly rape his wife in front of his youngest daughter, explaining that this was his way of displaying his love. A third father would leave the toilet door or bathroom door open when performing his ablutions. He would then display mock outrage toward his daughter for "perving" on him whenever she chanced upon him in these situations.

Such was the ownership, control, and conditioning imposed on these women's lives that at the time of presentation most struggled to conceptualize themselves as separate autonomous human beings. A total of 80% felt "fused" with their fathers, and 90% described feeling that their body did not belong to them. All of them had an introjected version of their father as one of their alters. Yet despite this, no less than 90% had given serious contemplation to killing their father, and indeed one as an adolescent had cut the brake lines of her father's car. Another had embedded a cricket stump into an abusive brother's head. At least three fathers had become aware of their daughters' plans to kill them.

The Manipulation of Sexual Arousal

The manipulation of orgasm seems central to the sorts of conditioning associated with this spectrum of abuse, and it forms a key component of the abuser's generation of shame to ensure the silence of the victim. Congruent with Yates's 1982 finding, the average age at which these women first became orgasmic was 6. Most (70%+) experienced their father telling them that sexually they were better than their mother, and like the abuse victims described in the international press many experienced periods when sexual abuse occurred with a frequency that exceeded once a day. All of them experienced their father telling them to ask him for sex, and the great majority (80%) experienced their father as controlling the sexual feelings they were allowed to have and controlling the circumstances in which orgasm was experienced. Some described how it was never possible to achieve orgasm without thinking of the father. What was generally apparent with virtually all these women was the extreme control exerted by their fathers over virtually all areas of their lives, but particularly over their sexual functioning.

Most (60%) experienced sexual arousal as something that only occurred in association with abuse. For example, one acknowledged that the men she picked were psychologically a recreation of her father. With most, the father's semen became part of the introjected controlling father, with some impressing on their daughter a model that equated semen with them living inside their daughter. In 80% of cases the father took an active role in the creation of named alters, with such identity states performing particular sexual roles. A similar number reported their father actively inducing dissociative switching. Three fathers, like Tommy Thompson (Artley, 1993), had their daughter wear a special ring or bracelet. One such ring had the patient's initials displayed on a gold heart-shaped emblem and the reverse side inscribed with "Love Dad" and a date. Another, some 18 years after her husband had become aware of the abuse and it had been reported to police, found two pieces of jewelry deposited in their letter box engraved with "Daddy's girl," "I mean what I say," and "It's your fault." Most (70%) recalled having had the status of being the "favored child."

Such was the power of the attachment and so central was sex as the currency of relatedness that most (60%) were aware of occasions in which they set up scenarios that could be expected to result in their father having sex with them. For the 70% who married, sexual abuse by the father did not stop. Even absent or dead fathers lived on as introjected conditioning entities, and 80% set up sexual reenactments based around fathers. Virtually all (90%) were subjected to critical questioning regarding alternative sexual partners, and all experienced their father actively undermining any relationship with a prospective boyfriend.

Even a dead father's role was largely inherited by another individual from within the family or extended abuse grouping (e.g., one woman in her late 40s had already had two abortions associated with her sexually abusing violent brother). "He tells me I'm not allowed to tell anybody. He says that I deserve it . . ." Finding a safe partner in such circumstances is problematic, and of the seven who married at least once, three married someone who was flagrantly abusive and the fourth had an extremely brief marriage. Of the six women who had children of their own, two thirds knew or strongly suspected that their father had sexually abused at least one of their own children. At least 70% of fathers coerced their daughters into having some form of sexual contact with their own offspring or with a young relative.

Control Issues

Half of these women experienced outright financial theft on the part of a parent. This fit the pattern exemplified by the international group in which the father exerted enormous control over all aspects of living and imposed an isolationist regime. For example, as children, 50% were allowed only limited opportunities to play with other children. The rest had no opportunity at all. Only one, on a single occasion only, was allowed to have a friend sleep over.

Involvement with the Mental Health System

All of these women had experienced substantial suicidal ideation, and no less than 80% had survived serious suicide attempts. One had somehow twice survived jumps from close to the top of a multistory car park, the injuries making her permanently crippled. In taking out a restraining order on her parents, she stated, "I've [been] that stripped of my life, there's nothing left but to say everything. They've got me on Clozapine." A total of 70% had ended up in intensive care following a suicide attempt. Half the group had severe external scarring from self-harm, whereas 90% had self-harmed their genitals, reflecting deeply unresolved issues about a conditioned sexuality, attachment to their abusers, and associated self-hate. Moreover, 90% had, or continued to have, an eating disorder. A diagnosis of schizophrenia had previously been given to 40%. All but one had had multiple mental health unit admissions. At the most extreme, the youngest of the group had spent the majority of the previous decade hospitalized, having been admitted on more than 100 occasions during this period. Her extreme self-harm, suicide attempts, and loud intrusive voices had resulted in a diagnosis of chronic schizophrenia and treatment with Clozapine.

Finally, 40% of this group had been sexually abused by one or more doctors or therapists, and in 20% of cases this included a psychiatrist. One such psychiatrist was subsequently suspended from practice for his sexual involvement with another female patient.

Dissociative Phenomena

Reflecting the extremely high levels of dissociation in this group of women was an average initial Dissociative Experiences Scale score of 62 (Carlson & Putnam, 1993) for the nine who had initially completed it. Between 80% and 100% heard their father's voice internally, heard his voice and/or footsteps externally, experienced the sensation of being touched, and smelled and tasted things in the absence of external stimuli. In addition, 80% experienced voices as being louder than normal conversation and never experienced their head as silent. Nearly all had answered the voices out loud on occasion despite people being present. Most experienced substantial periods when they were in states that felt as if they were out of present time. Moreover, 90% experienced somatic sensations of vaginal intercourse when entirely alone, and no less than 50% were aware of experiencing orgasms in their sleep associated with dreams of their father. At least 40% on looking into a mirror would on occasion see their father's face, and a similar percentage would see a child's face.

The Fathers

Characteristically the fathers demonstrated extreme projection, extreme self-justification, pervasive self-focus, and a sense of total ownership exemplified by statements such as "I brought you into this world and I can take you out!"

One woman, a victim of multigenerational abuse, described her grandfather telling her, "You make good people do bad things." Her father would tell her, "You are a bitch on heat. You make people do it. It's your fault."

Any expression of regret for their actions on the part of the abusing fathers was rare. One, in the middle of being sexually abused as an adult, would repeatedly experience her father suddenly yelling out to his wife, "Annabelle! I must stop doing this!" Another father, thought by his daughter to have DID, not long before his death made a vague and oblique apology, stating, "Maybe I'm wrong. I don't remember everything. If I did do something, I'm sorry."

All 10 women had had at least some contact with police with respect to some aspect of their abuse. At the time of this writing two had successfully taken out aggravated violence orders against primary family abusers, and another had formally raised concerns with child safety authorities about her father's contact with a niece. A fourth had notified police about an individual known to her who had been collecting child sexual exploitation pictures, and he was duly convicted.

Corroboration

Evidence in addition to scars and internal injuries that corroborated the generally unwavering accounts of extreme abuse given by these 10 women was substantial. In the case of one I was able to interview at length the patient's sister and all of her adult children. Both of the older individuals had experienced similar abuse at the hands of her father and his associates. Three others found photos or video recordings that showed serious examples of their abuse. Elements of the extreme violence and abuse associated with the extended family of another were the subject of a number of newspaper articles. My interactions with various parents of these women gave no cause to doubt their account of what life was like in their particular family. The father of one who had been made a ward of the state as a child because of the abuse was hostile and abusive in the one nonprovocative phone contact I had with him. Another vacillated between being threatening and being ingratiating, whereas a third father caught himself out in a crucial lie that underscored his involvement in his daughter's abuse. Taking into account corroborative accounts, photos and videos showing abuse, utterances of parents, internal injuries/scarring, newspaper accounts, engraved jewelry, sworn court evidence, past medical records, and the internal consistency of accounts over time, there could be little doubt that these 10 women had been abused in ways consistent with their descriptions.

DISCUSSION

In comparing the content of what has been written regarding the adult incest scenarios in international press reports with the sort of data reported here, several observations emerge. Press reports are drawn largely from police briefings or court transcripts, and little of the average victim's subjective account appears. A great many of the issues canvassed here are essentially never going to be commented on in the popular press. The things that are described in press accounts regarding the father's assumed ownership of his daughter, using her as a sex slave, isolating the daughter, making death threats, or producing weapons; mothers failing to protect; child safety departments being ineffectual; the enormous difficulty daughters have in following through with a formal police report; the father doing things that are sadistic; the duration of the incestuous abuse and the number of occasions of incestuous abuse; as well as instances of fathers demonstrating extreme preoccupations with hardcore pornography, prostituting their daughter, abusing other children, and extending the focus of their abuse to the progeny of their own abused daughter; as well as multigenerational abuse are all entirely congruent with the sort of data presented here. In today's society extraordinary abuse can perpetually occur in family settings without triggering any helpful public awareness. Young in 1964 sagely commented on extremely abusive isolationist families:

> Opportunities to express individual interests, to satisfy curiosity normal for any child, to explore and pursue private projects usually a part of the learning experience of childhood were denied. *In effect, the children were withdrawn from the contacts and experiences which might have taught them that not all families were like theirs.* (p. 61, italics added)

Isolated, dominated, sexually stimulated and conditioned from infancy, the unprotected recipient of unending parental projection, and bonded to their abusers, who use a combination of fear, shame, and conditioning while taking up permanent introjected residency in their psyche, it is apparent at presentation that it has not been possible for the victims of such extreme abuse and deprivation to attain enough selfhood (see Middleton, 2005) *to achieve escape velocity from their ambivalently attached principal abusers, be they alive or dead.* As concerning as it sounds, Josef Fritzl probably did not need to build an underground enclosed prison behind eight locked doors in order to sexually abuse his daughter and father children to her without anyone intervening. The multigenerational abuse experienced by some adds credence to the observations of most of the women that at least one parent had themselves been sexually abused as a child and that many of these may have developed a dissociative disorder.

Sophisticated abusers, including some therapists, are adept at manipulating the vulnerabilities of women such as the 10 described here, who have been highly conditioned sexually since early childhood, who are very prone to reenactments, who experience sexual arousal in relation to abuse, and who have learned long ago the dire consequences of refusal. Sex for these women for large parts of their lives had been forced to become a central component of their attachment behavior. It thus becomes inevitable, in longer term therapy with such individuals, that such transferences are likely to emerge. At one time or another, 60% of these women spontaneously raised the issue of having sex with their therapist. This had nothing to do with anything said that could have remotely suggested such a possibility. For some the proposition came early, as if part of the conditioned way in which all relationships were commenced, whereas for others it came late and at a time when the impossibility of such a relationship was seemingly very clear. Such propositions seemed mainly about confirming for themselves that they were safe.

In this spectrum one encounters scenarios that do not make it into texts. One father used his daughter's mobile phone camera to photograph himself sexually abusing his (adult) daughter, though avoiding any shots that identified his face. Recently she recovered photos of herself as a seriously injured and malnourished 5- to 6-year-old that I myself saw. The ex-husband of another woman reported to me that their marriage went into terminal decline the day he unexpectedly returned home to find evidence that his wife had just had sex with her father in their marital bed. Another woman, in the hospital, struggling to effect a separation from her father, contrived a pretext for demanding immediate discharge. The underlying reason was her compulsion to seek out her father and have sex with him. Another woman wanted me present at the time she told her husband that incestuous abuse at the hands of her (now dead) father had continued through the earlier years of their marriage.

One woman, whose incestuous abuse had commenced at the hands of her maternal grandfather, stated that the precipitant of his death was a son arriving unexpectedly to find his father in the act of sexually abusing his 10-year-old daughter. An ugly scene developed. The next day the grandfather got the handgun that he used to terrorize his child victims and shot himself, his death being reported as the result of a heart attack. Another, visiting her parent's house, was going through some old family videos when to her shock she saw footage of her father exposing her as a young adolescent. Her mother's only comment was, "That was the way it was then . . ." The video was subsequently viewed by police and by the woman's current partner.

I have personally encountered a palpable resistance by at least some health professionals to the facts associated with ongoing incestuous abuse during adulthood on most occasions when I have publicly presented at a publicized forum on this subject. One or more will directly or indirectly make known their displeasure at having to listen to such material. The criticism is never that what is covered is not thought to be accurate but rather that it is confronting to the point of being traumatizing and that the individual (usually a therapist) would very much prefer not to know about it. Sometimes this point of view is conveyed with considerable anger. If the individual is asked how he or she thus deals with a patient with this sort of history, the response is invariably a rationalization for avoiding awareness of it. Yet as with all other forms of interpersonal abuse silence is the perpetrator's greatest ally.

CONCLUSIONS

Despite the emblematic patron saint of the mentally ill, St. Dymphna, being a young woman who died at the hands of her violent, entitled, and incestuous father, collectively the trauma field has not yet given a proportionate weighting to the reality that in many cases of DID one is not dealing with unlocking the internal barriers that were put up in the past to protect an individual from being overwhelmed by inescapable trauma but in reality one is dealing with an adult whose childhood abuse never ended and whose mindset incorporates the attachment needs of a heavily conditioned child entwined with the self-directed anger, shame, and despair of an adult. This is exemplified by what should in all probability have been the last words ever formulated by one of the 10 women described here, a text to her father stating, "Always Daddy's little girl," before she jumped from a multilevel car park.

REFERENCES

Artley, A. (1993). *Murder in the heart*. London, England: Hamish Hamilton.

BBC News. (2003, August 19). *Incest father of six jailed*. Retrieved from http://tiny.cc/ebwhn

Braun, B. G. (1985). The transgenerational incidence of dissociation and multiple personality disorder: A preliminary report. In R. P. Kluft (Ed.), *Childhood antecedents of multiple personality* (pp. 127–150). Washington, DC: American Psychiatric Press.

Bryant, N. (2009). *The Franklin scandal*. Waterville, OR: Trine Day.

Carlson, E. B., & Putnam, F. W. (1993). An update on the Dissociative Experiences Scale. *Dissociation, 6*(1), 16–27.

Courtois, C. A. (1988). *Healing the incest wound* (1st ed.). New York, NY: Norton.

Courtois, C. A. (2010). *Healing the incest wound* (2nd ed.). New York, NY: Norton.

Dell, P. F. (2009). The long struggle to diagnose multiple personality disorder (MPD): Partial MPD. In P. F. Dell & J. A. O'Neill (Eds.), *Dissociation and the dissociative disorders:* DSM-V *and beyond* (pp. 403–428). New York, NY: Routledge.

Dell, P. F., & O'Neill, J. A. (Eds.). (2009). *Dissociation and the dissociative disorders:* DSM-V *and beyond*. New York, NY: Routledge.

Ellenberger, H. (1970). *The discovery of the unconscious: The history and evolution of dynamic psychiatry*. New York, NY: Basic Books.

Frenkel, S. (2010). Goel Ratzon, Israeli 'harem messiah,' arrested in Tel Aviv. *The Times*. Retrieved from http://tiny.cc/ps2ax

Gardner, D., & Bowden, N. (2009, September 1). Jaycee Lee Dugard: My 'guilt' over bond with captor who fathered my two children. *Mail Online*. Retrieved from http://tiny.cc/p5hvhw

Goodwin, J. M. (1985). Credibility problems in multiple personality disorder patients and abused children. In R. P. Kluft (Ed.), *Childhood antecedents of multiple personality* (pp. 1–20). Washington, DC: American Psychiatric Press.

Goodwin, J. M. (Ed.). (1993). *Rediscovering childhood trauma: Historical casebook and clinical applications*. Washington, DC: American Psychiatric Press.

Greenhill, S. (2010, March 11). Childhoods stolen by the British Fritzl. *Daily Mail*. Retrieved from http://tiny.cc/25aqy

Groth, A. N. (1979). *Men who rape: The psychology of the offender*. New York, NY: Plenum.

Herald Sun. (2011, August 26). *Austrian horror house worse than Fritzl's*. Retrieved from http://tiny.cc/s8hvhw

Herman, J. L. (1981). *Father–daughter incest*. Cambridge, MA: Harvard University Press.

International Society for the Study of Dissociation. (2000). Guidelines for treating dissociative identity disorder (multiple personality disorder) in adults (1997). *Journal of Trauma & Dissociation, 1*(1), 117–134.

International Society for the Study of Trauma and Dissociation. (2011). Guidelines for treating dissociative identity disorder in adults, third revision. *Journal of Trauma & Dissociation, 12*(2), 115–187.

IOL News. (2008, April 29). *Incest victim says world ignored her plight*. Retrieved from http://tiny.cc/ze38e

Kluft, R. P. (1984). Multiple personality in childhood. *Psychiatric Clinics of North America, 7*, 121–134.

Kluft, R. P. (1986). Personality unification in multiple personality disorder: A follow-up study. In B. G. Braun (Ed.), *Treatment of multiple personality disorder* (pp. 29–60). Washington, DC: American Psychiatric Press.

Kluft, R. P. (Ed.). (1990). *Incest-related syndromes of adult psychopathology*. Washington, DC: American Psychiatric Press.

Kluft, R. P. (1994). Countertransference with MPD. In J. P. Wilson & J. D. Lindy (Eds.), *Countertransference in the treatment of PTSD* (pp. 122–150). New York, NY: Guilford Press.

Kluft, R. P. (1995). Six completed suicides in dissociative identity disorder patients: Clinical observations. *Dissociation*, *8*(2), 104–111.

Kluft, R. P. (2009). A clinician's understanding of dissociation: Fragments of an acquaintance. In P. F. Dell & J. A. O'Neill (Eds.), *Dissociation and the dissociative disorders:* DSM-V *and beyond* (pp. 599–624). New York, NY: Routledge.

Lunbeck, E., & Simon, B. (2003). *Family romance, family secrets: Case notes from an American psychoanalysis, 1912*. New Haven, CT: Yale University Press.

Mail Online. (2009, March 29). *Columbian 'Fritzl' accused of fathering ELEVEN children with his daughter during a 25-year rape ordeal*. Retrieved from http://tiny.cc/31uk6

Mail Online. (2010, March 13). *Fugees video director 'had six children with own daughters to preserve his own bloodline and survive Doomsday.'* Retrieved from http://tiny.cc/0eivhw

Marsh, S., & Pancevski, B. (2009). *I'm no monster: The horrifying true story of Josef Fritzl*. New York, NY: Berkley.

Michelson, L. K., & Ray, W. J. (Eds.). (1996). *Handbook of dissociation: Theoretical, empirical, and clinical perspectives*. New York, NY: Plenum.

Middleton, W. (2005). Owning the past, claiming the present: Perspectives on the treatment of dissociative patients. *Australasian Psychiatry*, *13*(1), 40–49.

Middleton, W. (2013). Parent-child incest that extends into adulthood: A survey of international press reports, 2007–2011. *Journal of Trauma & Dissociation*, *14*, 184–197.

Middleton, W., & Butler, J. (1998). Dissociative identity disorder: An Australian series. *Australian and New Zealand Journal of Psychiatry*, *32*, 794–804.

Middleton, W., Dorahy, M., & Moskowitz, A. (2008). The concepts of dissociation and psychosis: An historical perspective. In A. Moskowitz, I. Schäfer, & M. Dorahy (Eds.), *Dissociation and psychosis: Multiple perspectives on a complex relationship* (pp. 9–20). London, England: Wiley.

Nagpal, S. (2009, August 4). Life for Russian sex slave who killed stepdad after watching Fritzl's TV trial. *TopNews.in*. Retrieved from http://tiny.cc/ekivhw

Netter, S. (2009, November 20). Missouri sex abuse case gets even more grotesque. *ABC News*. Retrieved from http://tiny.cc/xB2Is

Pertossi, M. (2009, May 12). Man 'fathered his daughter's seven kids.' *The Age*. Retrieved from http://tiny.cc/umivhw

Pisa, N. (2009, March 28). Italian hid and raped daughter for 25 years. *Sky News*. Retrieved from http://tiny.cc/5vvev

Prince, M. (1906). *The dissociation of a personality*. New York, NY: Longmans, Green.

Putnam, F. W. (1989). *Diagnosis and treatment of multiple personality disorder*. New York, NY: Guilford Press.

Russell, D. E. (1986). *The secret trauma: Incest in the lives of girls and women*. New York, NY: Basic Books.

Sacco, L. (2009). *Unspeakable: Father-daughter incest in American history*. Baltimore, MD: Johns Hopkins University Press.

Salter, A. C. (2003). *Predators, pedophiles, rapists, and other sex offenders*. New York, NY: Basic Books.

Sawyer, D. (2011, July 17). A stolen life [Television series episode]. In G. Martz and K. Gray (Producers), *60 Minutes*. Sydney, NSW, Australia: Willoughby Studios of Channel Nine.

Simon, B. (1992). Incest—See under Oedipus complex: The history of an error in psychoanalysis. *Journal of the American Psychoanalytic Association, 40*, 955–988.

Summit, R. C. (1989). The centrality of victimization: Regaining the focal point of recovery for survivors of child sexual abuse. *Psychiatric Clinics of North America, 12*, 413–430.

The Blaze. (2011, February 9). *Convicted child molester beheaded by fellow inmates in Brazilian prison riot*. Retrieved from http://tiny.cc/4jyiuw

The Link. (2011, March 25). *German 'incest dad' jailed*. Retrieved from http://thelinkpaper.ca/?p=5734

The Telegraph. (2010). *Josef Fritzl's former home to be demolished*. Retrieved from http://tiny.cc/aqivhw

Yates, A. (1982). Children eroticized by incest. *American Journal of Psychiatry, 139*, 482–485.

Young, L. (1964). *Wednesday's children: A study of child neglect and abuse*. New York, NY: McGraw-Hill.

Dissociation and Symptoms of Culture-Bound Syndromes in North America: A Preliminary Study

COLIN A. ROSS, MD, ELIZABETH SCHROEDER, BA, and LAURA NESS, PsyD
The Colin A. Ross Institute for Psychological Trauma, Richardson, Texas, USA

The aim of this study was to determine whether classical culture-bound syndromes occur among psychiatric inpatients with dissociative disorders in North America. The Dissociative Trance Disorder Interview Schedule, the Dissociative Experiences Scale, and the Dissociative Disorders Interview Schedule were administered to 100 predominantly Caucasian, American, English-speaking trauma program inpatients at a hospital in the United States. The participants reported high rates of childhood physical and/or sexual abuse (87%), dissociative disorders (73%), and membership in the dissociative taxon (78%). They also reported a wide range of possession experiences and exorcism rituals, as well as the classical culture-bound syndromes of latah, bebainan, amok, and pibloktoq. Our data are consistent with the view that possession and classical culture-bound syndromes are predominantly dissociative in nature and not really culture-bound from the perspective of Caucasian, English-speaking America.

Dissociative trance disorder was included in an appendix to the *Diagnostic and Statistical Manual of Mental Disorders, Fourth Edition* (*DSM–IV*; American Psychiatric Association, 1994) as a culture-bound diagnosis

This research was supported by a grant from the Jude Jordan Foundation.

requiring further study. Subsequently, Guarnaccia and Rogler (1999) called for systematic study of culture-bound syndromes, including the degree to which they are dissociative in nature. Many of the classical culture-bound syndromes are included in the *DSM–IV* as subtypes of dissociative disorder not otherwise specified (During, Elahi, Taieb, Moro, & Baubet, 2011). Possession experiences and other sudden, time-limited alterations in identity, behavior, and mental state are widely regarded as dissociative in the literature on transcultural psychiatry (Bourguignon, 1976; Cardeña, van Duijl, Weiner, & Terhune, 2009; Huskinson, 2010; Krippner, 1997; Lewis-Fernandez, 1994; Suryani & Jensen, 1993; Swartz, 2011). In addition, *DSM* dissociative disorders and dissociation as measured by the Dissociative Experiences Scale (DES; Bernstein & Putnam, 1986; Carlson et al., 1993; van IJzendoorn & Schuengel, 1996; Waller, Putnam, & Carlson, 1996; Waller & Ross, 1997) have been described in a wide range of cultures (Baita, 2005; Dominguez, Cohen, & Brom, 2004; Fan et al., 2010; Kianpoor & Rhoades, 2005; Kleindorfer, 2005; Martinez-Taboas, 1995; Ross, 1997; Ross et al., 2008; Sar, Akyüz, Kundakci, Kiziltan, & Dogan, 2004; Sar et al., 2003; Saxena & Prasad, 1989; Tutkun et al., 1998; Van Duijl, Cardeña, & De Jong, 2005; Van Duijl, Nijenhuis, Komproe, Gernatt, & de Jong, 2010; Xiao et al., 2006).

In the context of this literature, we developed a structured interview called the Dissociative Trance Disorder Interview Schedule (DTDIS). The DTDIS inquires about a wide range of possession experiences and culture-bound syndromes and was designed to be coadministered with the DES and the Dissociative Disorders Interview Schedule (DDIS; Ross, 1997; Ross & Ellason, 2005; Ross & Halpern, 2009). The DTDIS is the first structured interview designed for the study of culture-bound syndromes and incorporates the *DSM–IV* diagnostic criteria for dissociative trance disorder into its questions. The DTDIS was created in order to provide a standardized interview for study of trauma, dissociation, and culture-bound syndromes.

Based on our prior clinical experience with North American dissociative disorders and our knowledge of the related literature (Bull, Ellason, & Ross, 1998; Ross, 1997, in press), we decided to administer the DTDIS, DES, and DDIS to a sample of 100 inpatients in a North American trauma program with high rates of trauma and *DSM–IV* dissociative disorders. From prior clinical and research experience, we expected that the participants would be predominantly Caucasian, American born, and English speaking; would have high rates of reported childhood trauma and dissociative disorders; and would endorse the typical DDIS profile for chronic, complex dissociative disorders (Ellason, Ross, & Fuchs, 1996; Ross, 1997, in press; Ross & Ellason, 2005). We made the following predictions:

1. The participants will report a wide range of possession experiences and symptoms of culture-bound syndromes despite being Caucasian, American born, and English speaking and will report involvement in

a wide range of shamanistic and ritual healing procedures, including exorcisms.

2. The possession experiences and symptoms of culture-bound syndromes will be positively correlated with scores on the DES and a number of different symptom scales on the DDIS.

We based these predictions on our overall view that the classical culture-bound syndromes are predominantly dissociative in nature and occur in North America, and therefore are not really culture bound or specific to the cultures in which they are classically said to occur (e.g., pibloktoq among the Inuit or latah in Indonesia and Malaysia).

METHOD

Participants

Consecutively admitted inpatients in a trauma program were approached and asked to participate. Of the 100 inpatients who agreed to participate, 79 were female and 25 were married; the average age was 41.6 years (*SD* = 10.9 years). A total of 89 participants responded to a question about nationality: 87 were American and 2 were from Hispanic countries; all 89 were residents of the United States and all gave English as their primary language. Of 88 participants who responded to the question about occupational status, 23 said that they were employed, 56 unemployed, 4 retired, and 5 homemakers; 31 said that they had been in jail in the past. Of 73 participants reporting their annual income, 3 earned $100,000 or more, 11 earned $50,000 to $99,999, 15 earned $25,000 to $49,999, and 44 earned less than $25,000.

All participants gave written informed consent, and the study was approved by the Medical Staff Committee of the hospital, which acts as the internal review board. All participants were covered by either Medicare or private insurance, and all met utilization review criteria for inpatient treatment, mostly because of acute suicidal ideation. This means that the participants were highly disturbed from a clinical perspective. Participants were administered the DDIS and DTDIS by the second author, who also handed them the DES and received it back from them after it had been completed.

Measures

The DES is the most widely used self-report measure of dissociation (Bernstein & Putnam, 1986; Carlson et al., 1993; Dell, 2002; van IJzendoorn & Schuengel, 1996). It has 28 items and has psychometric properties including split-half reliability and test–retest reliability, and it has been analyzed using a variety of advanced statistical techniques (Carlson et al., 1993). Besides yielding a total score that ranges from 0 to 100, the DES can be analyzed using a procedure called taxometric analysis (Waller et al., 1996; Waller & Ross, 1997). This analysis separates respondents into two discrete categories: those with pathological dissociative experiences (in the dissociative taxon) and those without.

The DDIS has been used in a series of research projects in North America, Turkey, and China (Fan et al., in press; Ross, Duffy, & Ellason, 2002; Ross & Ellason, 2005; Ross & Halpern, 2009; Ross et al., 1990, 2008; Ross & Ness, 2010; Sar & Ross, 2009; Xiao et al., 2006). It is a 131-item structured interview that inquires about a range of symptoms and *DSM–IV* diagnoses, as well as childhood abuse. The DDIS had good concurrent validity with the DES ($\kappa = 0.81$; Bernstein & Putnam, 1986), the Structured Clinical Interview for *DSM–IV* Dissociative Disorders ($\kappa = 0.74$; Steinberg, 1995), and a clinical interview ($\kappa = 0.71$) in an inpatient psychiatric hospital in the United States (Ross et al., 2002).

The DTDIS has not been used in any previous studies, and no data on its psychometric properties are available. The DTDIS was developed in order to gather standardized data on possession states and related experiences, including classical culture-bound syndromes such as amok, latah, bebainan, pibloktoq, and ataque de nervios. These syndromes overlap with one another and involve discrete episodes of behavioral dyscontrol, shouting, echolalia, confusion, crying, exaggerated startle, and, in the case of amok, attempts to kill others, which may be successful. Each is described in *DSM–IV* as being culture bound; for instance, pibloktoq is limited to Arctic Inuit populations, ataque de nervios occurs primarily in Puerto Rico, and latah occurs in Malaysia and Indonesia.

The DTDIS is divided into eight sections with a score that varies from zero to a maximum possible in each section. The number of items in each section is as follows: Traditional Treatment, 25; Identity Changes, 15; Environmental Precipitants, 16; Memory, 7; Dissociative Trance, 10; Cognition, 5; Physical and Somatic Symptoms, 16; *DSM–IV* Dissociative Trance Disorder, 6; DTDIS Total Score, 84; and DTDIS Symptom Score, 43. Seven of the section scores are added together to yield a DTDIS Overall Score that ranges from 0 to 84. The Symptom Score is calculated as follows: Total score – (Traditional Treatment + Environmental Precipitants). The diagnostic criteria for the classical culture-bound syndromes are imbedded in the seven symptom sections. The DTDIS makes *DSM–IV* diagnoses of dissociative trance disorder, trance subtype and dissociative trance disorder, possession trance subtype. The questions are close to verbatim transcriptions of the *DSM–IV* criteria.

Data Analyses

For the 100 participants, average DES total scores and the number of participants in the DES taxon were calculated. For the DDIS, average section scores were calculated, including Schneiderian symptoms, somatic symptoms, *DSM–IV* borderline personality disorder criteria secondary features of DID, and extrasensory perception (ESP)/paranormal experiences; also, the number of participants positive for somatization disorder, substance abuse, depression, borderline personality disorder, and the five dissociative disorders was tabulated, as was the number of people positive for a dissociative disorders of some kind. For the DTDIS, the average section scores and Overall Score were calculated. In addition, the number of participants responding "yes" to individual items was tabulated, as was the number of participants meeting criteria for each of the culture-bound syndromes and dissociative trance disorder.

These variables were entered into a Pearson correlation matrix with significance set at $p < .05$. Finally, these variables were entered into a regression analysis with the DTDIS Overall Score as the criterion variable.

RESULTS

Results for the DDIS diagnostic categories and symptom scales are shown in Table 1. For the DDIS questions concerning possession, the number of

TABLE 1 Dissociative Disorders Interview Schedule Findings Among 100 Trauma Program Inpatients

Variable	% Positive	Average score (*SD*)
Diagnosis		
Somatization disorder	24	
Substance abuse	61	
Major depressive episode	96	
Borderline personality disorder	72	
Dissociative amnesia	61	
Dissociative fugue	15	
Depersonalization disorder	45	
Dissociative identity disorder	46	
Dissociative disorder NOS	11	
Dissociative disorder of some kind	73	
Symptom cluster		
Somatic symptoms		9.9 (7.9)
Schneiderian symptoms		3.8 (3.2)
Borderline personality criteria		5.4 (2.2)
Secondary features of DID		6.2 (4.9)
ESP/paranormal		3.8 (3.3)
Conversion symptoms		1.5 (1.8)
Suicide attempts		1.7 (1.7)
Abuse history		
Physical abuse	73	
Sexual abuse	79	
Physical and/or sexual abuse	87	

Notes: NOS = not otherwise specified; DID = dissociative identity disorder; ESP = extrasensory perception.

participants answering "yes" was as follows: possession by a demon, 18; possession by a dead person, 8; possession by a living person, 7; and possession by some other power or force, 16.

The average DES score was 32.2 ($SD = 23.0$), and 78% of participants were in the dissociative taxon. The sample was thus typical of psychiatric inpatients with chronic, complex dissociative disorders and symptoms; severe childhood trauma; and extensive comorbidity in terms of DES and DDIS scores (Ross & Ellason, 2005).

In a Pearson correlation matrix, the DDIS symptom scales, the average DES score, and the DTDIS Total Score correlated strongly with one another, as shown in Table 2. The results of the regression analysis are shown in Table 3.

On the DTDIS, one person was positive for dissociative trance disorder, trance subtype and none were positive for dissociative trance disorder, possession trance subtype. The number of participants positive for each of the classical culture-bound syndromes on the DTDIS was as follows: latah, 11; amok, 11; bebainan, 26; pibloktoq, 3; and ataque de nervios, 0. Average scores on the DTDIS subscales were as follows: Traditional Treatment, 1.6

TABLE 2 Pearson Correlations Between Dissociative Disorders Interview Schedule Symptom Clusters, DES Scores, and DTDIS Total Scores Among 100 Trauma Program Inpatients

Variable	1	2	3	4	5
1. DES	—				
2. Schneiderian	.59***	—			
3. 2° DID	.86***	.59***	—		
4. ESP/paranormal	.34***	.43***	.37***	—	
5. DTDIS	.48***	.55***	.51***	.55***	—

Notes: DES = Dissociative Experiences Scale; Schneiderian = Schneiderian first-rank symptoms; 2° DID = secondary features of dissociative identity disorder; ESP = extrasensory perception; DTDIS = Dissociative Trance Disorder Interview Schedule.
***$p < .0001$.

TABLE 3 Regression Analysis with Dissociative Trance Disorder Interview Schedule Total Score as the Criterion Variable Among 100 Trauma Program Inpatients

Variable	β	Coefficient	*F* ratio	Probability
Schneiderian symptoms	0.33	2.441	17.593	.0001
ESP/paranormal experiences	0.24	1.745	8.521	.004
Somatization disorder	0.24	13.196	9.499	.003
Number of suicide attempts	0.22	2.964	8.186	.005
Constant		−6.326		

Notes: The total variance explained by the regression equation is 53.2%; the overall p for the regression equation is <.0001. ESP = extrasensory perception.

TABLE 4 Healing Methods Reported by 100 Trauma Program Inpatients

Question	Yes	No	Unsure
Exorcism or deliverance	14	84	1
Prayers	31	64	3
Other cure or healing	10	88	1
Herbs or medicines taken	6	10	0
Fasting	2	13	1
Things sucked out of or removed from your body	2	13	1
Healer gone into a trance	4	12	0
Spells cast	4	11	1
Soul retrieved from outside your body	3	11	2
Worked with your dreams	4	12	0
Animal sacrificed	2	14	0
Miracles occur	4	11	1
Incense	6	10	0
Dancing	1	15	0
Ritual music or sounds	6	10	0
Bathed in or washed with blood	1	15	0
Head shaved	1	15	0
Faith in a higher or lower power	12	4	0
Incantation	3	11	2
Scarification (ritual scarring)	4	12	0
Beating or other physical force	3	13	0
Having a hole drilled in your head	0	16	0

Notes: The Dissociative Trance Disorder Interview Schedule questions in Table 4 are formatted as, for example, "Have you fasted because you were possessed or controlled by an outside force?"

(*SD* = 3.5); Identity Changes, 3.4 (*SD* = 3.5); Environmental Precipitants, 2.6 (*SD* = 3.8); Memory, 2.1 (*SD* = 3.0); Dissociative Trance, 2.1 (*SD* = 3.2); Cognition, 1.5 (*SD* = 2.2); Physical and Somatic Symptoms, 3.5 (*SD* = 5.1); *DSM–IV* Dissociative Trance Disorder, 1.16 (*SD* = 2.0); DTDIS Total Score, 18.0 (*SD* = 23.6); and DTDIS Symptom Score, 13.8 (*SD* = 18.1).

Responses to individual DTDIS questions are shown in Table 4.

DISCUSSION

Our predictions were confirmed by the data. The participants reported high levels of childhood physical and/or sexual abuse (87%), dissociative disorders (73%), DES taxon membership (78%), and comorbidity. Their DES and DDIS profiles were typical of those of individuals with chronic, complex dissociative disorders. The participants were predominantly Caucasian, American born, and English speaking, and their DTDIS scores were highly correlated with selected DDIS symptom clusters. Also, the participants reported involvement in a range of exorcism procedures and shamanistic rituals (Eliade, 1964), including having objects sucked out of their bodies; having a healer enter a trance state during a ritual; engaging in soul retrieval, animal sacrifice, or ritual dancing; and being washed with blood. The most common exorcism procedures involved prayer, which is consistent with mainstream Caucasian American Christian practice. Clearly, however, stereotypically "primitive" or cross-cultural practices exist in North America and are not limited to specific ethnic groups such as Hispanic Santeria practitioners.

An additional unexpected finding was the fact that only one person met criteria for dissociative trance disorder, despite the wide range of different possession and culture-bound syndrome experiences. It appears that one of three things must be true: (a) The base rate of dissociative trance disorder is low in this population, (2) the DTDIS is not detecting *DSM–IV* dissociative trance disorder that exists in the population (false negatives), or (3) the *DSM–IV* criteria for dissociative trance disorder are not valid. At the moment, one can conclude only that both the DTDIS and dissociative trance disorder require further study.

Although our data are preliminary in nature, it appears that the classical culture-bound syndromes are not really culture bound. They occur among highly dissociative English-speaking Caucasian Americans. Calling these syndromes culture bound, then, may be an epidemiological error, and one that is based on American and *DSM* ethnocentricity. Just as mainstream clinicians often fail to diagnose dissociative disorders in North America, so too do they fail to diagnose the classical culture-bound syndromes. This is to be expected if the culture-bound syndromes are predominantly dissociative in nature and linked to the *DSM–IV* dissociative disorders.

One might conclude that categorizing latah, bebainan, amok, and pibloktoq as culture-bound syndromes is a form of cultural oppression: When these syndromes occur in cultures outside of Caucasian, English-speaking North America, they are regarded in the *DSM–IV* as "localized, folk, diagnostic categories that frame coherent meanings for certain repetitive, patterned, and troubling sets of experiences and observations" (American Psychiatric Association, 1994, p. 844). The implication is that these cultures are less sophisticated than the mainstream culture of the United States (Lewis, 1971), but our data suggest that the same social, cultural, and psychological forces operate in the United States. The data suggest that for a truly independent observer, English-speaking Caucasian Americans are just as culture bound as any other group in the world. The participants in our study reported a wide range of possession and related experiences and a wide range of ritual exorcism practices.

No participants met criteria for ataque de nervios or reported having a hole drilled in their head as a treatment for possession. This suggests that some syndromes and practices are not universal and may be more culture specific. However, although drilling holes in people's heads is not practiced as a delivery or exorcism technique in North America, our trauma program patients often report cutting on themselves in order to "let the bad feelings out." This could be viewed as a secularized, less radical version of drilling a hole through the skull to let demons out. It may be that there are no truly discrete, specific culture-bound syndromes but instead a range of variants, permutations, and combinations of syndromes and practices across cultures with some culture-specific details.

Some authors believe that the *DSM–IV* unnecessarily pathologizes culturally normal and approved practices (Huskinson, 2010). The fact that suicide attempts were a predictor of DTDIS scores in the regression analysis is not consistent with this viewpoint. The symptoms reported by the participants did not occur solely as part of an accepted religious practice; they were regarded as pathological and treated by nonmedical practitioners with a variety of shamanistic and religious methods usually thought of as primitive and culture bound.

Our study is preliminary because it is based on a single sample. Although this sample was adequate for testing our predictions, further research with the DTDIS should be conducted in a wide range of cultures, languages, and population samples, including both clinical and nonclinical groups. The psychometric properties of the DTDIS need to be established. Within North America, it would be interesting to administer the DTDIS to a variety of groups, including fundamentalist Christians who speak in tongues, patients with conversion disorders or pseudoseizures, mass murderers, sex trade workers, and other populations who might have high rates of dissociation and possession. Also, it will be interesting to determine whether outside North America the classical culture-bound syndromes are accompanied by *DSM–IV* dissociative disorders and severe childhood trauma as they were in our sample.

REFERENCES

Baita, S. (2005). Coping with childhood trauma and dissociation in Argentina. In G. F. Rhoades & V. Sar (Eds.), *Trauma and dissociation in a cross-cultural perspective* (pp. 35–53). New York, NY: Haworth Press.

Bernstein, E. M., & Putnam, F. W. (1986). Development, reliability, and validity of a dissociation scale. *Journal of Nervous and Mental Disease, 174*, 727–735.

Bourguignon, E. (1976). *Possession*. San Francisco, CA: Chandler & Sharp.

Bull, D. L., Ellason, J. W., & Ross, C. A. (1998). Exorcism revisited: Positive outcomes with dissociative identity disorder. *Journal of Theology and Psychology, 26*, 188–196.

Cardeña, E., van Duijl, M., Weiner, L., & Terhune, D. (2009). Possession/trance phenomena. In P. F. Dell & J. A. O'Neil (Eds.), *Dissociation and the dissociative disorders:* DSM-V *and beyond* (pp. 171–181). New York, NY: Routledge.

Carlson, E. B., Putnam, F. W., Ross, C. A., Torem, M., Coons, P., Bowman, E. S., . . . Braun, B. G. (1993). Predictive validity of the Dissociative Experiences Scale. *American Journal of Psychiatry, 150*, 1030–1036.

Dell, P. F. (2002). Dissociative phenomenology of dissociative identity disorder. *Journal of Nervous and Mental Disease, 190*, 10–15.

Dominguez, D. V., Cohen, M., & Brom, D. (2004). Trauma and dissociation in psychiatric outpatients. *Israel Journal of Psychiatry Related Sciences, 41*, 98–110.

During, E. H., Elahi, F. M., Taieb, O., Moro, M.-R., & Baubet, T. (2011). A critical review of dissociative trance and possession disorders: Etiological, diagnostic, therapeutic, and nosological issues. *Canadian Journal of Psychiatry, 56*, 235–242.

Eliade, M. (1964). *Shamanism*. Princeton, NJ: Princeton University Press.

Ellason, J. W., Ross, C. A., & Fuchs, D. L. (1996). Lifetime Axis I and II comorbidity and childhood trauma history in dissociative identity disorder. *Psychiatry, 59*, 255–261.

Fan, Q., Yu, J., Ross, C. A., Keyes, B. B., Dai, Y., Zhang, T., . . . Xiao, Z. (2010). Teaching Chinese psychiatrists to make reliable dissociative disorder diagnoses. *Transcultural Psychiatry, 64*, 483–490.

Guarnaccia, P., & Rogler, L. H. (1999). Research on culture-bound syndromes: New directions. *American Journal of Psychiatry, 156*, 1322–1327.

Huskinson, L. (2010). Analytical psychology and spirit possession: Towards a non-pathological diagnosis of spirit possession. In B. A. Schmidt & L. Huskinson (Eds.), *Spirit possession and trance* (pp. 71–96). New York, NY: Continuum International.

Kianpoor, M., & Rhoades, G. F. (2005). "Djinnati," a possession stare in Baloochistan, Iran. In G. F. Rhoades & V. Sar (Eds.), *Trauma and dissociation in a cross-cultural perspective* (pp. 133–145). New York, NY: Haworth Press.

Kleindorfer, S. O. (2005). Dissociative experiences in the People's Republic of China: An empirical and cross-cultural study. In G. F. Rhoades & V. Sar (Eds.), *Trauma and dissociation in a cross-cultural perspective* (pp. 81–94). New York, NY: Haworth Press.

Krippner, S. (1997). Dissociation in many times and places. In S. Krippner & S. Powers (Eds.), *Broken images, broken selves: Dissociative narratives in clinical practice* (pp. 3–40). Washington, DC: Brunner-Mazel.

Lewis, I. M. (1971). *Ecstatic religion: An anthropological study of spirit possession and shamanism*. Baltimore, MD: Penguin Books.

Lewis-Fernandez, R. (1994). Culture and dissociation: A comparison of ataque de nervios among Puerto Ricans and possession syndrome in India. In D. Spiegel (Ed.), *Dissociation: Culture, mind and body* (pp. 123–167). Washington, DC: American Psychiatric Press.

Martinez-Taboas, A. (1995). *Multiple personality: An Hispanic perspective*. San Juan, Puerto Rico: Puente.

Ross, C. A. (1997). *Dissociative identity disorder: Diagnosis, clinical features, and treatment of multiple personality* (2nd ed.). New York, NY: Wiley.

Ross, C. A. (in press). Trance and possession experiences in dissociative identity disorder: A preliminary study. *Journal of Trauma & Dissociation*.

Ross, C. A., Duffy, C. M. M., & Ellason, J. W. (2002). Prevalence, reliability, and validity of dissociative disorders in an inpatient setting. *Journal of Trauma & Dissociation, 3*(1), 7–17.

Ross, C. A., & Ellason, J. W. (2005). Discriminating among diagnostic categories using the Dissociative Disorders Interview Schedule. *Psychological Reports, 96*, 445–453.

Ross, C. A., & Halpern, N. (2009). *Trauma model therapy: A treatment approach for trauma, dissociation and complex comorbidity*. Richardson, TX: Manitou Communications.

Ross, C. A., Keyes, B. B., Xiao, Z., Yan, H. Q., Wang, Z., Zou, Z., . . . Zhang, H. (2008). A cross-cultural test of the trauma model of dissociation. *Journal of Trauma & Dissociation, 9*, 35–50.

Ross, C. A., Miller, S. D., Reagor, P., Bjornson, L., Fraser, G. A., & Anderson, G. (1990). Structured interview data on 102 cases of multiple personality disorder from four centers. *American Journal of Psychiatry, 147*, 596–601.

Ross, C. A., & Ness, L. (2010). Symptom patterns in dissociative identity disorder patients and the general population. *Journal of Trauma & Dissociation, 11*, 458–468.

Sar, V., Akyüz, G., Kundakci, T., Kiziltan, E., & Dogan, O. (2004). Childhood trauma, dissociation and psychiatric comorbidity in patients with conversion disorder. *American Journal of Psychiatry, 161*, 2271–2276.

Sar, V., Kundakci, T., Kiziltan, E., Yargic, L. I., Tutkun, H., Bakim, B., . . . Özdemir, Ö. (2003). Axis I dissociative disorder comorbidity of borderline personality disorder among psychiatric outpatients. *Journal of Trauma & Dissociation, 4*(1), 119–136.

Sar, V., & Ross, C. A. (2009). A research agenda for the dissociative disorders field. In P. F. Dell & J. A. O'Neil (Eds.), *Dissociation and the dissociative disorders:* DSM-V *and beyond* (pp. 693–708). New York, NY: Routledge.

Saxena, S., & Prasad, K. V. S. R. (1989). *DSM-III* subclassification of dissociative disorders applied to psychiatric outpatients in India. *American Journal of Psychiatry, 146*, 261–262.

Steinberg, M. (1995). *Handbook for the assessment of dissociation: A clinical guide*. Washington, DC: American Psychiatric Press.

Suryani, L. K., & Jensen, G. D. (1993). *Trance and possession in Bali*. Oxford, England: Oxford University Press.

Swartz, L. (2011). Dissociation and spirit possession in non-Western countries. In V. Sinason (Ed.), *Attachment, trauma and multiplicity: Working with dissociative identity disorder* (pp. 63–71). London, England: Routledge.

Tutkun, H., Sar, V., Yargic, L. I., Ozpulat, T., Yanik, M., & Kiziltan, E. (1998). Frequency of dissociative disorders among psychiatric inpatients in a Turkish university clinic. *American Journal of Psychiatry, 155*, 800–805.

Van Duijl, M., Cardeña, E., & De Jong, J. T. V. M. (2005). The validity of *DSM-IV* dissociative disorder categories in south-west Uganda. *Transcultural Psychiatry, 42*, 219–241.

Van Duijl, M., Nijenhuis, E., Komproe, I. H., Gernatt, H. B. P. E., & de Jong, J. T. (2010). Dissociative symptoms and reported trauma among patients with spirit possession and matched healthy controls in Uganda. *Culture, Medicine and Psychiatry, 34*, 380–400.

van IJzendoorn, M. H., & Schuengel, C. (1996). The measurement of dissociation in normal and clinical populations: Meta-analytic review of the Dissociative Experiences Scale. *Clinical Psychology Review, 16*, 365–382.

Waller, N. G., Putnam, F. W., & Carlson, E. B. (1996). The types of dissociation and dissociative types: A taxometric analysis of dissociative experiences. *Psychological Methods, 1*, 300–321.

Waller, N. G., & Ross, C. A. (1997). The prevalence and biometric structure of pathological dissociation in the general population: Taxometric structure and behavior genetic findings. *Journal of Abnormal and Social Psychology, 106*, 499–510.

Xiao, Z., Yan, H., Wang, Z., Zou, Z., Xu, Y., Chen, J., . . . Keyes, B. B. (2006). Trauma and dissociation in China. *American Journal of Psychiatry, 163*, 1388–1391.

Ethnic Syndromes as Disguise for Protest Against Colonialism: Three Ethnographic Examples

ELIZABETH HEGEMAN, PhD
John Jay College of Criminal Justice, City University of New York, New York, New York, USA

Historical connections are suggested between the domination of 1 culture by another and dissociative spiritual and religious responses to that oppression. Connections are drawn between colonial oppression, trauma, and 3 examples of dissociation and spirit possession: the Zar cult of Southern Sudan, "Puerto Rican syndrome" or ataque, and the Balinese trance dance. Discussed by means of these examples are the role and functions of spirit possession as a means of escape from unbearable reality, where it becomes a form of the expression of needs and desires forbidden by authorities, a way of entering an identity not subject to traditional authorities, and reenactment of traumatic experience.

Through many centuries of colonialism, different forms of dissociation have been associated with conquest and extreme acculturation. This connection is based on the great differentials in power between conqueror and conquered, and the abuse and exploitation that accompany these inequalities. Extreme oppression that destroys habitat and livelihood and displaces populations leads to the desperate need to escape an unbearable reality of starvation and loss of cultural meaning. When the Ghost Dance Religion

---

This research was supported by a grant from the Research Foundation of City University of New York, under the Professional Staff Congress Grants Program, City University of New York.

of the native peoples of the Great Plains in the United States arose, the buffalo they depended upon were diminished, and the native people were pushed westward away from the habitat they knew and to which they had adapted. In the Sun Dance ritual, warriors strung themselves up by thongs from a high pole while others danced to hypnotic, repetitive music for long stretches of time in order to bring back the buffalo. According to Mooney (1996), ecstatic experience, dancing to bring on trance, and the belief in a messiah who would return the old ways of life sprang up in many places in North America.

In a similar ritual of despair, Cargo Cults of the Pacific Islands also involved dancing and ecstatic states, throwing away seed for next year's crops, their only goal to bring back the ancestors and go back to the time before the bloody colonial occupation. Both of these religions are examples of reactions to conquest that have involved altered states, the belief in a messiah, magical protection from injury, and emphasis on the afterlife rather than this life. In fact, most if not all of the world's great religions have arisen under conditions of terrible persecution or enslavement—Christianity under the Romans, Judaism under Egyptian enslavement, and Buddhism under attack from Mongols and nomads from the north. We can speculate that in the early phases in the history of these religions, when starvation and violence were rampant, dissociation was a common feature of experience. At present, the fastest growing religious groups throughout the world are Pentecostal and charismatic (Anderson, 2004), emphasizing a focus on the afterlife and on ecstatic experience rather than the present day in an appeal to the disenfranchised.

DOES COLONIALISM LEAD TO SPIRIT POSSESSION?

The shock of physical pain or emotional betrayal challenges, even destroys, a person's sense of meaning and coherence. We are accustomed to individual dissociative responses to these and therefore may be likely to assume that when we encounter dissociative phenomena in other cultures, it is the direct result of some form of personal trauma. But the connections between trauma and dissociation are far more complex in the approximately 400 cultures studied by anthropologists, and an important difference is that dissociative experience can be part of shared community customs, with institutionalized meaning. According to Bourguignon (1979), 90% of the world's cultures have some form of belief in spirits, and 50% have a structured tradition of possession, often involving healing through trance. Care must be taken not to impose Western cultural meanings on others. There is evidence that some traditions of trance healing and spirit possession may predate colonial contact (Bourguignon, 1979). Although cultural conditions such as colonial domination create a fertile ground for dissociative response, the anthropological record is so rich and wide ranging that conclusive generalizations are hard to make. I argue in this article that even though dissociation and spirit possession may have predated colonial oppression, these practices have been so profoundly affected in their character and their role in the culture as the result of colonial domination so as to incorporate forms of unconscious resistance, satire, and reenactment in response to power.

THREE EXAMPLES OF CULTURALLY SANCTIONED DISSOCIATION IN RESPONSE TO OPPRESSION

There are some compelling examples in which the cultural material makes explicit reference to oppressive and colonial situations. In particular, traditions of spirit possession can represent getting out from under a repressive authority, can express important personal experiences of resistance and aspects of identity that are freer from the dominant culture. All three of the examples I discuss here involve gender oppression as well as cultural oppression. The first example is the Zar cults of Southern Sudan. Before the British conquest, the Ottoman Empire dominated from the north, and slave hunters from many countries scourged the area. Women were expected to submit to the authority of their husbands as well as the Ottoman and British occupiers, but the Zar cult tradition allowed women some forms of empowerment in having their own rituals, meetings, and spiritual identities. In the second example, *ataque de nervios* in the Hispanic culture of Puerto Rico, "good" women are not permitted direct expression of anger or aggression either at the personal level or at the political level. Puerto Rico experienced the control of Spain until the Spanish–American War in 1898 and has had a colonial relationship with the United States since then. *Ataque* as an "idiom of distress" is a form of protest against conditions a woman finds unbearable. In the third example, *latah,* gender antagonism and a form of reaction to misogyny are present in the postcolonial village life of Indonesia.

First I discuss spirit possession as a dissociative response to oppression. Spirits have the advantage of not being bound by ordinary limits. Though not accepted as normal in Western cultures, spirit possession is a familiar condition worldwide in which a person perceives a spirit taking executive power over his or her body. Becoming possessed may be welcome or unwelcome for a person; a trance state may be valued as evidence of the capacity to heal illness or mental problems, if the spirit and host are in harmony. But an anguished period of months has been described during which a person resists the call to shamanism, and the distress is only resolved when the person accepts his or her calling. *Int'waso* in South Africa and *Kwa-byung* illness in Korea are two well-described examples (American Psychiatric Association, 1994).

Often these customs clash with Western medicine. In *The Spirit Catches You and You Fall Down* by Fadiman (1998), a Hmong family welcomed its baby's seizures as trance, a sign of her spiritual abilities and future as a healer, while the doctors tried to treat her seizures vigorously with Western medicine the family feared and resisted.

The Zar Cult

For the people of the Southern Sudan (now known as Darfur), spirits are representatives of an invisible world populated by *djinn* that match the human world and normally stay separate from it. Although the initial symptoms of a woman's possession—headaches, irritability, preoccupation—may not be welcome, once the spirit has been identified through a ceremony that matches a particular drumbeat known to represent a particular spirit, a woman seeks out the possession of her spirit and her identity is enhanced by the social recognition that her spirit must be nurtured by being able to appear during Zar ceremonies and speak through her. Harmony is restored once the possessed woman has become reconciled with her guardian and the previously unwelcome spirit has found a home.

Anthropologist Boddy (2007) dates the Zar cult from the beginning of the Ottoman conquest in 1820–1821. During the ethnographic present, Boddy (1989, 2007) describes women meeting all day and evening to feast, play drums, and become possessed by personal guardian spirits who become the means of the women's expression of desires and also the agents of satire of the colonial powers. A woman's guardian spirit must be satisfied with the gifts he or she demands, or the threat of infertility will be visited on the male lineage. The culture area where Zar is practiced is also the part of the world where the most extreme form of genital surgery is performed on girls—not only the clitoris but all of the external labia are removed, and the genital opening is sewed up, leaving only a very small hole for menstrual blood to come out. The woman's body then comes to represent the cultural ideal of being closed—like the courtyard of a house surrounded by high walls.

This practice is carried out on 7- to 9-year-old girls under unsanitary conditions, without anesthesia, while female relatives hold them. According to Boddy (1989), girls experience "more shock than pain" (pp. 49–50), and Boddy describes the practice in only a few paragraphs. Anthropologists may tend to normalize the customs of the people they study, partly because the culture itself normalizes the custom but also out of identifications with the culture and in order to avoid any guilt or cognitive dissonance that might come from recognition of pain members of the culture inflict on one another. It may be assumed that girls are likely to dissociate under these conditions of fairly intense physical pain, and perhaps the rituals of spirit possession are connected with this trauma.

The impact of English colonial power has been felt strongly in this area, with military headquarters established at Khartoum and the inhabitants employed in the army. Boddy gives a structural/economic analysis of the role of women's spirit possession in the colonial setting—she maintains that the demands of the spirits drove husbands into the money economy of the labor market, making the men available to work on colonial projects such as railways and roads and as mercenaries. It was believed that if a man does not supply the items the guardian spirit demanded his wife would be barren. In a lineage-based tribal culture, this was a dreadful fate for the whole family. Before the British conquest, perfume or cloth might have been the sort of request the spirits made. From the point of view of the possessed woman, these demands of her spirit are empowering, giving her the chance to control her husband by (not necessarily intentionally) appropriating the power of the possessing spirit and threatening her husband by withholding her fertility. She could not do this outside the medium of spirit possession without retaliation and loss of face.

The fascinating connection of spirit possession with colonialism comes in the form of a seeming satire. After the British conquest, spirits demanded things emblematic of the colonial military power, like a pith helmet, a riding crop, or jodhpurs. When one woman became possessed by the Zar she would put on this clothing and strut about, imitating the British soldiers. Some of the possessing spirits carry the names of British generals, such as Gordel (General Gordon) and Karoma (Lord Cromer), who are overly fond of rum and smoke cigarettes, like their British models. In this culture where women were not sequestered, they witnessed British behavior directly, and they also had access to goods that were stolen or spoils of war. Identification with the aggressor seems to be the psychic mechanism for this behavior, where even in trance the impact of colonial culture and its symbols was felt.

In sum, although in Sudan a tradition of spirit possession seems to have predated colonialism, it was modified to express affects and identifications after colonial conquest. For women doubly oppressed by their gender role and by the Ottoman and British colonial rule, the Zar tradition became a way of exerting power and influence by supernatural means. It also integrated dissociative experience in the form of trance into an accepted social ritual. So spirits are a perfect form of plausible deniability in that they can express feelings and desires, especially anti-authority ones, without the possessed person being held accountable for intentional opposition.

In a very recent study of posttraumatic stress disorder in two refugee camps in Chad, among a comparable cultural group to the ones Boddy studied, Hinton and Lewis-Fernandez (2011) identify two locally designated idioms of distress, both of which overlap with posttraumatic stress disorder and major depression. The authors do not mention either Zar or Boddy's ethnographic works, but that might be because their concern was to identify symptoms in order to assist aid workers in the refugee camps and to consider the cross-cultural validity of posttraumatic stress disorder as a diagnosis. It would be interesting to find out whether Zar practices were still in place and whether these recent idioms of distress were as effective as before in turning symptoms into a culturally accepted and adaptive form.

"Puerto Rican Syndrome"

Another example illustrates the phenomenon of culturally based spirit possession: Puerto Rican Syndrome or *ataque de nervios*. According to Gherovici (2003), this form of dissociation is structured by cultural expectations and illustrates the phenomenon of culturally normalized spirit possession. As described by Gherovici, *ataque de nervios* represents the cry for help of Puerto Rican women who, because of their gender, do not have access to direct forms of aggression. *Ataque de nervios,* like Zar possession, is recognized by psychiatrists and psychologists as an ethnic syndrome particular to one cultural group but not corresponding to any single recognized mental health diagnosis. Like many of the 25 idioms of distress listed in the *Diagnostic and Statistical Manual of Mental Disorders, Fourth Edition* (American Psychiatric Association, 1994), *ataque* is most often triggered by a stressful event and manifests dissociative symptoms: an altered state of awareness, episodes of fainting or apparent seizure, and a felt sense of being out of control. Someone may experience amnesia for what happens during the *ataque,* but afterward he or she goes back to normal functioning fairly soon. Although quite widespread—14% of a community sample and 75% of a mental health population reported being affected—*ataque* is not regarded as a mental illness by Hispanics themselves (Gherovici, 2003). As with Zar and the Balinese trance dance (discussed next), *ataque,* as a reflection of possession/trance states, is regarded by the Western or medical view as pathological, whereas in the culture itself it is understood as an important form of communication. If the possessed person (usually a woman) apprentices herself to a healer, she will even become respected for her ability to heal through her ability to contact the spirit world.

Gherovici (2003) emphasizes the role of socioeconomic factors and cultural oppression in analyzing the meaning of *ataque*. She maintains that *ataque* will occur when other modes of expression of anger and distress are blocked and offers case material to support this view. What blocks these expressions is the likelihood of punishment or retaliation by an oppressive authority; a typical episode might occur in a factory, army, or family situation where unfairness cannot be protested openly. The very name "Puerto Rican syndrome" by which the phenomenon was called in the middle of the 20th century was a form of denigration-by-diagnosis of a condition that those belonging to the ethnic group would recognize as a cry for help and respond accordingly. A typical treatment by an *espiritista* healer would involve support for the forbidden affects as well as a new potential identification with the possessing spirit in a welcoming community of healers-in-training. But note that the cure does not necessarily involve the conscious redirection of the anger or resentment at the authority—the true object is still disguised.

An Example of Dissociation Within the Family: The Balinese Trance Dance

This example discusses a painful trauma within the family, rather than the direct result of colonialism. It is included because of the fascinating connection Mead and Bateson make between the trauma of weaning and the reappearance and reenactment of the theme in the cultural practice of ritual. Mead and Bateson (1937) show "the return of the dissociated" hatred of the weaning mother in their 1937 film *Trance and Dance in Bali*. It would not be hard to locate Bali in the colonial model, as it has been conquered militarily and culturally many times, but this example, like Zar, shows the possible connections between the intimate personal experience of pain and betrayal appearing in shared community ritual. Mead and Bateson first show the apparent cruelty of the weaning mother, who pretends to nurse and cuddle another child while her own toddler (who has had free access to the breast until this moment) screams and cries in frustration, finally slipping off into the blank face of dissociation and making the hand movements that might be choreiform signs of abnormal neurological activity but that are typical of traditional Balinese dance. Mead and Bateson then show the pageant of the trance dance, in which the whole village takes part. The plot is of the struggle between a witch whose gaze can kill (and who cackles in the same way the teasing, weaning mother does) and a group of men who eventually overpower her and protect the village. Mead and Bateson show how each part of the trance dance represents a reenactment of the dissociated childhood fear and rage at the traumatic, but culturally normal, procedure in which the weaning mother betrays and rejects her toddler. Their theory holds that the community ritual incorporates and reenacts the painful betrayals of family life, specifically demonstrating the childhood aggression against the witchy, betraying sadistic mother. Because the practices of weaning are universal—sometimes hot pepper is smeared on the nipples—the story of the ritual is compelling and engaging for the whole community. This example has in common the important connection between a painful condition—helplessness, physical pain, loss, and so on—and the symbolic representation enacted in a trance state later in life, perhaps as part of a community group.

Another feature of the Balinese trance dance is that trance is not limited to specialized persons like shamans or dancers in the pageant. Any member of the community may go into trance and enact some part of the theme. Surprising to outside witnesses is that no one is injured during the wild dancing of people propping the point of a sharp knife (*kris*) against their breastbone. This may be a demonstration of the containment of rage originally directed at the other but now directed against the self, the only form of internal self-preservation available to the weaning toddler.

CONCLUSION

If we look for a traumatic origin for the source of dissociation, perhaps the felt sense of unfairness or powerlessness would qualify. The microaggressions of disrespect under subtle or overt domination are in themselves traumatic. The subordinate person accepts his or her role to a point, but no further. Yet does the person who becomes spirit possessed consciously intend to express opposition to authority? Gherovici (2003) maintains that consciousness, or awareness of political meaning and a determination to fight against domination, is manifest in some forms in the Puerto Rican community. Boddy takes the implicit position that women possessed by Zar spirits are not conscious of any political or power significance of their participation in this women-only activity. There is no evidence in her description of the culture or Zar practice that women are aware of engaging in a power play by becoming possessed, nor is there evidence in Gherovici's account that Puerto Rican women are intentionally falling to the floor, foaming at the mouth, and speaking in tongues. But the social reactions of the community to each group show sympathy, receptiveness, and supportiveness of the changes in role that come with spirit possession, which implies that recognition of unfairness is latent in the community. And, the elements of satire by the woman in a Zar possession state are unmistakable. The dissociative reenactments in these three traditions allow for the expression of forbidden affect in disguised form and lay the groundwork for new roles and new self-definitions incorporating what was forbidden under more authoritarian political regimes.

We can tolerate and account for these contradictions and changes in self-definitions if we adopt a more complex view of the self than is customary in Western and European cultures. The possessed woman can experience some satisfaction, power, and enhancement of identity without sacrificing her good name, or her reputation as a good (obedient) woman, and the weaning toddler self-state inside the grownup trance dancer can get some catharsis and expression of rage at the enraging mother in disguised form. In recent psychoanalytic thought, Bromberg (2006) and Howell (2005) have elaborated the theory of self-states to show how the self includes contradictory forms of self-experience, establishing how the developing self can wall off (dissociate) overwhelming pain or betrayal in order to allow another part of the self to continue to function in an apparently normal way. The person with dissociative identity disorder is unaware of and ordinarily has no access to these memory states unless triggered into a trance. Bucci's (1997) research on multiple code theory lays the basis for a neurological understanding of trance states and memory access. Bucci's work suggests that more complex models of the self allow for ways of incorporating a fuller understanding of these ethnographic examples and their significance in self-development in Western culture.

In sum, when we examine these three examples, the ethnographic record has great potential for helping us understand the political meaning of dissociative experience in response to oppression. Zar, *ataque*, and the Balinese trance dance all show the important capacity of rituals incorporating dissociation to connect individual experience to the group. Pain and betrayal at the individual level become shared cultural forms that express the meanings of that experience, in disguised form. In other words, the personal becomes political through rituals of possession and trance, both through the content of what is expressed in the material produced under trance and in the possession state itself as a way to escape an identity that no longer works, even if the escape is only temporary. In the cultural environment under colonial domination, old identities may not work, and dissociation plays a role in helping people create new ones. Given the danger of isolation, alienation, and madness that can come from dissociation, shared rituals are a saving grace in the face of oppression. Through them, we may witness culture in the making.

REFERENCES

American Psychiatric Association. (1994). *Diagnostic and statistical manual of mental disorders* (4th ed.). Washington, DC: Author.

Anderson, A. (2004). *An introduction to Pentecostalism: Global charismatic Christianity*. Cambridge, England: Cambridge University Press.

Boddy, J. (1989). *Wombs and alien spirits*. Madison, WI: University of Wisconsin Press.

Boddy, J. (2007). *Civilizing women: British crusades in colonial Sudan*. Princeton, NJ: Princeton University Press.

Bourguignon, E. (1979). *Psychological anthropology: Introduction to human nature and cultural differences*.Orlando, FL: Harcourt School Press.

Bromberg, P. (2006). *Awakening the dreamer: Clinical journeys*. Mahwah, NJ: Analytic Press.

Bucci, W. (1997). *Psychoanalysis and cognitive science: A multiple code theory*. New York, NY: Guilford Press.

Fadiman, A. (1998). *The spirit catches you and you fall down*. New York, NY: Farrar, Straus & Giroux.

Gherovici, P. (2003). *The Puerto Rican syndrome*. New York, NY: Other Press.

Hinton, D. E., & Lewis-Fernandez, R. (2011). The cross-cultural validity of post traumatic stress disorder: Implications for *DSM-5*. *Depression and Anxiety, 28*, 783–801. doi:10.1002/da.20753

Howell, E. (2005). *The dissociative mind*. New York, NY: Routledge.

Mead, M., & Bateson, G. (1935–1937). *Trance and dance in Bali* [Ethnographic film edited and narrated by Mead and Bateson]. New York, NY: American Museum of Natural History.

Mooney, J. (1996). *The ghost dance*. North Dighton, MA: JG Press.

Dissociation and Identity Transformation in Female Survivors of the Genocide Against the Tutsi in Rwanda: A Qualitative Research Study

DENISE H. SANDOLE, PsyD and CARL F. AUERBACH, PhD
Department of Psychology, Yeshiva University, Bronx, New York, USA

This qualitative research study deals with female survivors of the 1994 genocide against the Tutsi in Rwanda. It examines dissociation and identity change in these women before, during, and after the genocide. Three theories were used to frame the findings. The 1st was assumptive world theory (R. Janoff-Bulman, 1992), which postulates that traumatic events may shatter people's everyday assumptions about the world. The 2nd was catastrophic dissociation theory (G. Boulanger, 2007), which refers to the gradual breakdown of the self as it repeatedly "experiences its psychic foundations in ways that do not happen in the average expectable life" (G. Boulanger, 2008, p. 646). The 3rd was structural dissociation theory (O. Van der Hart, E. R. S. Nijenhuis, & K. Steele, 2006), which postulates that when people encounter events that they cannot integrate into their mental lives, their personality may fragment and divide. The data were transcripts of interviews with 30 female genocide survivors. Data analysis revealed that these women experienced trauma-induced identity transformations. Before the genocide, they existed as a "Civilized Self,"

The authors are grateful to Foundation Rwanda for providing them with the interview material and to the Rwandan survivors who shared their stories.

with a stable identity in a secure, assumptive world. During the genocide, they existed as a "Survivor Self," the massive trauma of the genocide having disrupted their prior self-experience and identity. After the genocide, they existed as an "Aftermath Self," in which their Civilized and Survivor Selves coexisted in an unintegrated, dissociated form.

The 1994 genocide against the Tutsi in Rwanda was one of the most intensive episodes of mass violence in human history. During a period of only 100 days, 800,000 Rwandan Tutsis and moderate Hutus were slaughtered. The genocide has also been described as a "gendercide," or "femicide," because rape was used as an instrument of war. It is estimated that between 250,000 and 500,000 Rwandan women of all ages were subject to sexual violence, including gang rape, sexual slavery, rape with weapons or sticks, mutilation of reproductive body parts, and intentional transmission of HIV/AIDS ("Shattered Lives," 1996). In the aftermath of the genocide, these women have been dealing with "overwhelming problems . . . including social stigmatization, poor physical and psychological health, unwanted pregnancy and poverty" ("Shattered Lives," 1996).

This study examines the transformative impact of gendercide on Rwandan women. Our approach begins with Herman's (1992) observation that survivors of wartime rape experience themselves as being "changed irrevocably" (p. 86). The woman's sense of self has been invaded and "systematically broken down" (p. 93). The result is a "contaminated identity" that is immersed in "shame, self-loathing, and failure" (p. 94).

In order to further develop Herman's insight, we used three other theoretical frameworks: assumptive world theory (Janoff-Bulman, 1992), catastrophic dissociation theory (Boulanger, 2007), and structural dissociation theory (Van der Hart, Nijenhuis, & Steele, 2006). Assumptive world theory postulates that traumatic events violently disconfirm and shatter people's prior assumptions about the world and their confidence in "the absolutisms of everyday life" (Stolorow, 2007, p. 16), leaving them disoriented, fearful, and vulnerable. Catastrophic dissociation theory (Boulanger, 2007, 2008) extends this by observing that massive psychic trauma may result in a "collapse of the self" by disrupting the psychic functions that maintain ordinary experience. The survivor has the "subjective experience of having lost touch" with her former self, ultimately becoming "unfamiliar to herself" (Boulanger, 2007, p. 98). Also useful in understanding the psychic effects of massive trauma is structural dissociation theory (Van der Hart et al., 2006), which postulates that the personality may fragment and divide when people are exposed to events so intensely negative and emotional that they cannot be integrated into their ongoing mental life.

Although it is known that wartime rape is intended to "destroy the identity of the victim" (Skjelsbaek, 2006, p. 375) along with her crucial social bonds (Amowitz et al., 2002), "very little" is known about what it is like "to be a victim of ethnically-based war rape" or how this experience might alter the victim's sense of self in the aftermath (p. 381). Furthermore, "little attempt has been made to deconstruct the actual process by which the adult self collapses" from severe traumatization (Boulanger, 2008, p. 643). The present study utilized the three theoretical frameworks mentioned previously to understand the process by which wartime rape affected women's sense of self and identity before, during, and after the genocide.

METHODS

Research Design

A qualitative grounded theory methodology was utilized in this research for three reasons. First, pragmatically speaking, the research materials were interviews conducted with female survivors, and these naturally lent themselves to qualitative data analysis. Second, the qualitative methodology allowed us to focus on understanding the survivors' subjective experience as revealed in the interviews. Third, there are two different schools of grounded theory arising from a difference between its two founders, Barney Glaser and Anselm Strauss (Glaser & Strauss, 1967). After their work together, Glaser (1978) developed a coding method in which theory emerges from data, unconstrained by any prior theoretical assumptions. Strauss, in contrast, developed a method in which the investigator uses a broad theoretical framework as a guide throughout the coding and interpretation process (Strauss & Corbin, 1990). Because our research used three theoretical frameworks, the Strauss method of grounded theory was used rather than an alternative method such as interpretive phenomenology (Giorgi & Giorgi, 2003). This choice allowed us to incorporate our theoretical frameworks into the data analysis.

Materials

The 30 interviews that were utilized for data analysis were provided to us by Foundation Rwanda, a U.S.-based nongovernmental organization that works to support female survivors of the genocide and their children. The interviews were conducted in 2008 for the purposes of media documentation; therefore, we did not provide input into the development of the interview pro forma. The interviews asked 12 open-ended questions that took the survivors through a narrative account of their genocide experience. The beginning questions asked about the survivors' lives before the genocide, the middle questions asked about the survivors' experiences during the genocide, and the final questions asked about the survivors' present lives. We note that the interview questions did not explicitly ask about identity but that the survivors brought the topic up spontaneously. In our view, this indicates the importance of identity to them. The participants were interviewed in their native language, Kinyarwanda, through interpreters at their Rwandan homes or at nearby survivor support centers, through which Foundation Rwanda gained access to many of their participants. A complete list of the questions may be obtained from us on request.

Participants

Thirty Rwandan females who survived wartime rape provided detailed descriptions of their genocidal experiences to Foundation Rwanda. The participants' ages ranged from 26 to 46, with a mean age of 32.8 years. At the time of the 1994 genocide, 56% of participants were 17 or younger and 30% of participants were the sole survivor of their entire immediate families. Despite the traditional role expectation of marriage in Rwandan society pre-genocide, 63% of participants remained unmarried post-genocide. Moreover, 100% of participants bore at least one child resulting from wartime rape; 70% of these children did not know that they were born from wartime rape, nor did they know the whereabouts of their biological fathers. A total of 40% of participants reported that they were HIV positive as a result of their wartime rape. In addition, 53% of participants reported that they participated in female survivors' groups and found them to be helpful. Finally, 33% of participants revealed that their Foundation Rwanda interviews were the first time they had ever spoken about their experience of wartime rape.

Data Analysis

The goal of the data analysis was to understand the transformative impact of wartime rape endured by female survivors of the 1994 genocide, as revealed in their interviews. The specific procedure was based on a grounded theory methodology developed by Auerbach and Silverstein (2003) for exploring the relevance of theoretical frameworks to a given phenomenon. It involves developing a system of categories that organizes the content of the interview transcripts into repeating ideas, themes, and theoretical constructs. In the first step of the data analysis, the first author read the transcripts with the following research question in mind: How can the experience of the female survivors be understood in terms of trauma and dissociation theory? From this reading, three broad narrative phases emerged, which were organized by both of us according to assumptive world theory, catastrophic dissociation theory, and structural dissociation theory. Following this initial reading, the first author began to underline text that bore on these three phases (relevant text). Then the relevant text was reviewed in order to develop ideas expressed by more than one participant (repeating ideas). Similar repeating ideas were then organized into themes. These themes typically included more than one repeating idea, although occasionally we judged one idea to be sufficiently important to be a theme in its own right. The themes were in turn grouped into theoretical constructs, formulated so as to be consistent with our three theoretical frameworks. To ensure the reliability of the coding, the first author did the coding independently, after which the second author reviewed the results, and then together we came to a consensus on the final coding. It should be noted that the coding process involved a hermeneutic circle (Gadamer, 1994), in which the results of each step were used to revise the results of the previous steps until a coherent picture emerged. As the final step of the data analysis, the theoretical constructs were organized into a theoretical narrative that told the story of the participants' transformative identity experience before, during, and after the genocide.

RESULTS

The results of the data analysis are presented in Table 1, which displays the 16 repeating ideas, eight themes, and three theoretical constructs derived from the interviews. These constructs were then used to form a theoretical narrative (see the Discussion) describing the women's sense of self before, during, and after the genocide. Theoretical constructs are indicated in italicized, underlined text. Themes are indicated in italicized text. Repeating ideas are indicated in quotation marks. The ratios (*x*/*y*) report the proportion of research participants who endorsed each repeating idea. Percentages (%) represent the percentage of participants endorsing each theme. This section describes the themes. The repeating ideas that define the themes are given in Table 1.

I. *Civilized Self* (Pre-Genocide)

Theme 1. Expected Order of Life Events (i.e., Marriage Then Children; 37%). More than a third (37%) of participants began their narrative by describing the sequential order of life events that had been the norm before genocide. As part of a traditional society, the Rwandan women expected to live at home with their parents and siblings until a proper suitor made an introduction and proposed marriage.

Theme 2. Family and Community Belonging (53%). More than half (53%) of the research participants defined their pre-genocide life in terms of belonging to a tight-knit, elaborate family system: "We had a distant family of relations of not less than around 100 people and we all settled in the same village around the same hill."

TABLE 1 Theoretical Constructs, Themes, and Repeating Ideas

I. *Civilized Self*

Expected Order of Life Events (i.e., Marriage Then Children; 37%)

1. "I was just a girl, not married." (5/30)
2. "Before genocide I was married. I had a husband. We lived happily . . . I had just got married and [then] we had just got one kid." (6/30)

Family and Community Belonging (53%)

1. "Right before genocide in our village all people were friendly." (2/30)
2. "We were thirteen in my family, father and mother, seven boys and three other girls. I was the fifth born." (9/30)
3. "We had family networks, there were structures of support . . . the villages had extended lineages so if you had a problem, you had people to come to your rescue. If you had something to celebrate, you had people to celebrate with you. It was a functional community before genocide." (5/30)

Multiple Roles and Functions (37%)

1. "My father was a director and my mother was a nurse . . . so it was a routine of life of what I may call a middle class family today. Mother, father working, children going to school, that was the life. Once in a while, going out to have fun." (3/30)
2. "My family was not a very rich family we depended on agriculture. My parents, my father and mother did farm. They provided food and school fees for us and we were able to go to school." (6/30)
3. "I finished post primary and then I went to study auto mechanics. I was a mechanic actually . . . my husband we loved each other. He was also, he had trained in auto mechanics and we agreed since we were doing the same job one of should continue and the other stays home to look after children." (2/30)

II. *Survivor Self*

Assumptive World Shattered (100%)

1. "My fiancé was killed. The man that killed my fiancé is actually the one who came to say he was going to protect me." (22/30)
2. "We went in a church nearby because we thought that the church was safe. All my family were killed in that church except myself." (8/30)

Severe, Continual Trauma and Unimaginable Acts of Survival (100%)

1. "They raped us for about a month. From April through May, up to the end of May. They come, they take you, they do what they want to do with you—that was sex. When they finished, they killed some, they left some, some couldn't walk—it was havoc in this village." (30/30)
2. "They thought maybe I was dead, but at night, I don't know how . . . I started getting dead bodies off myself . . . and managed to get up from the mass grave to the ground again." (30/30)

Reduction to One Ethnic Label (100%)

1. "They killed people, they killed, they killed whoever they could immediately see that he's a Tutsi." (30/30)

III. *Aftermath Self*

Unable to Return to Civilized Self (100%)

1. "These children distorted my life. The experience of rape distorted my ambitions. Now I am called a woman but I am not married to any man. I would have been something, someone. But I can't be that. I'm a woman but I don't have a husband." (30/30)

Isolated and Unsupported (100%)

1. "I am alone. I don't have any surviving relative apart from my old mother. From his family [son's biological father], they are all there. But they don't accept he is their son. They don't care about him." (22/30)
2. "I don't talk about my feelings. But in me I have heartache, bitterness, anger that I have no one to express to. I have managed to always suppress and live with it." (8/30)

Notes: Figures in parentheses represent either the percentage or ratio of participants who identified this theme or idea.

Theme 3. Multiple Roles and Functions (37%). More than a third (37%) of participants spoke of the multiple ways in which they related to their pre-genocide world. They were not just a Tutsi but rather a woman, mother, daughter, sister, worker, student, Rwandan.

II. *Survivor Self* (During the Genocide)

Theme 4. Assumptive World Shattered (100%). As the genocide spread across the country, these Rwandan women (100%) found themselves in another world, one in which pre-genocide norms and assumptions were no longer reliable. The participants described two main assumptions that were shattered during the genocide. The first involved family and community relationships. When threatened with the first incidents of violence in early April 1994, the women initially thought that they could count on these familiar relationships for safety. The second shattered assumption involved another common path to refuge: church. During the genocide, many Rwandans assumed that they would be safe if they took shelter in a Catholic church, as no one would dare to harm them there, but that was not the case.

Theme 5. Severe, Continual Trauma and Unimaginable Acts of Survival (100%). These Rwandan women (100%) endured not only one incident of rape but in most cases multiple incidents, typically in the form of sexual slavery in which they were held in captivity for long periods. The Rwandan women endured multiple sexual assaults, murder attempts, and the loss of entire families and communities over many consecutive months. Given that one seventh of the entire Rwandan population was killed in the early 1990s, these women survived against incredible odds.

Theme 6, Reduction to One Ethnic Label (100%). All participants (100%) described how they were viewed by others in terms of just their Tutsi identity during genocide. Other descriptors, such as former classmate, girlfriend, pregnant woman, devoted Christian, and sister-in-law, disappeared. As one woman told it,

> Earlier before genocide I had a boyfriend, but he was Hutu. So I went and knocked at his door asking them to open for me. He opened the door, but his relatives, his parents, said send the cockroach away. We don't need the cockroach in the house.

III. *Aftermath Self* (After the Genocide)

Theme 7. Unable to Return to Civilized Self (100%). Once the genocide ended, these Rwandan women (100%) told us how they tried to return to their former, pre-genocide worlds but were unable to do so. One woman described in great detail what she lost and how those losses define her daily existence post-genocide:

> I lost; I thought I had lost all life. I had lost virginity. I had lost my education . . . So when I looked at what had happened to me I thought there was no future . . . Now after the war many came and some men, and men that I would have loved, each one was telling me they wanted to be my husband. Now that hurt me (even) more because I knew I was no longer a girl to be someone's wife.

Theme 8. Isolated and Unsupported (100%). The participants in this study described an experience of being alone and without support in their post-genocidal world. These women directly associated their current isolation and hardships to their genocidal rapes, resultant pregnancies, and HIV infections. The participants also reported that, at the time of these interviews, they had not sought any emotional support in managing their genocidal rape experiences. They shared how their silence and disconnection placed a burden on them: "The challenge that I have is that I am alone with my problems, I do not share with anyone what I go through. It's me and my son. For me that it is the biggest challenge."

DISCUSSION

Theoretical Narrative

The aim of the present study was to understand the experience of female survivors of the 1994 genocide against the Tutsi in terms of three theoretical frameworks: assumptive world theory, catastrophic dissociation theory, and structural dissociation theory. These approaches were used to develop theoretical constructs that describe three stages of the survivors' experiences before, during, and after the genocide, namely *Civilized Self, Survivor Self,* and *Aftermath Self.*

The first, pre-genocide stage is the *Civilized Self.* This stage describes the women's assumptive world prior to the genocide. This world was a relatively safe and secure place with a set of norms typical of a traditional collectivist society. Participants identified themselves as young girls or married women whose assumptive world was marked by an *Expected Order of Life Events (i.e., Marriage Then Children; Theme 1),* as well as a vast network of *Family and Community Belonging (Theme 2).* The latter element included a large immediate family, extended family lineages, and interactional and interdependent community members that related to one another via *Multiple Roles and Functions (Theme 3).*

Soon after the genocide began, the Rwandan females shifted from the *Civilized Self* into the second phase, the *Survivor Self.* This phase is well described by assumptive world theory and catastrophic dissociation theory. For the Rwandan females, the *Survivor Self* emerged after *Severe, Continual Trauma and Unimaginable Acts of Survival (Theme 5),* including multiple rapes, loss of loved ones, and severe torture and violence. The Rwandan women had initially relied on their assumptive world to cope, turning to family and community connections and the church for safety. They soon realized that these assumptions no longer existed, that their *Assumptive World Had Been Shattered (Theme 4)* by genocide. The emergence of their *Survivor Self* helped these women stay alive by protecting their *Civilized Self* from the terror of *Severe, Continual Trauma* by performing *Unimaginable Acts of Survival (Theme 5),* an experience that corresponds to Boulanger's (2007) catastrophic dissociation. When the women were branded and hunted for being a Tutsi "cockroach" and *Reduced to One Ethnic Label (Theme 6),* survival became the only operational mode of functioning. Their nuanced, subjective experience no longer existed; they were reduced to dehumanized objects.

After the genocide, the women experienced themselves as an *Aftermath Self.* This phase of the post-genocidal self is well described by structural dissociation theory. Because of what they had suffered during the genocide, the women found themselves *Unable to Return to Their Civilized Selves (Theme 7).* They were often ostracized by society and/or withdrew from society, becoming *Isolated and Unsupported (Theme 8)* as they raised their children on their own. This contributed to a complex post-traumatic experience that included emotional distress, a physical sense of danger, chronic medical ailments, unmet basic needs, an uncertain future, and isolation from an indifferent world. To help reduce these problems, the participants provided some idea for possible interventions: support groups, access to specialized medical treatment, employment opportunities, education for their children, and recognition of their suffering and survival (local/international).

Limitations

The design of this study, particularly the fact that the interviews were conducted by Foundation Rwanda for media rather than research purposes, resulted in four important limitations. First, we were not involved in the sample selection process. This means that we do not know how representative these women are of the entire population of female survivors, which limits the generalizability of our conclusions. Second, the interview questions were not developed for research purposes, the result of which is that we lacked some demographic information about the participants. Third, we did not ourselves interview the participants, with the result that questions relevant to dissociation and identity were not directly asked. Fourth, we were not able to do member checks (Meadows & Morse, 2001), which entails the sharing of results with the original participants to see whether their experience was accurately reflected. We note, however, that while the second author was working on a different project, he informally shared the results with members of several different Rwandan survivor organizations, who found the results applicable to their own experiences.

Clinical Implications

These results have at least two important clinical implications. One is that the information provided about this population clearly identifies both the women and their children as a population at risk. If Rwandan society does not address their needs, mental health and otherwise, they are likely to become a permanently marginalized subpopulation of Rwandan society. At a more general level, clinicians working with patients who have experienced genocide or other severe, prolonged traumas might benefit from applying the Civilized–Survival–Aftermath Self model. The model would help clinicians more fully conceptualize these cases as well as provide psychoeducation to their patients that would help normalize their experiences, especially their struggle to return to their former, familiar selves.

Future Research

The results of this study should be followed up both theoretically and clinically. Theoretically speaking, it seems important to elaborate and develop the model suggested by the data. This can be done by doing more focused qualitative interviews with more precisely defined samples from this population, as well as other traumatized populations. It is important to note, however, that this is not an easy group to study, so that what is desirable in principle may not be feasible. In any event, the qualitative interviews could be supplemented by quantitative measures in a mixed methods design (Morse & Niehaus, 2009).

In terms of further clinical studies, we again point out how much the present study has identified a population at risk. We draw attention to "the 1995" children, the children born of genocidal rape. Some of the participants said that "we love each other . . . we are friends" in describing their relationship with their child, whereas others said more ambivalently "I don't hate my son. I don't love him either." It would be beneficial to interview these children and their mothers to better understand their experiences and perceptions and to develop possible treatment models specific to their needs. This research is currently being planned.

REFERENCES

Amowitz, L., Reis, C., Lyons, K. H., Vann, B., Mansaray, B., Akinsulure-Smith, A., . . . Iacopino, V. (2002). Prevalence of war-related sexual violence and other human rights abuses among internally displaced persons in Sierra Leone. *Journal of the American Medical Association, 287*, 513–521.

Auerbach, C. F., & Silverstein, L. B. (2003). *Qualitative data: An introduction to coding and analysis*. New York, NY: New York University Press.

Boulanger, G. (2007). *Wounded by reality: Understanding and treating adult onset trauma*. Mahwah, NJ: Analytic Press.

Boulanger, G. (2008). Witness to reality: Working psychodynamically with survivors of terror. *Psychoanalytic Dialogues, 18*, 638–657.

Gadamer, H. G. (1994). *Truth and method* (J. Weinsheimer & D. G. Marshall, Trans.). New York, NY: Continuum.

Giorgi, A. P., & Giorgi, B. M. (2003). The descriptive phenomenological psychological method. In P. M. Camic, J. E. Rhodes, & L. Yardley (Eds.), *Qualitative research in psychology: Expanding perspectives in methodology and design* (pp. 243–274). Washington, DC: American Psychological Association.

Glaser, B. (1978). *Theoretical sensitivity: Advances in the methodology of grounded theory*. Mill Valley, CA: Sociology Press.

Glaser, B., & Strauss, A. L. (1967). *The discovery of grounded theory: Strategies for qualitative research*. Chicago, IL: Aldine.

Herman, J. L. (1992). *Trauma and recovery: The aftermath of violence—From domestic abuse to political terror*. New York, NY: Basic Books.

Janoff-Bulman, R. (1992). *Shattered assumptions: Towards a new psychology of trauma*. New York, NY: Free Press.

Meadows, L., & Morse, J. M. (2001). Constructing evidence within the qualitative project. In J. M. Morse, J. Swanson, & A. Kuzel (Eds.), *The nature of qualitative evidence* (pp. 187–202). Thousand Oaks, CA: Sage.

Morse, J. M., & Niehaus, L. (2009). *Mixed method design: Principles and procedures*. Walnut Creek, CA: Left Coast Press.

Shattered lives: Sexual violence during the Rwandan genocide and its aftermath. (1996). Retrieved from the Human Rights Watch website: http://www.hrw.org/legacy/reports/1996/Rwanda.htm

Skjelsbaek, I. (2006). Victim and survivor: Narrated social identities of women who experienced rape during the war in Bosnia-Herzegovina. *Feminism and Psychology, 16*, 373–403.

Stolorow, R. D. (2007). *Trauma and human existence: Autobiographical, psychoanalytic, and philosophical reflections*. New York, NY: Taylor & Francis Group, LLC.

Strauss, A., & Corbin, J. (1990). *Basics of qualitative research: Grounded theory procedures and techniques*. Thousand Oaks, CA: Sage.

Van der Hart, O., Nijenhuis, E. R. S., & Steele, K. (2006). *The haunted self: Structural dissociation and the treatment of chronic traumatization*. New York, NY: Norton.

Transference-Focused Psychotherapy with Former Child Soldiers: Meeting the Murderous Self

NEL DRAIJER, PhD
Department of Psychiatry, VU University Medical Center/GGZinGeest, Amsterdam, The Netherlands

PAULINE VAN ZON, MA
Psychotraumacentrum Zuid-Nederland/Reinier van Arkel Groep, s'Hertogenbosch, The Netherlands

This article describes the application of transference-focused psychotherapy (TFP) to the treatment of former child soldiers suffering from dissociative identity disorder. It focuses on the problems with aggression faced in psychotherapy. TFP provides a psychodynamic, object relations model to understand the aggression arising in psychotherapy, focusing on the transference and countertransference in the here and now of the therapeutic relationship. Aggression is considered an essential and vital inner dynamic aimed at autonomy, distancing, and the prevention of injury and dependency. In extremely traumatized patients there may be aggressive and oppressive inner parts that want total control—identifying with childhood aggressors—thus avoiding vulnerability. According to TFP it is vital that this aggression is addressed as belonging to the patients themselves in order to reach some form of integration, balance, and health. This is illustrated in a case description.

The authors thank Dr. Frank Yeomans, PhD, for his very helpful remarks.

Aggression and anger are highly prevalent in combat-related posttraumatic stress disorder (PTSD) and negatively influence treatment outcome (Yehuda, 1999). Yet theories and treatment of PTSD focus predominantly on fear as the central emotion (Orth & Wieland, 2006). Anger and aggression are largely neglected in the literature on the treatment of traumatized individuals, including refugees (Ehntholt & Yule, 2006; Nicholl & Thompson, 2004). Similarly, severe aggression in dissociative identity disorder (DID) patients is often not a central focus (but see Chu, 1998; Mills, 2005). Managing split-off aggression in DID is even more problematic than in PTSD given its dissociated, egodystonic ("not me!") character.

It is our clinical experience in treating traumatized refugees that the use of state-of-the-art treatments for PTSD, such as narrative exposure therapy, eye movement desensitization and reprocessing, or testimony therapy, is ineffective and can even be retraumatizing as long as the therapeutic relationship is dominated by feelings of distrust, guilt, and shame that result in aggression and/or dissociation. Lack of emotion regulation and dissociation in the interpersonal context should have priority in psychotherapy, because they cause more functional impairment than PTSD symptoms. Past studies on emotion regulation in complex PTSD, such as anger and anxiety management, have focused on treatments containing components of psychoeducation, cognitive and behavioral aspects, and medication or a combination of these components (Chemtob, Novaco, Hamada, Gross, & Smith, 1997; Cloitre, 2009; Glancy & Saini, 2005; Saini, 2009; Yehuda, 1999). Approaches such as cognitive behavior therapy to control anger and anxiety may be successful in treating the situational aspects of anger and fear expression but typically not their underlying dispositions.

In working with adult refugees who were former child soldiers, using a staged-approach treatment with supportive, psychoeducational, and emotion regulation techniques resulted in little success. Because of their extreme interpersonal fears in contact with the therapist, these patients have great difficulties absorbing and processing new information and thus are unable to fully acquire emotion regulation strategies.

In this article we therefore address the following issues: How can therapists handle severe and split-off aggression in such patients? How should they handle oppression of the therapist by the patient and the extreme fears this induces in the therapist? How can therapists meet the "murderous self" and assist to integrate this self into the broader spectrum of aggressive affects with appropriate mastery?

FORMER CHILD SOLDIERS

UNICEF (2007) defined a *child soldier* as

> any person below 18 years of age who is or who has been recruited or used by an armed force or armed group in any capacity, including but not limited to children, boys and girls, used as fighters, cooks, porters, messengers, spies or for sexual purposes. (p. 7)

Child soldiers are used by both rebel armies and government troops. Africa has the largest number of child soldiers. Most of these children are forcibly recruited and abducted by armed groups. Others join these groups for the purposes of survival or to avenge slain family members (Betancourt et al., 2010; Schauer & Elbert, 2009).

The consequences of being a child soldier are considerable. These youths grow up in extreme and savage conditions in the jungle in which only the strongest survive. They form the bottom of the pecking order, making them the target of constant abuse, molestation, and harassment. These children are deprived of necessary care and protection from family and community and miss key services such as health care and education. The majority of child soldiers have been victims, witnesses, and/or perpetrators of severe violence and cruelties, such as combat situations, bombings, decapitations and amputations, burning people alive, and rape (Betancourt et al., 2010). After war, they are further vulnerable to reintegration failure because of not only being exposed to traumatic events but also being blamed and stigmatized because of their affiliation in the conflict (Schauer & Elbert, 2009). After arriving in The Netherlands, they are subjected to a lengthy and often exhausting asylum procedure. Once again, they are confronted with an inability to fully participate in society because of the minimal rights they are granted during the asylum procedure. They suffer from the loss of their social role, future possibilities, and their own cultural surroundings, such as language of origin, customary food, and social networks.

Prolonged exposure to toxic forms of violence, especially in childhood, has devastating long-term consequences. In response to threat, aggressive states are quickly and dramatically alternated with fearful flight or avoidance states. Because children are often physically incapable of fighting off their captors or fleeing a situation, the most common reaction to traumatic events is to detach themselves from the external and internal worlds through dissociation, experiencing numbing, depersonalization, and derealization (Schauer & Elbert, 2009). Youths who are exposed to such a degree of violence and threat are often unable to complete developmental tasks such as forming safe attachment relationships, a stable and integrated concept of self and others, and the competence to self-regulate emotion and behavior (Van der Kolk, 2005).

The reaction of many former child soldiers to repeated and prolonged interpersonal trauma may be best described by concepts such as complex trauma or developmental trauma disorder (Cloitre, 2009; Klasen, Daniels, Oettingen, Post, & Hoyer, 2010; Van der Kolk, 2005). The symptom profile refers to the presence of PTSD with additional disturbances in the domains of affect regulation, interpersonal relatedness, and self-identity. In addition to complex PTSD, these patients often suffer from depression and DID, in which both the memories of atrocities as well as participating perpetrator parts are totally split off from awareness. In the literature on dissociation these self-states (or alters) are described as "protector parts": emotional parts of the personality that are "fixated in the protective 'fight' subsystem, and attempt to manage the difficult emotions of rage and anger and to avoid feelings of hurt, fear or shame" (Van der Hart, Nijenhuis, & Steele, 2006, p. 82).

In treating former child soldiers, clinicians are confronted with oppression and dissociation in and outside of psychotherapy. Relatively minor stressors can trigger classic fight, flight, or freeze reactions, manifested by severe aggression and/or regressed dissociative states. These patients have difficulties controlling aggressive impulses, they perceive violence as a legitimate means of achieving one's aims, and they have insufficient skills to handle daily life without aggression. Clinicians are pulled into the reenactments of old trauma scenarios and become part of a wild therapeutic dance of approach and avoidance that can feel like war. They are faced with severe transference and countertransference problems.

TRANSFERENCE-FOCUSED PSYCHOTHERAPY (TFP) AND ITS APPLICATION

TFP is an evidence-based, manualized, psychodynamic treatment based on object relations theory (Clarkin, Yeomans, & Kernberg, 2006; Clarkin, Levy, Lenzenweger, & Kernberg, 2007; Doering et al., 2010; Yeomans, Clarkin, & Kernberg, 2002). It was developed to treat patients suffering from severe personality disorders, that is, with a borderline personality organization (Kernberg, 1984). *Borderline personality organization* refers to a psychological structure characterized by identity diffusion (a fragmented and fluctuating sense of self: oscillation of self-and-other representations and emotions linked between them) and "primitive" defenses (splitting, denial, and projective identification) with reality testing generally intact but prone to distortions under stress. The patient communicates not only verbally and nonverbally but also via projective identification (so-called belly talk), in which untolerated emotional states are externalized and induced in and sensed by the therapist.

The aim of TFP is to integrate these conflicting inner self-and-other states into a more coherent personality structure. The basic assumption of TFP is that human beings are social animals (who want to bond and be autonomous as well), whose inner worlds consist fundamentally of relational elements, dyads, consisting of images of self and other (the object) and the linking emotion. In borderline personality organization this inner world is divided into all-good and all-bad dyadic elements that are perceived as being in conflict with each other and kept apart through the process of splitting. In severely traumatized patients this basic division is further accentuated by dissociation. The theoretical questions about how splitting and dissociation interrelate and whether splitting itself is a dissociative, trauma-related phenomenon are beyond the scope of this article. In fact, in severely traumatized patients splitting and dissociation are totally intertwined. Nevertheless, the key idea is that splitting is driven by conflict: the conflict between the tendency to approach, to seek intimacy, and to bond versus the tendency to avoid contact and dependency and to defend against being hurt or controlled (i.e., the dynamics of love vs. aggression).

The all-good dyads consist of longing and perfect loving relationships with an ideal object, such as perfect mothers or fathers. These all-good dyads, because they are not integrated with realistic shortcomings and disappointments, are unrealistic and can lead to pathological frustration and a flip into the reverse all-bad dyads. All-bad dyads consist of images of persecutory/dominating relationships based on a mix of past subjective reality, one's own aggressive affects, identification with aggressors, and strong fears. In relationships, and in psychotherapy, the inner dyads oscillate: The anxious victim inside fearing retaliation by an overpowering other can suddenly switch into a dominating force attacking the now-weak other. If the therapist is experienced as a bad object, the patient may attack to protect himself or herself from being overpowered—thus enacting aggression without full awareness of being aggressive. This model of object relations thinking has the therapist exploring these projections empathically with the patient, looking as if through the patient's eyes. This perspective is very helpful in understanding and handling the constant push and pull in moment-to-moment interactions in the treatment of patients with personality disorders as well as severe dissociative disorders (Draijer, 2009, 2010a, 2010b).

TFP interventions consist of *exploring* the inner world of the patient and his or her view from that world on the therapist. To be able to do this it is particularly important to fully experience the transference *in the here and now* (What is the patient making of me?), empathically following the patient in his or her creation of the therapist, containing the dyad expressed in it, and presenting this to the patient. Thus, an intervention might be constructed as follows: "When I properly listen to you, it is as if you see me as a cruel and dominating person. That must be a very scary situation for you." When patients experience being understood properly by the containment of having the relationship articulated the way they perceive it, they suddenly calm down, even if in an angry state of mind, and are able to start reflecting on what is happening.

Once the reflective functioning of the patient begins to improve—which can take quite a while—the task for the therapist is to *confront* the patient carefully with inconsistencies and oscillations between dyads, raising the patient's empathic curiosity for his or her own inner world. An example intervention would be the following: "That is interesting. Just a few minutes ago our conversation seemed quite intimate and you shared your sadness with me, apparently perceiving me as a safe and reliable listener, but suddenly it seemed that you perceived me as a threat you have to protect yourself against by reclaiming total power. How do you combine these two states of mind?"

And finally, when the patient is able to reflect and experience the therapeutic relationship as supportive at least some of the time, it is the task of the therapist to *interpret* the defensive layering of opposing dyads. Interpretation in TFP is a process that leads to presenting the positive and negative dyads simultaneously to the patient, relating them. For example, "Could it be that your anger is so extreme, distancing you from me, because you feel so vulnerable when you realize that you long deeply for a safe relationship with a reliable parental figure?" or "Could it be that you seem to prefer to see me as totally unreliable, because perceiving me as trustful and reliable makes you feel so terribly sad about your losses? Could it be that—by doing this—you protect your heart against losing a loved one for a second time?" So interpretation is about "you and me" in the here and now; it is not etiological.

This whole step-by-step interactional and interpretational process (Caligor, Diamond, Yeomans, & Kernberg, 2009) results in the gradual mitigation of anger and rage and eventually in the integration of the personality.

In TFP the patient is held responsible for his or her own recovery; this means that in the beginning of treatment a contract is made about (self-) destructive acting out, and the therapist explains to the patient that this behavior is in opposition to a development toward health. When the patient might point out that he or she only knows one solution for conflict—to use violence—the therapist holds him or her responsible to prevent it: "All feelings are welcome and respected, even murderous rage, as long as we can talk about it and not act on it." When the patient has noticed a tendency to act out, or when he or she actually does, the patient is asked to mention it first thing in the next session. To prevent repetition of the cycle of abuse "the soldier needs to learn how to talk."

TFP ILLUSTRATED IN CASE MATERIAL

Ishmael is 24-year-old man from Sierra Leone who has been in The Netherlands since 2003. The first time the therapist met him, Ishmael had unsuccessfully been in psychotherapy for 3 years in which stabilization and support were the key focus. It soon became clear that Ishmael was highly ambivalent about treatment: motivated but scared of the intimacy inherent in psychotherapy. Ishmael's biggest fear was losing control of his aggression when being triggered and harming an innocent person. He had gotten into fights with others, including his girlfriend.

He met criteria for DID, PTSD, and depression, as well as personality disorder not otherwise specified. He suffered from amnesia and brief psychotic episodes, including auditory comments and visual hallucinations. He had been suicidal occasionally and had been hospitalized once. He reported feelings of severe distrust, guilt and shame, extreme loneliness, a sense of not belonging, and a sense of being dehumanized: "Sometimes I feel I am more an animal than a human being."

Ishmael was born in Sierra Leone. He describes his early years as moderately happy. At the age of 8 the rebels killed his mother in front of him and he was captured. He has never seen his father and sister since. Ishmael was forced by the rebels to stay with them in the jungle as a child-slave. There he experienced and witnessed innumerable cruelties and was forced to participate in them. After 5 years he was able to escape and managed to stay alive in Freetown. Currently he is in the middle of an asylum procedure.

The main problem in the first phase of psychotherapy was his inability to remain psychologically present while relating to others. This would manifest in the form of dissociation (e.g., switching into other states of mind, being absent) or in extreme dominance, aggression, and oppression of the therapist. He reported paranoid feelings: having extreme fears of being abused, exploited, or humiliated and not being cared for. He was unable to use the affect regulation techniques that were taught to him. When exposed to his aggression the therapist often felt overwhelmed by fear and struggled to reflect on what was going on. TFP offered a framework that made sense in understanding these confusing forces, the pushing and pulling, the reenactments.

Moving to TFP marked the transition from a one-person model of understanding the patient and his symptoms to a two-person model of understanding the patient and the dynamic interpersonal forces he experiences. When asked about the differences in approach after this transition, the first thing that came to the therapist's mind was: "So much more contact and understanding of what he is going through, since I empathically explore and see through his eyes the person he is making of me. Dissociation and aggression became understandable as a means to regulate distance and intimacy in our relationship."

Using Clarkin et al.'s (2006) overview of the dominant dyads in the transference and countertransference, we illustrate some of these in this psychotherapy (see Table 1). The following transference–countertransference interaction demonstrates the dynamic nature of dyadic relationships. In

TABLE 1 Dominant Dyads in Transference–Countertransference

Patient	Therapist
Controlling, omnipotent self	Weak, slave-like other
Abused victim	Sadistic attacker/persecutor
Out-of-control, angry child	Incompetent, useless parent
Dependent, gratified child	Perfect provider
Friendly, submissive self	Doting, admiring parent

reaction to his vulnerability in sharing with the therapist one of his most traumatic experiences, and becoming sad, the patient suddenly switched into a different state. The therapist experienced the following:

> I feel overwhelmed by his sudden shift to aggression. His eyes sharpen and in a derogative manner he says, "Can't you see? There is fighting everywhere around you." His gaze hardens and becomes indifferent. His lips slightly curl in a sadistic smile. It seems that I am part of the reliving of a violent and cruel traumatic experience in which we are facing each other in a combat situation. I no longer see the Ishmael I know; I see an extremely dangerous and threatening rebel who's capable of anything. I wonder if he sees the same threat in me. I feel confused. My body is warning me that there is danger and I am hyperaroused. I catch myself looking at his hands, wondering if he could attack. Right now I want to stay sharp, but chaos takes hold of me. I am no longer able to reflect on what is going on and am drowning in a flood of fear. In the meantime I'm desperately searching for my therapeutic framework and tools but they seem to be washed away. I feel paralyzed and helpless. I can't win this battle, he's stronger, and I surrender to him . . . Is this what he wants to achieve with his aggression?
>
> I point out his aggression and ask what is happening inside of him. He seems startled; his aggression suddenly disappears, he denies being angry or afraid; now he is the one who's confused and vulnerable. I am suddenly the perpetrator and he is the victim. I don't want to be the perpetrator. There's confusion again.

Reconstructing what happened afterward in supervision, we see an aggressive defense against sadness and vulnerability, as well as the reenactment of trauma, but in the reversed, dominant position, scaring the therapist to a terrifying submission and confusion. The patient seems to evoke in the therapist the extreme fear that he is unable to verbalize. There is an oscillation between the sadistic attacker/persecutor and the abused victim. The task of the therapist is to tolerate this almost unbearable fear.

If the therapist is able to survive this fear and to keep reflecting on what is happening between her and the patient, taking a respectful and neutral stance, she is increasingly able to contain the bad object projected onto her and to try to engage the patient in reflecting on or symbolically holding what had previously existed as a raw, unsymbolized affect state. The therapist's empathic curiosity engages the patient in seeing that the intense state that overwhelms him may exist in a broader context of other internal states and thus not comprise the whole of reality or of the relationship, thus modifying the object, especially in its intensity and its one-dimensional quality. Room for reflection, be it just a second or two, and tolerance for affect are slowly but gradually growing, as all affects are accepted, tolerated, and contained by the therapist. In the patient a process takes place in which he slowly brings together the attacker he fears and the empathic and reflecting other he experiences and may secretly long for—both of which are reflections of internal states within him. This is thought to be an integrative process. Thus, the persecutory objects and self-states in the patient become gradually detoxified (Scharff & Tsigounis, 2003).

Some time later the therapist struggles with overwhelming feelings of powerlessness and sadness, empathizing with the patient. Now the patient seems to be more able to tolerate his vulnerable state as well as being connected with the therapist. Now the therapist notes the following:

> Ishmael expresses intense feelings of worthlessness related to atrocities he experienced as a victim. He longs for peace of mind and death. I feel his self-loathing and pain. Unable to tolerate it, I try to change his guilty and shameful perspective on himself but notice it does not fit his needs. He lets me know that he has no room for it. I tell him that I understand that wanting to change his perspective was a futile attempt to deal with my own feelings of powerlessness that his sadness induced. I add: "We could let the sadness exist here as we sit together, without having to talk about it." He remarks that he would like that, especially because there is nowhere else where he can just let his sadness exist. Our eyes meet and his sadness hits me. He sees that my eyes become moist and I say that his sadness affects me. For a moment he turns his head away but then meets my gaze again and I can see that he allows his sadness to exist in my presence. There is an intense moment of meeting. At the end of the session, Ishmael tells me that through experiencing and sharing his sadness he feels "more connected" and less lonely.

From a dyadic perspective, the therapist's feelings of powerlessness and sadness come from how the patient is interacting with and perceiving her (i.e., projection and projective identification). In this instant the therapist first wanted to comfort the patient prematurely and get away from the sadness, acting out the way the patient regularly does. Then the patient was aware of the sadness in the therapist, as she was willing to sit it out with the patient, tolerating the sadness together. This being there in the sadness with him together restored his tolerance for connection, for relatedness, for the mother in him that he had lost.

After 18 months of TFP the therapist notices a remarkable increase in and tolerance for intimacy and vulnerability in the therapeutic relationship. This development represents access to the previously split-off libidinal segment of the patient's internal world. He is more able to verbalize and tolerate painful experiences and strong emotions. There are fewer oscillations between emotional states and there is less black-and-white thinking. The aggression has become less wild, destructive, and scary and seems to be gradually melting away. Aggressive feelings, thoughts, and fantasies are openly shared in therapy. Ishmael is better able to regulate emotions and to assert himself nonviolently.

At the symptom level there are fewer nightmares, fewer flashbacks/reliving states of terror, less dissociation, less avoidance of traumatic material, less distrust, and fewer feelings of guilt and shame. Auditory comments and visual hallucinations have receded. With respect to DID there is more differentiation between then and now. Emotional states are less fragmented and less separated by amnesia. Severe traumatic experiences concerning atrocities no longer are told only through the murderous self but now are also told in sad and more reflective states. Ishmael lives a less isolated life; he has more contact with the outside world through his volunteer work, hobbies, and even a budding friendship.

DISCUSSION

In the treatment of former child soldiers from Africa with DID, TFP helps to address the aggression of these patients and their tendency to seek total control and dominance over or oppression of the therapist. It is a helpful object relations model to understand the severe problems with split-off aggression, as well as the sudden and confusing switches in the mental states of the patient, addressing transference–countertransference, the therapeutic dance of push-and-pull interactions and reenactments between patient and therapist, instead of addressing primarily symptoms situated in the patient.

This touches also on the discussion of working either from a one- or two-person psychology perspective in understanding and treating extreme trauma. The case described here moved from a one-person perspective with limited success (focusing on symptoms and psychopathology perceived solely *in* the patient) to a two-person psychological model in which the focus was on the dynamics as perceived *between* the patient and the therapist in the form of splitting, projective identification, and oscillating self-and-other states. This helped the patient to emotionally regulate, to start mentalizing, to socialize, and to integrate more, both internally and externally. Instead of following the traditional phase-oriented trauma therapy, affect regulation was strengthened by focusing on enhancing secure attachment in the therapeutic relationship.

This represents a move from PTSD seen primarily as an anxiety disorder toward (complex) PTSD (and DID) perceived primarily as relational disorders characterized by isolation, loneliness (disconnection), distrust of others, lack of soothing, lack of comforting inner relationships, rage toward mankind, shame, and guilt. Complex stress-related disorders such as DID are disorders of personality, identity, and affect regulation, relational disorders altogether. Psychodynamic models work in the here and now of the therapeutic relationship.

After 18 months of TFP we observed improved affect regulation as well as mentalization and relatedness in this patient. The mechanism of change in the improved affect regulation could be hypothesized in the fine attunement by the therapist to, and containment of, the dominant dyads and the emotional states linked to them in the here and now of the interaction. Supporting this hypothesis is a study by Levy et al. (2006) that showed a development toward improved reflective functioning and security of attachment in borderline patients after 1 year of TFP. More secure attachment leads to better affect regulation (Schore, 2005). One could argue that TFP is similar to mentalization-based therapy. The major difference is that in TFP the oscillation, the conflict between different dyads, is central. Moreover, as the transference is addressed, the therapist takes part in the dance and is less of a coach; TFP is more experiential than cognitive. Finally, TFP respects aggression as a central dynamic force.

Views on aggression and how to treat it diverge considerably. Some treatment models do not address it at all (assuming that it comes from an 'alien self'), others solely try to control it (more cognitive–behavioral types of anger management) or suppress it (e.g., through medication); however, in TFP it is considered essential and vital (and in a way healthy) in the inner dynamics.

We have the clinical impression that in severely traumatized patients in whom aggression does not surface in treatment directly, aggression may be channeled through nightmares and self-harm. In this way it is projected onto (inner) perpetrators as a safe way to experience aggression (externalizing it internally). Such patients also have (aggressive) oppressive parts who want total control—arising from identification with their childhood aggressors. From a TFP perspective, in order to reach some form of integration, balance, and health it is essential that the patient's aggression is addressed and acknowledged to belong to the patient himself or herself. We observe that not all patients are able or willing to face this, and they feel that there is no way forward but to stay oppressed by holding onto their identity as a victim, perpetually attacked by projected aggression.

The TFP therapist takes part in the dance but tries to keep reflecting on what happens between them. The therapist does this in a respectful way, remaining neutral toward the conflicts in the patient, accepting what is put forward into him or her. To use the metaphor of a harbor: All ships are allowed in; no ship needs to stay at sea (i.e., all feelings and mental states, however negative they may be, are welcome in the relationship with the therapist). The therapist then acts as a reflecting mirror in which the patient sees a more integrated image of himself or herself than what he or she is projecting. The containment of aggression and hatred is a precondition on the road toward the integration of good and bad. The murderous self needs to be seen, respected, welcomed, and appreciated for what it means to the entire person: It is the keeper of horrible memories and it watches over the patient to avoid being hurt again. This aspect of self is extremely lonely (dehumanized) and convinced that no one will ever like it or be close to it. If this dangerous and hateful part of the patient feels that it is understood, respected, and appreciated, the patient's hate slowly starts to melt (see Draijer, 1999). Only then is there room for mourning and deep sadness. Patients who have killed need to mourn, and rituals of mourning and regret may be introduced.

Finally, for the therapist to learn to make himself or herself emotionally available to the inner world of the patient, to participate in this dance and to recognize it and reflect on it in order to make an intervention, supervision is a *conditio sine qua non*. To develop this emotional availability, this mental skill and awareness of induced feelings and processing them into an intervention, the therapist needs a safe and accepting relationship with a supervisor.

CONCLUSION

Extreme aggression and a self-state of a killer—particularly in males—pose severe problems for patients with dissociative disorders, alienating them from other people, preventing intimacy, and inducing fear in their psychotherapists. This problem is hardly addressed in the theory or research on PTSD, and treatment focuses primarily on anxiety.

Anger and aggression are central to severe traumatization, causing patients to feel guilty, bad, and isolated, leaving them struggling for control and alienating them from fellow humans. This is particularly the case when patients have been forced to kill. In the treatment of former child soldiers with DID suffering from split-off aggression, TFP helps to address these aggressive parts and their tendency to seek total control over, or oppression of, others, including the therapist. It also helps free patients from their internal oppression.

REFERENCES

Betancourt, T. S., Borisova, I. I., Williams, T. P., Brennan, R. T., Whitfield, T. H., de la Soudiere, M., . . . Gilman, S. E. (2010). Sierra Leone's former child soldiers: A follow-up study of psychosocial adjustment and community reintegration. *Child Development*, *81*, 1077–1095.

Caligor, E., Diamond, D., Yeomans, F. E., & Kernberg, O. F. (2009). The interpretive process in the psychoanalytic psychotherapy of borderline personality pathology. *Journal of the American Psychoanalytic Association*, *57*, 271–301.

Chemtob, C. M., Novaco, R. W., Hamada, R. S., Gross, D. M., & Smith, G. (1997). Anger regulation deficits in combat-related posttraumatic stress disorder. *Journal of Traumatic Stress*, *10*(1), 17–36.

Chu, J. A. (1998). *Rebuilding shattered lives*. New York, NY: Wiley.

Clarkin, J. F., Levy, K. N., Lenzenweger, M., & Kernberg, O. F. (2007). Evaluating three treatments for borderline personality disorder. *American Journal of Psychiatry*, *164*, 922–928.

Clarkin, J. F., Yeomans, F. E., & Kernberg, O. F. (2006). *Psychotherapy for borderline personality: Focusing on object relations*. Arlington, VA: American Psychiatric Publishing.

Cloitre, M. (2009). Effective psychotherapies for posttraumatic stress disorder: A review and critique. *CNS Spectrums*, *14*(1), 32–43.

Doering, S., Hörz, S., Rentrop, M., Fischer-Kern, M., Schuster, P., Benecke, C., . . . Buchheim, P. (2010). Transference-focused psychotherapy v. treatment by community psychotherapists for borderline personality disorder: Randomised controlled trial. *British Journal of Psychiatry*, *196*(5), 389–395.

Draijer, N. (1999). Pathologische haat en traumatisering; de worsteling met afstand, nabijheid en herinnering [Pathological hatred and traumatization: The struggle with approach, avoidance and memory]. In G. F. Koerselman & W. Tilburg (Eds.), *Haat* [*Hatred*] (pp. 55–74). Tricht, Netherlands: Foundation Psychoanalysis and Psychiatry.

Draijer, N. (2009, November). *Transference focused psychotherapy (TFP) techniques in the treatment of DID*. Preconference workshop at the International Conference of the International Society for the Study of Trauma and Dissociation, Washington, DC.

Draijer, N. (2010a, April). *Transference focused psychotherapy (TFP) techniques in the treatment of DID*. 2nd International Conference of the European Society for Trauma and Dissociation, Belfast, Ireland.

Draijer, N. (2010b, October). *An object-relational approach to problematic (counter) transference, working with patients with severe trauma related disorders (DID, C-PTSD, BPD)*. Workshop at the International Conference of the International Society for the Study of Trauma and Dissociation, Atlanta, GA.

Ehntholt, K. A., & Yule, W. (2006). Practitioner review: Assessment and treatment of refugee children and adolescents who have experienced war-related trauma. *Journal of Child Psychology and Psychiatry*, *47*, 1197–1210.

Glancy, G., & Saini, M. A. (2005). An evidenced-based review of psychological treatments of anger and aggression. *Brief Treatment and Crisis Intervention*, *5*(2), 229–248.

Kernberg, O. F. (1984). The Structural Interview. In O. F. Kernberg, *Severe personality disorders: Psychotherapeutic strategies* (pp. 27–51). New Haven, CT: Yale University press.

Klasen, F., Daniels, J., Oettingen, G., Post, M., & Hoyer, C. (2010). Posttraumatic resilience in former Ugandan child soldiers. *Child Development*, *81*, 1096–1113.

Levy, K. N., Clarkin, J. F., Yeomans, F. E., Scott, L. N., Wasserman, R. H., & Kernberg, O. F. (2006). The mechanisms of change in the treatment of borderline personality disorder with transference focused psychotherapy. *Journal of Clinical Psychology, 62*, 481–501.

Mills, J. (2005). *Treating attachment pathology*. Oxford, England: Rowman & Littlefield.

Nicholl, C., & Thompson, A. (2004). The psychological treatment of post traumatic stress disorder (PTSD) in adult refugees: A review of the current state of psychological therapies. *Journal of Mental Health, 13*(4), 351–362.

Orth, U., & Wieland, E. (2006). Anger, hostility, and posttraumatic stress disorder in trauma-exposed adults: A meta-analysis. *Journal of Consulting and Clinical Psychology, 74*, 698–706.

Saini, M. A. (2009). Meta-analysis of the psychological treatment of anger: Developing guidelines for evidence-based practice. *Journal of the American Academy of Psychiatry and the Law Online, 37*, 473–488.

Scharff, J. S., & Tsigounis, S. A. (2003). *Self-hatred in psychoanalysis: Detoxifying the persecutory object*. New York, NY: Brunner-Routledge.

Schauer, E., & Elbert, T. (2009). *The psychological impact of child soldiering*. Retrieved from http://www.fotres.ch/index.cfm?action=act_getfile&doc_id=100518

Schore, A. N. (2005). Attachment, affect regulation, and the developing right brain: Linking developmental neuroscience to pediatrics. *Pediatrics in Review, 26*, 204–211.

UNICEF. (2007). *Paris principles: Principles and guidelines on children associated with armed forces or armed conflict*. New York, NY: Author.

Van der Hart, O., Nijenhuis, E. R. S., & Steele, K. (2006). *Structural dissociation and the treatment of chronic traumatization*. New York, NY: Norton.

Van der Kolk, B. A. (2005). Developmental trauma disorder: Towards a rational diagnosis for chronically traumatized children. *Psychiatric Annals, 35*, 401–408.

Yehuda, R. (1999). Managing anger and aggression in patients with posttraumatic stress disorder. *Journal of Clinical Psychiatry, 60*(15), 33–37.

Yeomans, F. E., Clarkin, J. F., & Kernberg, O. F. (2002). *A primer of transference focused psychotherapy for the borderline patient*. Northvale, NJ: Jason Aronson.

Boundary Modifications in the Treatment of People with Dissociative Disorders: An International Perspective

ADAH SACHS, MA

Clinic for Dissociative Studies and The Bowlby Centre, London, England

This article examines the prevalence and types of modifications to professional boundaries that occur in the treatment of people with dissociative disorders (DDs) and considers some of the implications of the findings. The study is based on the replies of 163 professionals to a 20-question survey. The survey compared the boundaries that each practitioner kept with patients/clients (P/Cs) who suffered DDs to their boundary practice with all of their other P/Cs (non-DDs). Boundaries were deemed modified when professionals treated their DDs P/Cs differently than their other P/Cs. Professionals' general boundaries were not examined. The results showed a marked tendency for the modification of professional boundaries when treating people with DDs. These results appeared to be independent of country or profession but were more pronounced among the more experienced professionals. Areas of greatest modifications were identified. The prevalence of these modifications points to their potential importance in understanding some features of DDs.

The field of mental health, which inherently deals with people's vulnerabilities, places great importance on professional boundaries. The subfield of trauma and dissociation, with its constant brushing against the forensic, is particularly sensitive to this issue, and views regarding the ethical, legal, and clinical merits of various practices vary greatly and are often polarized.

Differences in culture, country, profession, training organization, registering body, and trends further complicate questions regarding boundaries.

The idea for this study came from numerous colleagues and supervisees whom I have heard confess, "This case, I don't even take to supervision." The clinicians in question were fully trained, experienced, registered professionals. The cases they referred to were of patients/clients (P/Cs) with dissociative disorders (DDs). The reason for these confessed statements was that in the cases in question these clinicians had acted in ways that differed from their normal practice in regard to boundaries, and they felt anxious about the potential of finding themselves in violation of their professional guidelines. Yet they considered that the changes to their normal boundaries were necessary and that they could not have carried out their *duty of care* toward their P/Cs while maintaining their normal professional boundaries. A case in point is one on which I have recently been consulted in which a clinician was facing allegations of misconduct by the health service for continuing to see privately, but for no charge, a DDs patient who had been discharged from the service.

It has been my subjective impression that such conflicts and risk taking are not rare in the treatment of P/Cs with DDs. This pilot study examines whether evidence can be found to support this subjective impression. It also measures the prevalence and type of modifications to professional boundaries in the treatment of people with DDs and observes some of the characteristics of the professionals who reported them.

DEFINITIONS

In this article, the term *professional boundaries* is broadly used to describe the normal standard of contact that professionals observe with their P/Cs. The article does not attempt a view regarding what this standard should be. The term *boundary modifications* refers to any differences between the professional boundaries that professionals observe with their DDs P/Cs compared with their practice with any other P/Cs. This study measures these modifications regarding 20 specific questions. Boundary crossing, boundary breaking, and boundary violations are not examined.

THE CENTRAL PRINCIPLE

The complexity and wide variation of views regarding the correctness and suitability of different boundary practices makes it difficult to agree upon a baseline against which professional boundaries could be measured. The *central principle* of this study was thus to compare the normal boundaries of each professional with the boundaries of that same professional when he or she works with DDs P/Cs. Professionals who kept, crossed, or violated boundaries with both P/Cs groups (DDs and non-DDs) in the same manner were deemed, for the purpose of this study, to show no boundary modifications. With this principle in mind, differences in views, values, principles, and practices between the wide variety of professionals could be largely bypassed, as each professional was only compared to himself or herself in his or her work across the two P/Cs groups.

It should be emphasized that the thorny questions of what constitutes keeping, crossing, breaking, or violating clinical boundaries (and indeed the numerous definitions of *boundaries*) are not the subject of this article, and the study does not attempt a view on this, nor does it examine controversies regarding these concepts. (For a sample of the extensive writing on boundaries controversies across several professions, see Chu, 2011; Doel et al., 2010; Gabbard & Nadelson, 1995; Galton, 2006; Guthheil & Gabbard, 1998; Poole & Cook, 2011; Pope & Keith-Spiegle, 2008).

METHOD

The Participants

To participate in this study, one had to work or to have worked with both DDs and non-DDs populations (at least one case from each group), be a registered professional or a registered trainee-professional, and be invited to the study as a member of a participating professional organization. As participants were asked to potentially place themselves at risk by reporting professional boundary violations (with either P/Cs group), the survey was designed to be strictly anonymous in order to minimize response bias. To further ensure confidentiality, no details on the participants were required other than their membership in the invited professional organizations and their professional registration status. Background questions were optional. Participants were notified that the material gathered might be published.

To ensure the suitability and genuineness of the respondents, participation was offered only to members of specific professional groups. These groups were chosen to provide a wide range of professional attitudes and a wide geographical spread. Participation in the study was proposed to the appropriate committee, board of directors, or chairperson of seven professional bodies (see below). Following approval, these organizations invited their own members through their normal channels of communication (e.g., members' online bulletin, password protected) to take part in the survey. Online access to the survey was granted by a group-designated password. Each person could reply once. People who belonged to more than one group could only reply once, at their discretion. Only completed surveys were used in the study. Approximately 400 responses were received, of which 163 were usable.

Responses were collected in five groups, as follows: United Kingdom: The Bowlby Centre; Association of Christian Counsellors; Institute for the Arts in Therapy and Education ($n = 30$); Israel: Trauma and Dissociation Israel, an association of trauma therapists ($n = 15$); Europe: Association of German-Speaking Trauma Therapists ($n = 14$); International: International Society for the Study of Trauma and Dissociation (ISSTD) membership ($n = 56$); and International: dissociative identity disorder specialists, individually invited ($n = 48$); total $N = 163$.

The Instrument

The study aimed to establish whether there are notable differences between the boundaries that professionals keep in their work with the two groups (DDs and non-DDs) of P/Cs. The instrument used was a 20-question survey that explored clinicians' actual practice (not views or values) with both groups. A number of experienced colleagues reviewed the initial list. The final list (see Appendix) was constructed to reflect areas that are frequently discussed in boundaries discourse (e.g., contact between sessions), as well as a few that are more unusual (e.g., looking after your P/C's children or pets). An optional section, not used in the scoring, explored background parameters: profession, country of practice, percentage of DDs P/Cs in one's practice, and additional comments.

Scoring

According to the central principle of this study, the scoring did not evaluate the strictness of the boundaries of each professional but the differences between the practices that each professional applied to the two groups (DDs vs. non-DDs). Each of the survey questions (see Appendix) had five possible answers, which in the scoring process received numerical values from 0 to 3. Each question was answered twice: once for the DDs group and once for the non-DDs group. The numerical discrepancy between the two answers to the same question was scored and is the subject of this study. The score for DDs P/Cs is referred to as A and that for non-DDs P/Cs as B. The difference between them (A minus B) is the C score. When the answers to A and B were the same, the C score for that question was 0. A positive C score (+C) means A > B; a negative C score (–C) means A < B.

RESULTS

The 20 C scores for each respondent were aggregated to give a total C score per respondent. Out of the 163 respondents, 138 (85%) had a positive total

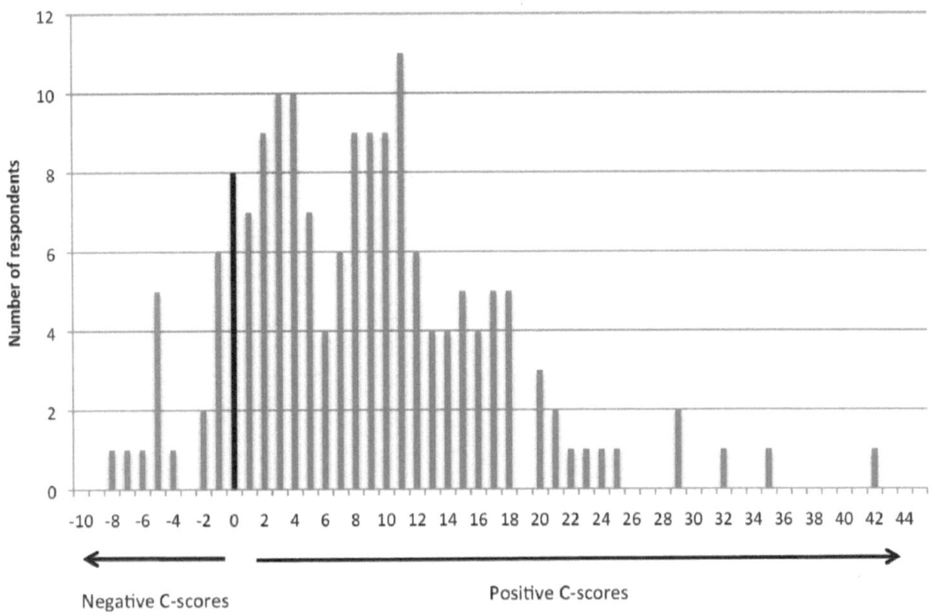

FIGURE 1 Distribution of C scores by respondent.

C score (i.e., the total of their answers for the DDs group was higher than the total of their answers for their non-DDs cases). Their scores ranged from 1 to 42 out of 60 possible points. Seventeen (10%) of the respondents had a negative total C score (i.e., answers for the non-DDs group were higher than those for the DDs group). Their scores ranged from 1 to 8 points out of 60 possible. Only 8 (5%) respondents reported total C = 0 (i.e., no overall difference in practice with the two groups; see Figure 1).

Out of 3,260 C scores (20 questions × 163 respondents), approximately two thirds were C = 0 (the same answer for both the DDs and non-DDs groups). The last third, however, were consistently weighted toward the DDs group (the answer for the DDs group greater than the answer for the non-DDs by at least one step, e.g., from "rarely" to "sometimes"). Positive C scores were reported 1,061 times out of 3,260 (32%); negative C scores were reported 133 times (4%). The ratio of +C answers to –C answers was 8:1. These ratios varied for each question but never reversed: For each question, instances of positive C were always markedly higher than instances of negative C (see Table 1).

Some Differentiations

Given the relatively small sample size (N = 163), further division into subgroups may have provided misleading results. There were, however, a few subgroups that appeared potentially interesting and worthy of reporting.

TABLE 1 Distribution of C Scores by Question

	Number of responses per C score								
Question No.	−3	−2	−1	**All −ve**	0	**All +ve**	+1	+2	+3
1	0	0	8	**8**	51	**104**	54	43	7
2	0	0	3	**3**	111	**49**	31	13	5
3	0	0	1	**1**	139	**23**	14	6	3
4	0	2	4	**6**	93	**64**	37	23	4
5	0	0	7	**7**	83	**73**	47	24	2
6	0	3	5	**8**	118	**37**	23	13	1
7	0	0	2	**2**	122	**39**	25	11	3
8	0	3	5	**8**	120	**35**	23	12	0
9	1	4	9	**14**	101	**48**	35	13	0
10	0	0	9	**9**	128	**26**	20	6	0
11	0	0	4	**4**	106	**53**	25	20	8
12	0	0	4	**4**	88	**71**	46	21	4
13	0	1	5	**6**	104	**53**	33	18	2
14	0	1	7	**8**	103	**52**	41	9	2
15	0	0	6	**6**	95	**62**	34	22	6
16	0	0	18	**18**	111	**34**	28	3	3
17	0	0	11	**11**	116	**36**	23	10	3
18	0	0	1	**1**	105	**57**	39	16	2
19	0	0	4	**4**	84	**75**	54	17	4
20	0	2	3	**5**	88	**70**	45	21	4
Total	1	16	116	**133**	2,066	**1,061**	677	321	63

By country. The sample provided a wide geographical cover. As well as the country-specific groups (United Kingdom, German-speaking Europe, and Israel), the international spread included Canada, most states in the United States, eight European countries, and a small sample from Australia, New Zealand, and Africa. The average C scores by country were very similar: German-speaking Europe, 6.1; Israel, 6.5; United Kingdom, 7.2; international ISSTD membership, 7.7. Only minor geographical or national differences were noted in this study.

By profession. Across the most frequently reported professions in this study, psychiatrists and medical doctors showed the highest average +C scores (14 and 12.8, respectively) and art therapists and psychologists the lowest (4.4 and 4.3, respectively). Counselors, psychotherapists, and social workers were almost identical, in the middle range (9.5, 9.2, and 8.8, respectively).

Considering the variations in these results, several factors are noted as potential explanations. The majority of psychologists in this study were from the United States. Two of them commented that they were required by insurers to be available out-of-hours to *all* of their P/Cs when asked. If such is the requirement of all U.S. psychologists, then their scores may be artificially determined (by funding providers rather than their own clinical choices). Indeed, the psychologists' distribution picture showed elevated bottom-scores for both A and B groups (= fewer than average "never" answers for *all* P/Cs). In regard to the art therapists, 50% of them in this study were also trainees. The C score result may thus reflect their level of experience (see the next section) rather than their profession.

The psychiatrist and medical doctor groups had the highest average C scores in this study. Notably all of them scored the highest on Question 19 (placing oneself at risk personally or professionally in work with his or her DDs P/Cs). Their overall high C scores thus seemed to occur despite a high sense of risk rather than as a reflection of a relaxed attitude toward boundaries.

By level of experience with DDs. One background question was "What is the percentage of DDs P/Cs in your practice?" Respondents who answered "over 50%" showed markedly higher C scores than their colleagues for most questions. Worryingly their average C score to Question 20, "Reached a point of burnout," was 30% higher.

Of the practitioners with less experience, two trainee art therapists who had negative C scores (= answers for the DDs group lower than for the non-DDs group) reported in their comments that the therapy with their DDs P/Cs had broken down. What is interesting is that both believed that it had to do with their boundaries being too loose. In the absence of a larger sample one can only wonder whether these comments and the low C scores reflect the fact that trainees who are under evaluation for qualifying, as well as the least experienced, are potentially the most anxious about boundary modifications.

By severity of cases. This study did not evaluate the severity of cases. However, the group of practitioners who specialized in the treatment of dissociative identity disorder (and was thus likely to represent professionals who work with the most severe cases) showed the highest +C scores on 15 out of the 20 questions and the highest overall average +C score (11, compared with 7.7 for the ISSTD general membership).

By index questions. Although the replies to all of the survey questions were weighted toward boundary modifications with the DDs group, there were five questions for which less than 55% of respondents maintained their normal boundaries with their DDs P/Cs. These questions indicate areas in which practice with DDs P/Cs has in fact departed from the practice with other groups and may require new guidelines (see Table 2).

DISCUSSION

This pilot study was carried out on a small scale and limited to a descriptive analysis of the results. The findings, nevertheless, do appear to present a picture. They show an almost universal tendency, reported by 85% of practitioners in the survey, for professionals to modify some of their normal boundaries when working with DDs P/Cs (compared with 10% of respondents who reported modifying their boundaries with non-DDs P/Cs).

TABLE 2 C Scores for the Index Questions

	Distribution of C scores		
Have you ever . . .	Negative C scores	0	Positive C scores
1. Conducted significant work with your P/C outside your normal working hours?	4%	31%	65%
5. Conducted sessions on the phone, or in any other place other than your usual office?	5%	50%	45%
12. Kept contact (e.g., on the phone) with your P/C while you were on holiday?	2%	54%	44%
19. Risked yourself professionally or personally?	3%	51%	46%
20. Reached a point of burnout?	3%	52%	45%

Notes: P/C = patient/client.

The wide prevalence of boundary modifications reported by professionals in their work with DDs, especially among the more experienced and more qualified practitioners, challenges the notion that such modifications are aberrations or deviations from normal practice. In particular, the five index questions point to areas in which practitioners' boundaries get modified 50% of the time, thus changing the meaning of what is "normal" in practice with DDs.

Most commonly in this study boundary modifications were found to be linked with practitioners' availability: offering time outside normal working hours, outside the office, and during practitioners' holidays. It is noteworthy that these boundary modifications not only are at odds with the respondents' normal practice but are also greatly inconvenient and were often accompanied by the additional stresses of secrecy and risk taking (Questions 18 and 19) and a high burnout rate (Question 20). Clearly these types of modifications cannot be seen as self-serving, and they beg the question why.

My hypothesis is that these frequent boundary modifications may reflect a feature in people with DDs that actually requires different boundaries in several areas and that most professionals, especially the more experienced ones, tend to recognize and respond to this need. This hypothesis may explain the findings of frequent boundary modifications in work with this group despite the high cost to practitioners. It may also explain the relative consistency of this phenomenon despite the many variations among the professionals.

Limitations of This Study and Suggestions for Further Research

This pilot study focused only on actual practice differences and did not explore practitioners' insights into or reasoning regarding the discrepancies in their practice with the two groups. A follow-up study of professionals' views regarding their boundaries with the two groups is warranted.

The absence of respondents' profile information may have also obscured important information. A larger scale study could provide a more complex, accurate, and reliable picture.

If, as the hypothesis suggests, people with DDs require changes in boundaries, evidence for this may be found through a treatment outcome study. Such a study would need to define parameters for measuring treatment outcome (and the timescale involved) and compare these parameters in P/Cs whose treatment used different types of boundaries.

The results of this study also point to a need for theoretical principles (as opposed to empirical reasons) that could explain, and perhaps guide, any boundary modifications in the work with people with DDs.

It is my view that given the prevalence of boundary modification in the work with DDs P/Cs and in the light of the risks and stresses that are associated with unclear boundaries, an in-depth study of this phenomenon should be a matter of priority to the field of DDs.

CONCLUSIONS

Difficulties in maintaining professional boundaries are usually regarded as a sign of lack of experience, confidence, rigor, or sophistication in one's training or practice. The main findings of this pilot study, however, form a different picture in the case of working with DDs P/Cs. With these P/Cs, boundaries are reported to be modified very frequently, at a high cost to practitioners, and more so by the more qualified and experienced professionals. These findings suggest that boundary modifications in working with DDs do not reflect incompetence and, given their wide prevalence, cannot even be seen as a deviation from normal practice.

Based on the findings of this study I hypothesize that boundary modifications in work with DDs may reflect a feature of people with DDs to which experienced professionals respond by modifying their normal boundaries. Further empirical outcome research as well as theoretical exploration is needed in order to elucidate this feature and its implications for improved practice with this group.

REFERENCES

Chu, J. (2011). *Rebuilding shattered lives* (2nd ed.). Hoboken, NJ: Wiley.

Doel, M., Allmark, P., Conway, P., Cowburn, M., Flynn, M., Nelson, P., & Tod, A. (2010). Professional boundaries: Crossing a line or entering the shadows? *British Journal of Social Work, 40*, 1866–1889.

Gabbard, G., & Nadelson, C. (1995). Professional boundaries in the physician-patient relationship. *Journal of the American Medical Association, 273*, 1445–1449.

Galton, G. (2006). *Touch papers: Dialogues on touch in the psychoanalytic space*. London, England: Karnac.

Guthheil, T., & Gabbard, G. (1998). Misuses and misunderstandings of boundary theory in clinical and regulatory settings. *American Journal of Psychiatry, 155*, 409–414.

Poole, R., & Cook, C. (2011). Praying with a patient constitutes a breach of professional boundaries in psychiatric practice. *British Journal of Psychiatry, 199*, 94–98.

Pope, K., & Keith-Spiegle, P. (2008). A practical approach to boundaries in psychotherapy: Making decisions, bypassing blunders, and mending fences. *Journal of Clinical Psychology, 64*, 638–652.

APPENDIX

The Survey Questions

Please answer each question once for each category (DDs and non-DDs). Answer N/A only if the question is meaningless for you for *both* groups (e.g., Question 2 if you are a medic).

In your professional capacity, have you ever done any of the following (tick one in each category):

1. Conducted significant work with your patient/client (P/C) outside your working hours?
   DDs P/Cs
   N/A never rarely sometimes often
   Non-DDs P/Cs
   N/A never rarely sometimes often
2. Accompanied your P/C to a doctor or to hospital?
3. Taken your P/C with you on holiday?
4. Invited your P/C to stay at your home for the night, for their safety?
5. Conducted sessions on the phone, or in any place other than your usual office?
6. Visited your P/C at their home?
7. Breached your P/C's confidentiality in any way (as defined by your professional body's guidelines)?
8. Withheld information from relevant professionals at your P/C's request?
9. Accompanied your P/C at a police interview or to court?
10. Met members of your P/C's family or friends?
11. Looked after your P/C's child, other relatives or pets?
12. Kept contact (e.g., on the phone) with your P/C while you were on holiday?
13. Given your P/C presents or money?

14. Had physical contact (nonsexual, nonmedical) with your P/C?
15. Advocated for your P/C?
16. Declined to charge for your work or parts of it?
17. Decided to end the work with your P/C unilaterally or abruptly?
18. Kept any of your interactions with your P/C a secret?
19. Risked yourself personally or professionally?
20. Reached a point of burnout?

Notes: DDs = dissociative disorders.

Seeking Asylum—Trauma, Mental Health, and Human Rights: An Australian Perspective

LOUISE NEWMAN, BA, MBBS, PhD

Centre for Developmental Psychiatry & Psychology, Monash University, Clayton, Victoria, Australia

Asylum seekers represent a highly traumatized group with experiences of systematic oppression, loss, displacement, and exposure to violence. Around the world many are viewed with distrust and anxiety. The Australian response to asylum seekers is one that has used prolonged detention with significant negative impact on mental health. This has prompted much social debate and the involvement of clinicians and researchers in advocating for the human rights of asylum seekers. This article reviews the impact of mandatory prolonged detention on the mental health of asylum seekers and the significance of this for recovery and adaption. It concludes that the mandatory detention of high-risk and oppressed groups compounds trauma, with a potential long-term negative impact on mental health.

Experiences of political oppression, traumatic loss, displacement, social breakdown, and attempted genocide underlie much global movement of peoples and many attempts to find a safe haven. These factors have both immediate and transgenerational effects on nations, specific groups, and individuals. Being a bereaved, displaced, and traumatized person with an uncertain future characterizes the contemporary asylum seeker. Many exist in this state for decades.

The plight of the asylum seeker produces strong responses in potential host nations, ranging from empathic and supportive approaches to harsh and restrictive policy. In a global context, responses to asylum seekers reflect anxiety, disavowal of trauma, and an attitude of blaming the traumatized for their own situation. These responses are arguably very similar to the complex range of responses seen to emerge in the situation of other traumas such as child abuse and domestic violence, in which trauma may be denied or minimized (Crittenden, 2008). The difficulty of thinking about and responding to trauma and negative attitudes toward victims is well known and may be understood as a deficit in the capacity to bear and acknowledge the reality of abuse.

This article focuses on the response to asylum seekers in Australia, where immigration law revolves around the mandatory detention of all so-called unauthorized arrivals. Detention may be prolonged and includes children and torture sufferers.

ASYLUM SEEKERS: A GLOBAL CONTEXT

In 2009 the United Nations Refugee Agency classified an estimated 43.3 million people as refugees, asylum seekers, displaced persons, or stateless. Many flee political and social oppression, human rights violations, war, and conflict. Asylum seekers are individuals who are seeking protection and classification as refugees in terms of the United Nations Refugee Agency definition. These individuals have universally experienced multiple traumatic events, including violence, loss, and displacement (Porter & Haslam, 2005). Silove (1999) described the impact of mass violence and community breakdown in situations of humanitarian crisis as disrupting core adaptive systems or psychosocial domains needed for functioning. These adaptive systems include safety and security, maintenance of interpersonal relationships, effective mechanisms for administering justice, the capacity to maintain beliefs and identity, and the ability to express aspirations that confer meaning. Asylum seekers fleeing trauma and persecution face fundamental disruption to their sense of safety and attachment and to systems of meaning and belief, with significant implications for psychological functioning (Newman, Dudley, & Steel, 2008). The prolonged nature of asylum claims also contributes to mental health issues (Ryan, Kelly, & Kelly, 2009).

Responses to asylum seekers around the globe show some variation. People fleeing regional wars and mass human rights violations may be internally displaced or in temporary shelters for prolonged periods. The review of asylum claims may take several years. Although the detention of asylum seekers and irregular entrants may occur in many settings, most countries do not use detention as a first option. Most countries, including Argentina, Brazil, Venezuela, Austria, Denmark, and The Netherlands, have a presumption against detention in law, policy, or practice (Sampson,

Mitchell, & Bowring, 2011). Several countries, including Denmark, Finland, Sweden, and New Zealand, legally require that alternatives to detention be examined (such as community processing of asylum claims). The New Zealand Immigration Act (2009), for example, outlines conditions to avoid detention, such as reporting requirements. Australia is unique in requiring in law the detention of all unauthorized arrivals for an indefinite period and in using remote detention facilities (Human Rights and Equal Opportunity Commission, 2008).

SEEKING ASYLUM IN AUSTRALIA

Australia received approximately 6,500 asylum seekers in 2010. All asylum seekers arriving by boat without documentation are detained in designated security facilities. Detention is therefore arbitrary and indefinite. It applies to both children and adults. Although detention is said to be for administrative purposes, such as health and security checks, it is also seen by the government to have significant value as a deterrent, sending a message that unauthorized boat arrival does not result in freedom in or entry to Australia. The mandatory detention of asylum seekers is unique to Australia and continues to be a focus of widespread public policy debate and concern.

More recently, it has been proposed that asylum seekers be sent to another country, such as Malaysia, where their claims for asylum in Australia may be heard. This raises the issue of Australia's obligations as a voluntary signatory to the United Nations Refugee Convention as well as concerns about a broader commitment to advocacy for human rights and protection in the Asian regions. Immigration detention then serves both local and regional political agendas and has become the focus of a discussion about human rights commitment in Australia and the country's role in providing leadership in this area for a region in which there are ongoing concerns about rights and protection.

Service provision and access to health and mental health services are problematic in remote areas of Australia. The use of remote islands ("offshore processing") has served to render the plight of asylum seekers invisible and has distanced the issue from the conscience of the general public. Anxiety in some parts of the community about the number arriving has hindered more reflective assessment of the reasons behind and impact of asylum seeking—the motives, ambivalence, and psychological consequences of loss and displacement are not often part of the political coverage of the issues. It is in this context that psychological research has played a significant part in the asylum seeker debate and continues to raise key issues of ethical and human rights commitment.

DETENTION AND MENTAL HEALTH

Mental health is a core public health issue for refugees. A recent meta-analysis found that more than 30% of refugees experience posttraumatic stress disorder and depression (Steel et al., 2009). Poor mental health manifests in self-harm and suicidal behavior, interpersonal violence, social isolation, and poor social functioning and adaptation (Mollica et al., 1993; Oquendo et al., 2003; Silove, 1999). Mental disorder in refugees arises from a mix of factors, including (a) repeated exposure to traumatic experiences in the country of origin; (b) stresses encountered in the period of transition and asylum seeking; and (c) post-migration experiences, such as insecure residency, fear of repatriation, and socioeconomic discrimination.

In Australia mental health professionals have played a major part in raising clinical and ethical concerns regarding the impact of mandatory detention, and particularly its impact on child development. For many of these professionals the need to intervene and advocate on behalf of detainees raised serious questions about the boundaries of professional behavior and the moral responsibility to oppose damaging government policy. Gathering evidence about the mental health impacts of detention became an important strategy in this debate.

A 2004 Human Rights and Equal Opportunity Commission report on children in detention noted the negative developmental effects of detention on children and the failure of Australia to respect its obligations under the international human rights treaties to which it has subscribed. It also noted the potential long-term effects of traumatic exposure with the risk of ongoing mental disorder. The report noted the difficulties faced by parents in the detention environment and the way in which parental depression and despair affect children, resulting in attachment difficulties (Human Rights and Equal Opportunity Commission, 2004). Several clinical reports have described children with attachment and developmental disorders (Mares & Jureidini, 2004; Mares, Newman, Dudley, & Gale, 2002).

The case of 5-year-old SB, an Iranian child in detention with his family, received considerable public attention and raised community awareness of the plight of detained children. SB was held in remote detention for an 11-month period and was exposed to riots, self-harming behaviors, and suicide attempts. He was described as becoming withdrawn and anxious and having nightmares. The family was transferred to a metropolitan center where SB witnessed a significant suicide attempt and became withdrawn and mute, deteriorating to a state where he refused all oral intake and was hospitalized. SB required several admissions for rehydration, and every time he was returned to the detention facility his condition deteriorated. He was assessed by several child psychiatrists who all indicated that returning the child to such a traumatic environment would result in relapse. They advised that he be released into the community with his mother. This was declined by the then Minister for Immigration, who was concerned that this would set a precedent for the release of children from detention. Predictably, SB's condition deteriorated and he was placed in community foster care separated from his mother. As he continued to deteriorate his mother was released 4 months after the separation and his father 8 months later. SB was found to be a genuine convention refugee. This is an example of harm to a child resulting from inflexible, oppressive government policy in which clinicians felt that they had an obligation to be open about the child's plight and to act as advocates. The whole issue of the nature of medical and psychiatric recommendations about treatment and the placement of detainees became very difficult, with clinicians arguing that in some cases the environmental contribution to disorder was so great that the only possibility of recovery lay in release and community placement. In some cases the government accused detainees of simulating illness and psychiatric conditions to gain release and failed to acknowledge the reality of psychological distress and the toxic environment.

The response of the detention system to individuals seen as simulating psychiatric disturbance was highlighted by the case of CR, an Australian permanent resident found to have been held unlawfully in detention for a period of 10 months. CR was suffering from a severe and chronic psychotic disorder and was acutely unwell, speaking her native language (German) when she was detained. She was placed initially in prison and then in immigration detention, as it was assumed that she was an illegal person. Her condition deteriorated and she was housed in a behavioral management unit, largely in isolation. She became behaviorally disorganized to the point that she was incoherent, smearing feces and removing her clothes. The detention system did not recognize this as possible mental illness, and she did not receive adequate psychiatric assessment or any treatment. CR was treated as "badly behaved" and disruptive and was only released to care when recognized by family members in a media article. This case raised serious issues about the culture of the detention system, which focused on behavioral control and made assumptions about detainees, including their attempts to be manipulative and deceitful. The report that followed this incident looked at the provision of mental health services and support in detention and stressed the need for ongoing independent monitoring of service standards and provision of appropriate levels of care. This report prompted the establishment of an independent advisory body comprising representatives of medical and health professional bodies (Detention Expert Health Advisory Group, 2005) that continues to function to provide advice to the department regarding the health and mental health needs of asylum seekers, including approaches to reduce the risk of self-harm and suicide.

CLINICAL RESEARCH

The relationship between mental health and human rights was brought into focus by the findings of several studies that detention and lack of resolution of refugee status undermine psychological well-being and contribute to ongoing deterioration (Silove et al., 2007; Steel et al., 2004; Steel & Silove, 2001).

A recent systematic review of studies investigating the impact of immigration detention on the mental health of children, adolescents, and adults identified high levels of mental health problems in detainees (Robjant, Hassam, & Katona, 2009). Time in detention was found to be associated with severity of distress. Anxiety, depression, and posttraumatic stress disorder were commonly reported (more than 85% of detainees), as were self-harm and suicidal ideation (Newman, Proctor, & Dudley, 2011).

The prolonged nature of detention, with its associated uncertainty about the future and persistent anxiety, is regarded as a major contributing factor to mental deterioration, depression, and increasing hopelessness (Green & Eagar, 2010; Steel et al., 2004). In this context, self-harm is simultaneously a form of protest and an expression of frustration and sometimes of suicidal ideation. The question of suicidal intent is often difficult to assess, and the detention system has tended to label all such behavior as manipulative and lacking in serious intent, ignoring the ambivalence and complex feelings involved. Several reports have noted high rates of self-harm among detainees and forms of symbolic protest, such as sewing the lips together (Steel et al., 2004). Governments typically deny an association between the conditions of detention, protest behavior, and mental distress and reiterate that this behavior relates to manipulation and character pathology. There is a clear lack of understanding of the psychological implications of asylum seeking within a punitive system and also a difficulty in acknowledging the reality of mental distress and the need for support.

There is evidence for an initial improvement in mental health shortly after release, although mental health effects may be prolonged, extending well beyond the point of release into the community. Factors such as the length of time in detention, negative experiences and traumatic exposure during detention, and the process of establishing refugee claims are all significant and compounding components of the asylum-seeking experience. The role of preexisting trauma and the impact of persecution, displacement, and loss also contribute to risk and mediate outcome. This raises issues of the meaning of individual diagnosis and formulation of difficulties when the environment of detention and the refugee determination process itself is a major factor in producing distress. This evokes questions about the issue of what sort of psychological treatment will be useful if the individual remains in a situation in which recovery is not possible. The toxic environment of the detention center, with its often rigid culture and priorities, acts to increase distress, confusion, and overall rates of mental health problems.

Detainees frequently express distress at their powerless position and at the prevailing culture of disbelief and blame in the detention centers. Asylum seekers have made an active and often difficult decision to leave home, culture, and family, and for unaccompanied minors the burden of carrying on their culture and future is significant.

To find that the system is one of rules and bureaucratic regulation that erodes individual autonomy and sense of control is deeply disturbing and unexpected. Unrealistic wishes about rapid processing and release may compound this situation so that the asylum seeker feels powerless and abandoned. For survivors of torture and trauma the situation is even more serious and distressing as a result of what is experienced as a traumatizing regime. Traumatic responses may be triggered by unempathic, intrusive, and rigid responses to high levels of distress and anxiety. In these situations encounters between staff and asylum seekers can become conflictual and come to represent anger and a sense of frustration toward the immigration system.

Steel and colleagues (2004) studied 10 of 11 families in a remote center using standardized instruments for diagnostic assessment. Every adult was found to have major depression, and most reported suicidal ideation. All children were diagnosed with at least one psychiatric disorder, and most met diagnostic criteria for more than one. Half of the children had posttraumatic stress disorder. Assessment of the lifetime prevalence of mental disorder found a low level of preexisting psychiatric symptoms, supporting the view that detention itself results in mental disorder. A striking feature of this study was the high reporting of negative experiences within the detention system, including abusive and harsh treatment and the witnessing of self-harm and suicidal behavior.

Length in detention has emerged as a major contributing factor to mental deterioration, physical symptoms, and hopelessness (Green & Eagar, 2010). An early study by a detained medical practitioner in Villawood detention center (Sultan & O'Sullivan, 2001) found that severity of depressive symptoms increased with the length of time in detention and deteriorated to a state of cognitive deficit, pervasive mistrust, and psychotic symptoms. A major concern remains that there is a lack of understanding of detention-related deterioration and an assumption that these conditions are responsive to treatment within detention, without resolution of the individual's status. The prescription of psychotropic medication in detention (antidepressants and antipsychotic drugs) is arguably not likely to result in any significant improvement in the mental health of the detained population.

Recent work reviewing medical records of detainees again found that length of time was related to health problems and in particular noted complex physical health presentations, medical service utilization, and mental health diagnoses increasing at the 12-month period. Rates of disorder are low in the early periods of detention and extremely high after 18 months in detention (Green & Eagar, 2010). Although this relationship is now accepted by the government it remains difficult to adhere to only brief periods of detention (the current policy is 90 days) and to facilitate community processing of particularly vulnerable groups, such as survivors of torture and children. Community placement of vulnerable asylum seekers, if based on a model of personal autonomy and participation, may be one way to prevent deterioration and increasing distress and reduce rates of self-harm. The occurrence of six suicides across the detention system from September 2010 to November 2011 is clearly extremely concerning and requires rethinking the policy of mandatory detention (Newman et al., 2011).

The research outlined here has played a significant role in the asylum seeker debate and calls for reform of immigration law in Australia. The results have been used to counter the prevailing systemic tendency to deny or minimize the negative impact of detention and to point to high levels of psychiatric morbidity, particularly posttraumatic stress disorder, arising from the detention experiences. Asylum seekers do arrive with preexisting traumatic exposure and loss that impacts on rates of distress, but research suggests that it is the experience of detention itself that is most significant. This raises issues of the capacity to provide treatment in this environment and can result in clinicians feeling disempowered and deskilled. Reassurance and simplistic approaches to dealing with anger, frustration, and depression have limited utility, particularly when self-harm and behavioral disturbance have been seen as politically motivated bad behavior. This has resulted in the under-recognition of serious mental distress and disorder and difficulty in creating a more psychologically supportive environment that may reduce cognitive and emotional dysfunction. Treating professionals have little control over the length of time an asylum seeker spends in detention and are often in the position of observing deterioration with very little in the way of intervention to influence this. The limitations of the traditional clinical role are evident and place clinicians in a position in which ethical dilemmas are unavoidable.

CLINICAL AND ETHICAL DILEMMAS

Many clinicians have described feeling a lack of efficacy in dealing with detained populations. Speaking on behalf of those with little power and maintaining a stance of support for the best interests of the detainee becomes important in a situation in which a traditional treatment approach has limited utility. Documentation of health issues over time and case notes supporting the clinical argument for release into the community have been used in many cases in which clinicians have been concerned about the well-being of a detained asylum seeker. The statement that within a damaging environment treatment is fundamentally problematic is powerful but puts clinicians in an ethical dilemma in which they are potentially clinically compromised. Supporting nonprofessional advocates and volunteers has also been an important role for professionals, with many not experienced in dealing with high levels of distress and suicidality (Mares & Newman, 2007).

For mental health clinicians the traditional model of trauma and recovery is challenged in the detention context. In many situations history has shaped a group's understanding of trauma and practices have developed that aim to preserve the memory of traumatic events and prevent the repetition of trauma in the future. Groups impacted by attempted genocide frequently engage in active processes of traumatic construction, memory recording, and communication of history to the next generation. Although this seeks to offer protection to future generations, it also provides a mechanism for how the next generation may be directly impacted by the unresolved trauma of its parents. In many of these situations it is not readily apparent that individual psychological models such as that of posttraumatic stress disorder have much utility or add to an understanding of the needs of traumatized groups. Trauma for asylum seekers occurs in a particular sociopolitical context and has motivated the attempt to find a safe haven and reestablish social functioning and identity. There will also be cultural variations in the expression of distress and the experience of trauma, and there is a need to explore this in a framework that is broader than that of Western diagnostic approaches. This should also translate into interventions at the sociopolitical level that transcend the individualistic psychological models of Western psychology and take into account a group's history, culture, and models of trauma and recovery.

CURRENT ISSUES AND CONCLUSION

Increasing numbers of boat arrivals into Australia have prompted a political debate about factors influencing asylum seeking and those that might deter it. Many seek asylum in response to political oppression and prolonged discrimination and have preexisting psychological vulnerabilities, often associated with a history of torture and trauma. Concerns have again been raised about the mental damage and compounding of trauma caused by detention. It seems that the evidence previously gathered on these issues has not been referred to as a guide in current planning. Attempts to provide psychological support and increase mental health services to detainees face the challenges discussed previously, which coalesce around the difficulties of treating in a damaging environment. Increasing numbers of failed asylum seekers and long-stay cases will have a major impact on the operation of detention centers and rates of protest, disturbance, and mental disorder. Attempted suicides and suicidal behavior are increasing, and comments have again been made that bad behavior will not be tolerated and asylum seekers will face criminal charges in some situations. The challenge appears to be one of recreating some level of psychological and empathic understanding of the plight of the asylum seeker and of the impact of mandatory detention. A trauma-informed model of care is essential and should underlie policy reform and service provision.

REFERENCES

Crittenden, P. M. (2008). *Raising parents: Attachment, parenting, and child safety*. Abingdon, England: Routledge/Willan.

Green, J. P., & Eagar, K. (2010). The health of people in Australian immigration detention centres. *Medical Journal of Australia, 192*(2), 65–70.

Human Rights and Equal Opportunity Commission. (2004). *A last resort? National inquiry into children in immigration detention*. Retrieved from www.hreaoc.org.au. Sydney, Australia: Author.

Human Rights and Equal Opportunity Commission. (2008). *Immigration detention report: Summary of observations following visits to Australias immigration detention facilities*. Retrieved from www.hreaoc.org.au. Sydney, Australia: Author.

Mares, S., & Jureidini, J. (2004). Psychiatric assessment of children and families in immigration detention—Clinical, administrative and ethical issues. *Australia and New Zealand Journal of Public Health, 28*, 520–526.

Mares, S., & Newman, L. K. (2007). *Acting from the heart: Australian advocates for asylum seekers tell their stories*. Sydney, Australia: Finch.

Mares, S., Newman, L. K., Dudley, M., & Gale, F. (2002). Seeking refuge, losing hope: Parent and children in immigration detention. *Australasian Psychiatry, 10*(2), 91–96.

Mollica, R., Donelan, K., Tor, S., Lavelle, J., Elias, C., Frankel, M., & Blendon, R. J. (1993). The effect of trauma and confinement on functional health and mental health status of Cambodians living in Thailand-Cambodia border camps. *Journal of the American Medical Association, 270*, 581–586.

Newman, L. K., Dudley, M., & Steel, Z. (2008). Asylum, detention and mental health in Australia. *Refugee Survey Quarterly, 27*, 110–127.

Newman, L. K., Procter, N. G., & Dudley, M. J. (2011). Suicide and self-harm in immigration detention. *The Medical Journal of Australia, 195*(6), 310–311.

Oquendo, M. A., Friend, J. A., Batsheva, H., Brodsky, B. S., Burke, A. K., Grunebaum, M. F., . . . Mann, J. J. (2003). Association of comorbid posttraumatic stress disorder and major depression with greater risk for suicidal behavior. *American Journal of Psychiatry, 160*, 580–582.

Porter, M., & Haslam, N. (2005). Predisplacement and postdisplacement factors associated with mental health of refugees and internally displaced persons: A meta-analysis. *Journal of the American Medical Association, 294*, 602–612.

Robjant, K., Hassam, R., & Katona, C. (2009). Mental health implications of detaining asylum seekers: Systematic review. *British Journal of Psychiatry, 194*, 306–312.

Ryan, D. A., Kelly, F. E., & Kelly, B. D. (2009). Mental health among persons awaiting an asylum outcome in Western countries: A literature review. *International Journal of Mental Health, 38*(3), 88–111.

Sampson, R., Mitchell, G., & Bowring, L. (2011). *There are alternatives*. Melbourne, Australia: International Detention Coalition.

Silove, D. M. (1999). The psychological effects of torture, mass human rights violations and refugee trauma: Towards an integrated conceptual framework. *Journal of Nervous & Mental Disease, 187*, 200–207.

Silove, D. M., Sinnerbrink, I., Field, A., Manicavasagar, V., & Steel, Z. (1997). Anxiety, depression and PTSD in asylum-seekers: Associations with pre-migration trauma and post-migration stressors. *British Journal of Psychiatry, 170*, 351–357.

Silove, D. M., Steel, Z., Susljik, J., Frommer, N., Lonergan, C., Chey, T., . . . Bryant, R. (2007). The impact of the refugee decision on the trajectory of PTSD, anxiety and depressive symptoms among asylum seekers: A longitudinal study. *American Journal of Disaster Medicine, 2*(6), 321–329.

Steel, Z., Chey, T., Silove, D. M., Marnane, C., Bryant, R., & van Ommeren, M. (2009). Association of torture and other potentially traumatic events with mental health outcomes among populations exposed to mass conflict and displacement. *Journal of the American Medical Association, 302*, 537–549.

Steel, Z., Momartin, S., Bateman, C., Hafshejani, A., Silove, D. M., Everson, N., & Mares, S. (2004). Psychiatric status of asylum seeker families held for a protracted period in a remote detention centre in Australia. *Australian and New Zealand Journal of Public Health, 28*, 527–536.

Steel, Z., & Silove, D. M. (2001). The mental health implications of detaining asylum seekers. *Medical Journal of Australia, 175*, 596–599.

Sultan, A., & O'Sullivan, K. (2001). Psychological disturbances in asylum seekers held in long term detention: A participant-observer account. *Medical Journal of Australia, 175*, 593–596.

The Franklin Scandal: The Cover-Up of Child Abuse and its Analogues to Dissociative Identity Disorder

NICK BRYANT

The Franklin Scandal *is a book that carefully documents the cover-up of a nationwide pedophile network that pandered children throughout the United States. Nebraska legislators attempted to expose the network in 1989 and 1990, but the legislators' efforts were followed by a rash of mysterious deaths and the overpowering responses of federal and local law enforcement, including the FBI and Justice Department, which effected an immaculate cover-up of the trafficking network. The events delineated in* The Franklin Scandal *include parallels to the amnestic barriers that exist between a dissociated alter personality and the host personality in Dissociative Identity Disorder (DID) in the respect that societal institutions entrusted with the task of protecting children instead functioned, in effect, as an "alter" invested in disavowal of these crimes, dissociated from the larger society that seeks to protect children. As the cover-up of child abuse affected by these institutions proliferated, the child-protective laws and values of the body politic and citizenry were thwarted, much as abuse-denying, abuser-aligned "alters" can thwart life-affirming, self-protective functions in individuals with DID.*

In Dissociative Identity Disorder (DID), the primary feature is the presence of two or more distinct personality states, self-reported or observed by others, resulting in a failure to recall everyday events and/or important autobiographical information, and/or traumatic events (American Psychiatric Association, 2013). DID is also characterized by an impaired continuity in the sense of self and the self's sense of agency (American Psychiatric Association, 2013). In a comprehensive review of the literature, Dalenberg et al. (2012) argue convincingly that DID is "a response to antecedent traumatic stress and/or severe psychological adversity" (Dalenberg et al., 2012, p. 1).

Many individuals with DID have personality states that can psychologically influence the larger psyche to be amnestic for their abuse or to deny their abuse in order to enhance their psychological survival. However, these initially "helping" personality states turn to abuser-identified persecutory intra-psychic entities over time, which ultimately become disruptive to the individual's psychological integrity (Sar & Öztürk, 2009).

By analogy, just as a traumatized individual's internal world can be characterized by entities dislocated from the whole, recent history tells us that the larger society also includes powerful subgroups, such as the leadership of religious institutions and the Boy Scouts, who should have worked to protect children, but instead protected the children's abusers by disavowing the children's abuse, which, in the context of the larger society, parallels the denial that exists in DID.

These subgroups and their effective disavowal of child abuse over decades begs the question of whether or not Americans wish to deny the reality of child abuse or have Americans' awareness of child abuse been limited by the effectiveness of these powerful subgroups to suppress this knowledge? The scandal involving Jerry Sandusky and Penn State and the subsequent outrage that it fostered indicates that Americans do not wish to deny the reality of child abuse. But, rather, Penn State had the ability to suppress the knowledge of child abuse over years. Penn State's effort to preserve and protect its power and prestige acted much like an abuser-aligned alter personality within the larger psyche, a society that views child abuse as anathema to its laws and mores.

The Franklin Scandal (Bryant, 2009), which was the culmination of a seven-year investigation into a child trafficking network, embodies the emergence of two competing and largely dissociated forces: federal and state authorities who engaged in the cover-up of child abuse and the citizenry who seeks to protect abused children.

The Franklin Scandal essentially begins with Lawrence (Larry) King of Omaha, Nebraska. King was an African American, and the media reported that he had climbed out of a working-class background to become a hugely successful entrepreneur. Throughout the 1980s, the middle-aged King, tall and corpulent, had been described as a Republican Party "high-roller" (Keary, 1988). He was Vice Chairman for Finance of the National Black Republican Council, a sanctioned affiliate of the Republican National Committee. King also ardently campaigned for the 1988 presidential bid of his personal friend George H.W. Bush. King had an array of diverse business ventures, but his primary day job was manager of Omaha's Franklin Community Federal Credit Union, which was created to provide loans for Omaha's underserved black community.

The first documented alleged victim of Lawrence King-related child abuse to come forward was Eulice Washington. She had been placed in the foster home of Jarrett and Barbara Webb as an eight-year-old—Barbara Webb was a cousin of Lawrence King. The Webbs eventually adopted Eulice and her two sisters as well as two other children. Three foster children also lived in the Webb home.

The children in the Webb home told social services personnel of repeated "beatings" and "whippings" at the hands of the Webbs (Carpenter, 1985). In fact, a physician who treated one of the children said that a "rubber hose" most likely produced the welts on his back (Carpenter, 1986). After years of social services' documented findings of abuse by the Webbs, the children in the Webb household were ultimately placed in various foster homes, but child abuse charges were never leveled against the Webbs.

After Eulice Washington's liberation from the Webb home, she told her new foster mother that Jarrett Webb had repeatedly molested her. She even passed a "polygraph" administered by the Nebraska State Patrol (NSP) on her accusations (Carpenter, 1986), but Jarrett Webb was never prosecuted for his purported molestation of Eulice Washington.

Washington also told her foster mother that Lawrence King had flown her and several Boys Town students (Boys Town is the distinguished Catholic orphanage on the outskirts of Omaha) to pedophilic orgies in Chicago and New York City. In March of

1986, a Boys Town youth worker interviewed Eulice Washington and penned a very detailed report about her allegations regarding Boys Town students and Lawrence King. The youth worker discovered that a Boys Town employee who she did not "trust" was tasked with looking into the allegations (Bryant, 2009, p. 58). Boys Town also allegedly informed the NSP and Federal Bureau of Investigation (FBI) about Eulice Washington's allegations.

At this point, social workers, NSP personnel, and officers within Nebraska's state judiciary were aware of the alleged abuse within the Webb household, but no child abuse charges were brought against the Webbs. Boys Town claims that the NSP and FBI were also informed of Eulice Washington's allegations regarding Lawrence King, but she was not interviewed by either investigative entity. Thus, Eulice Washington and the children in the Webb household represent the first documented disruption in the normal continuity of a society to protect its children from abuse. The failure to appropriately respond to the allegations arising in the Webb household by institutions entrusted to protect children is the first manifestation of a societal subgroup that was an abuse-disavowing, abuser-aligned nascent "alter." The guardian ad litem for Eulice Washington would later testify at a grand jury that the county prosecutor did not prosecute Jarrett Webb, because he did not believe Eulice Washington's allegations (Transcript of testimony, Douglas County Grand Jury, 1990). So, in essence, the abuse was ignored and thus omitted as a reality from the collective memory of the authorities and also the society.

Approximately two years after Eulice was polygraphed by the NSP, the Omaha Police Department (OPD) investigated Lawrence King and a photographer associated with King, Rusty Nelson, for "possible child pornography" (Hoch, 1988). But, despite the OPD uncovering leads and filing multiple crime reports, the investigation was inexplicably discontinued (Bryant, 2009, pp. 66–69).

About a month after the OPD's first documented investigation of Lawrence King for alleged child abuse, Shawneta Moore, a 15-year-old girl at an Omaha psychiatric hospital, disclosed to hospital personnel, including her psychiatrist, that she had been enmeshed in a child prostitution and pornography ring since she was nine years old. She also disclosed ritualistic forms of abuse, including multiple perpetrators committing homicide.

Moore's psychiatrist phoned the OPD, and an OPD officer was dispatched to the hospital to interview Moore. Moore eventually related to the OPD officer that Lawrence King was "involved" in her abuse and the abuse of other children (Carmean, 1988). Although the OPD officer found Moore to be "credible," the OPD did not interview her again (Bryant, 2009, p. 76). Moore's essentially ignored allegations by the OPD represent another disruption in the normal continuity of a society protecting its children from sexual abuse. By ignoring Moore's allegations, the OPD was, in effect, also omitting her abuse from the collective memory of the larger society.

Nebraska's Foster Care Review Board is a state agency that reviews the plans, services, and placements of children in foster care to ensure their optimum welfare, and members of the Foster Care Review Board had become aware of several allegations regarding Lawrence King's abuse of children. The Foster Care Review Board submitted a report to the Nebraska Attorney General of a "child exploitation ring" on July 20, 1988.

Although the Nebraska Attorney General's office was alerted about the abuse allegations whirling around King, the Nebraska Attorney General's office investigator who was assigned to investigate the child abuse allegations would confess that he did not conduct an interview of a single alleged victim (Transcript of testimony, Franklin Committee Hearing, 1989). The inaction by Nebraska Attorney General's office with regard to Lawrence King-related child abuse allegations compounded the neglect of the aforementioned agencies, and, thus, the chasm widened between the abuse-disavowing alter protecting the alleged child molesters and the laws and mores of the body politic.

THE FAILURE OF THE FRANKLIN COMMUNITY FEDERAL CREDIT UNION

On November 4, 1988, five months after the Foster Care Review Board alerted state authorities about their concerns regarding Lawrence King-related child abuse, federal agents descended on the Franklin Community Federal Credit Union, and the National Credit Union Administration would ultimately conclude that King had looted $39.4 million from the credit union (Dorr, 1988).

A few weeks after the Franklin Credit Union was raided by federal agents, Nebraska state senators in Lincoln, the state's capital, had seen enough Franklin Credit Union press about missing millions and cooked books to conclude that something was seriously awry. The senators unanimously approved Legislative Resolution 5, which called for a state senate subcommittee, the "Franklin Committee," to investigate the Franklin Credit Union's failure.

Senator Loran Schmit, who chaired the state senate's Banking Committee, drafted Resolution 5. Schmit was a third-generation corn farmer and a 21-year veteran of the state legislator. The 60-year-old Schmit was Nebraska's version of a rural Renaissance man: he had earned a B.S. in Agriculture from the University of Nebraska, and he juggled various business ventures.

As chairman of the state senate's Banking Committee, Senator Schmit had witnessed major banking improprieties in Nebraska throughout the 1980s, and he initially thought that the Franklin Credit Union was merely one more example of Nebraska's banking industry malfeasance. "You can't get rid of that much money without someone knowing about it," said Schmit the day he introduced Resolution 5 (World-Herald Bureau, 1988).

Shortly after Schmit introduced Resolution 5, he said he received an anonymous phone call that foreshadowed the suppressive forces that the "Franklin Committee" would be challenging: the caller urged Schmit not to pursue an investigation into the Franklin Credit Union under the auspices of being a "good Republican," because he said it would "reach to the highest levels of the Republican Party." (Bryant, 2009, p. 79) Schmit, however, was undeterred.

Senator Ernie Chambers, the 52-year-old Democrat representing North Omaha, immediately jumped on the Resolution 5 bandwagon. Chambers was the only senator voting for the investigation into the financial collapse of the Franklin Credit Union who was aware of the child abuse allegations regarding King, because members of the Foster Care Review Board had edified him about the allegations.

After Resolution 5 was passed, members of the Foster Care Review Board testified in front of the emerging Franklin Committee, and the Committee members heard shocking tales of interstate child trafficking and extreme child abuse that had been perpetrated with impunity, even though authorities within law enforcement were aware of the allegations.

The Foster Care Review Board members' testimony in front of the Franklin Committee ushered the King-related child abuse allegations into public consciousness, and the *Omaha-World Herald*, *Lincoln Journal*, and *The New York Times* followed with articles on the allegations. *The New York Times* described the allegations as "lurid" (Robbins, 1988).

The *Lincoln Journal* ran an article on Franklin-related child abuse that quoted Nebraska Attorney General Robert Spire and OPD Chief Robert (Bob) Wadman. "We did receive some sensitive information in July," said Attorney General Spire (Rutledge, 1988). "My office acted promptly and professionally and nothing was sat on" (Rutledge, 1988). OPD Chief Wadman spoke of a thoroughly conducted investigation and denied a lack of action by the OPD: "Every step that should have been taken was taken" (Rutledge, 1988).

But, in reality, Shawneta Moore had been interviewed only once by the OPD, and Eulice Washington had never been interviewed by the OPD or the Attorney General's office. Previously, the Nebraska Attorney General's office and the OPD simply ignored the child abuse allegations, but now those agencies were proactively engaging in deceit to cover up the child abuse allegations.

The Franklin Committee members quickly realized that they would be navigating through law enforcement disavowals as they investigated the child abuse allegations. So their first major order of business was to appoint a chief legal counsel, and he quickly conscripted a Lincoln Police Department officer to serve as the Committee's investigator.

At the beginning of July 1989, the Franklin Committee was required to deliver an "Interim Report" to the state's legislature to secure additional funding, and the Committee's counsel was tasked with writing the report. In the Interim Report, the Committee's counsel said that the Committee's investigation of the Lawrence King-related child abuse allegations would be wrapping up at the end of August. But Senator Schmit absolutely would not sign off on the Committee discontinuing its investigation of the child abuse allegations by the end of August, and he added an addendum to the report stating that the child abuse allegations would continue to be investigated after August.

The Committee ultimately ruptured over the direction of the report. Three senators, and the Committee's counsel and investigator resigned in the wake of Senator Schmit's addendum. An *Omaha World-Herald* article reported on the Committee's rupture. The article quoted the Committee's investigator, who said that Schmit had remarked to him that there was "pressure to stop the investigation." In the article, Schmit confirmed the pressures: "I have gotten phone calls threatening me," he said. "I've been told to leave it alone or my kids were going to be orphans" (Flanery, 1989).

After the resignations, the Franklin Committee conscripted a Lincoln, Nebraska-based attorney as the Committee's counsel, and, at the behest of the Committee's new counsel, the Committee hired Lincoln, Nebraska-based private investigator Gary Caradori to be its investigator. Caradori had a stellar record in both the military and also in the NSP before forming Caracorp, his private investigation firm.

Though Caradori was the chief executive officer of a large security and investigative firm, he was a seasoned and relentless detective, and his passion was finding missing persons, particularly abducted children and teenage girls enmeshed in drugs and prostitution. Over the years, various newspapers had published articles on Caradori's investigations.

Whereas the Franklin Committee's initial investigator had conducted an investigation into state law enforcement's investigation of Lawrence King-related child abuse allegations, Caradori was committed to carrying out his own patented investigation. Early in his investigation, Caradori received a call from a friend who was an OPD lieutenant, and his friend cautioned him of the looming danger ahead, saying that "the sexual component of Franklin had been covered up from the start" (Bryant, 2009, p. 105).

Caradori immersed himself in the Franklin investigation with his usual determination. His initial foray included reading the reports, memos, and all the previous documentation and testimony collected by the Franklin Committee. From the onset of Caradori's investigation, several obstacles confronted Caradori and his staff. Many of Caradori's "Investigative Reports" from August and September of 1989 note that he faced widespread distrust and a pall of fear as he attempted to cultivate confidential informants or simply interview individuals who had previously volunteered information, because they suspected that the Franklin Committee was merely serving the function of a continuing cover-up.

In addition to widespread distrust, Caradori also encountered enemies that he had not anticipated. He suspected his phones were tapped, because when he arranged meetings over the phone FBI agents would already be at the designated place when he arrived. In an interview conducted with Caradori's wife, she stated that a friend of Caradori's who worked for the phone company checked out his phones and confirmed that they were tapped (Bryant, 2009, p. 106).

Despite these problems, Caradori soldiered on to locate victims and follow the money trail. To follow the money trail, Caradori originally received help from the National Credit Union Administration (NCUA). After the Franklin Credit Union was closed, the NCUA had set up a "reconstruction office" in Omaha to decipher the whereabouts of the missing millions (Bryant, 2009, pp. 107–108). The stacked boxes there contained thousands of checks, invoices, receipts, etc. The NCUA initially granted Caradori access to the reconstruction office, and he was allowed to make copies of documentation he deemed relevant to his investigation.

At the NCUA reconstruction office, Caradori and his investigative assistant, Karen Ormiston, managed to find boxes containing scores of receipts from various air charter services used by Lawrence King. The flight receipts rarely listed passengers, or would merely list "Larry King." The receipts also revealed that King charted planes on an almost weekly basis. Though King jetted to numerous locations throughout the country, his favored destination was Washington, DC.

The majority of the charter services were located outside the state of Nebraska, so they did not have to honor the Franklin Committee's subpoenas. In October 1989, however, Caradori made contact with the pilot of a charter service frequented by King (Caradori, 1989a). The pilot informed Caradori that he had piloted King, "two young males in their midteens," and a "young white female in her midteens" on a flight to Los Angeles (Caradori, 1989a).

In a later Investigative Report (Caradori, 1990a), Caradori described his meeting with a former employee of a charter service used by King. The woman disclosed that King used her charter service "once a week," and she remarked that King routinely traveled with a number of young men who dressed in expensive suits. She also said the young men never spoke, which she found "strange."

ADDITIONAL VICTIMS SPEAK OUT

Caradori's Investigative Reports describe him scouring the streets and bars of Omaha to cultivate informants. He heard numerous rumors corroborating King's abuse of children, and it enabled him to identify other alleged perpetrators. At this point in the investigation, it was not uncommon for Caradori to log over 100-hour weeks.

One of the names Caradori gleaned working the bars and cultivating confidential informants was Alisha Owen. At that time, 20-year-old Owen was serving a three to four year sentence at the Nebraska Facility for Women at York for bouncing checks. Caradori had no idea whether or not Owen would be a fruitful lead, and he consigned her to a low-priority lead as demonstrated by the fact that he contacted the prison's administration about Owen on October 11 (Caradori, 1989b), but he did not make a trek to York prison until October 30 (Caradori, 1989a).

Caradori and his investigative assistant, Karen Ormiston, arrived at York prison around 7:00 p.m. Earlier that afternoon, Caradori had phoned the prison's Associate Warden and requested to meet Owen in a location that offered a modicum of privacy, and prison personnel escorted Caradori and Ormiston to a conference room in the prison basement.

A pair of guards then ushered Owen into the room, and Caradori and Ormiston introduced themselves to her. Owen stood 5'4" and weighed 150 pounds in her brown state-issued prison garb. She had a thick mane of curly brown hair and hazel eyes. Her rounded face, tentative voice, and mannerisms had the qualities of a timid teenager, even though she had turned 21 years old the month before, and her adolescence had been a detour to her own private hell.

Though Caradori was gracious to Owen, he quickly cut to the chase. She was initially hesitant to discuss her past, but she later revealed to me that Caradori and Ormiston conveyed an integrity that allayed her suspicions and fears. Over the course of the next three hours, she confessed to her involvement with "former members of the Franklin Credit Union," and she specified perpetrators whose names had repeatedly surfaced throughout Caradori's investigation (Caradori, 1989a). At the conclusion of the interview, Caradori asked Owen if she would be willing to make a formal statement the following week. Owen said she needed to sound out her parents, because she felt that her cooperation would potentially endanger members of her family.

Later in the week, Owen's mother and father visited her at York—Owen and her mother then took a walk in the prison's yard. Owen told her mother that she had been one of the abused children in the "Franklin" case. Though Owen's mother was dumbfounded by her daughter's disclosures, she finally had an explanation of her daughter's peculiar behavior, starting at the age of 14. As Owen and her mother cried, her mother asked her daughter why she had not come to her parents for help. Owen said that she was convinced her parents would not have backed down from the powerful perpetrators and they would have been murdered.

After Owen met with her parents, she phoned Caradori and consented to be interviewed. The Committee's counsel drafted a waiver stating that Owen's statements were made freely and voluntarily without promises or threats, and she was under oath during her statement and would be subject to prosecution for perjured statements. On the morning of November 7, 1989, Caradori and Ormiston arrived at York and started videotaping Owen's statement around 11:30 a.m. Following a series of respites and breaks, they finished at 10:00 p.m.

In Caradori and Ormiston's interview synopsis, they state that Owen said she was 14 years old when she met "some Boys Town" students at an outdoor dance in August of 1983, and one of the Boys Town students invited Owen to a party the following Friday night (Caradori & Ormiston, 1989a, p. 1). On that Friday night, Owen said that the Boys Town student and a friend picked her up and drove her to a luxury apartment building. They arrived at the party between 9:30 p.m. and 10:00 p.m. The luxury apartment and the party were a world removed from Owen's working-class background and prior life experiences. Owen said that the party consisted of approximately six adults and 20 minors (Caradori & Ormiston, 1989a, p. 1). At the time of the first party she attended, Owen said she did not have a clue about the identities of the adults. But in a short time she understood the adults to include Lawrence King, then-*Omaha World-Herald* publisher Harold Andersen, and then-Omaha Police Chief Robert Wadman (Caradori & Ormiston, 1989a, p. 1).

Owen said that she quickly found herself in over her head. She worried about retribution against her family, and she felt that she could not turn to the police for help. She also said that one of King's henchmen repeatedly terrorized her by threatening her life and the lives of her family members too. She stressed to Caradori that her fear of retribution was very real—she had heard of kids who were either "sold or murdered" (Caradori & Ormiston, 1989a, p. 18). She explained that the threats were counterbalanced by financial rewards: Owen regularly received funds as a drug courier.

Owen named several perpetrators and victims, and she discussed being on two flights—one to Kansas City and one to Los Angeles—where King pandered her as an underage prostitute (Caradori & Ormiston, 1989a, p. 11). Owen also told Caradori that she had several sexual liaisons with OPD Chief Wadman (Caradori & Ormiston, 1989a, pp. 1–9). She provided a myriad of specifics, regarding places and times, when she discussed her liaisons with Chief Wadman. Owen also related stories of sadistic abuse, including bondage and the threat of mutilation with a knife.

After Caradori videotaped Owen for a second time on November 21, he started to search for Troy Boner, who Owen said had also been victim in King's pandering network. Caradori eventually made contact with Boner through his mother, and they agreed to meet at a restaurant in Omaha. As Caradori and Ormiston waited for Boner in the restaurant's parking lot, he pulled up in a green Gran Torino that was driven by his mother's boyfriend. The 22-year-old Boner, standing 6'3" and weighing 200 pounds, cautiously emerged from the car and shook hands with Caradori and Ormiston.

Caradori noted that Boner was noticeably agitated, and the restaurant was too congested to confer a feeling of privacy, so Caradori suggested a second restaurant nearby. Boner rode with Caradori and Ormiston, but he had his mother's boyfriend follow them. His mother's boyfriend stayed in the parking lot as Boner, Caradori, and Ormiston entered the second restaurant. The three situated themselves around a table and talked in "generalities" for five or ten minutes before Caradori provided Boner with a succession of details that were designed to convey to Boner that his information was "on target" (Caradori, 1989c). After half an hour, Boner decided to grant Caradori a formal, videotaped statement.

Caradori and Ormiston then drove Boner to a Residence Inn hotel in Lincoln, Nebraska, where Boner gave them a seven-hour videotaped interview. During Boner's videotaped statements, he corroborated Owen's information on numerous alleged perpetrators, including Lawrence King and OPD Chief Wadman (Caradori & Ormiston, 1989b, p. 7). Boner also corroborated Owen on many events, which included being flown to various locations to be used as an underage prostitute. Boner, too, discussed sadistic abuse, which included bondage and being burned by cigarettes.

Both Owen and Boner had mentioned that Danny King (no relation to Lawrence King) was another victim enmeshed in Lawrence King's alleged pedophile network. The following week, Caradori and Boner drove to Omaha and proceeded to Danny King's apartment. Boner knocked on the front door as Caradori stood next to him. Danny King let Boner into the apartment, and Boner briefly explained Caradori's intentions to King. Caradori noted that Boner and Danny King were alone for approximately "two minutes" before Caradori entered the residence (Caradori & Ormiston, 1989c, p. 1).

The 20-year-old Danny King—short, frail, and skinny—had a congenital throat condition, and he spoke in a guttural rasp. Danny King had a single mother, and he grew up with little supervision, whereas Owen came from an intact nuclear family and Boner came from a semi-intact family.

After Caradori dropped off Boner, he took Danny King to the Residence Inn hotel in Lincoln, Nebraska. Before Caradori drove Danny King to the Residence Inn, King asked Boner "Did you tell them everything?" And Boner replied, "Yes, I told them everything" (Caradori, 1989d). The following day, Caradori and Ormiston interviewed King for approximately six hours. During Caradori's interview of Danny King, he corroborated both Owen and Boner on perpetrators, events, and flights (Caradori & Ormiston, 1989c, pp. 5–10). Danny King, like Owen and Boner, disclosed extremely sadistic abuse too. He discussed being subjected to bondage and beatings.

The allegations of Owen and Danny King corroborated those of Shawneta Moore about abuse perpetrated by a school administrator, even though Owen and King had never previously met Moore. Moreover, Caradori's interviews of Owen, Boner, and Danny King corroborated Eulice Washington on chartered flights. Owen and Boner also corroborated Washington on the purported entanglement of Boys Town students in Lawrence King's pandering network.

In addition to Washington, Owen, and Boner's statements about Boys Town victims, Caradori indicated that a confidential informant of Caradori's provided him with the names of several Boys Town students who had been allegedly ensnared by King's pedophile network (Bryant, 2009, p. 122). Caradori found these revelations to be heartbreaking, because Boys Town had employed his father as a teacher.

By mid-December of 1989, Caradori had accrued approximately 21 hours of victim testimony from Owen, Boner, and Danny King (Bryant, 2009, p. 130). As the Franklin Committee members were confronted with Caradori's mounting evidence, they became increasingly perplexed about where to turn due to their distrust of state and federal law enforcement, because Committee members felt that those agencies had not properly pursued the child abuse allegations. The Franklin Committee tendered its concerns to the U.S. Attorney General's office, but they did not receive a response.

THE FEDERAL GOVERNMENT PROACTIVELY PARTICIPATES IN THE COVER-UP

The Committee ultimately submitted its 21 hours of videotaped statements to the offices of Nebraska's Attorney General and Nebraska's U.S. Attorney on December 27, 1989. State and federal law enforcement were now forced to act. They no longer had the luxury of defaulting to the position that the child abuse allegations had no substance. In addition to pledging immediate action by the NSP, Nebraska's Attorney General called upon the Douglas County judges (Omaha is located in Douglas County) to impanel a grand jury to probe the child abuse allegations. The U.S. Attorney for Nebraska later announced that a federal grand jury would probe the allegations too.

The announced state grand jury coincided with a rather unexpected event concerning Lawrence King when President George H.W. Bush visited Omaha to speak at a fundraiser for Nebraska's governor. King claimed President Bush was a personal friend, and he had previously hosted a "$100,000 gala" for the newly nominated Bush at the 1988 Republican Convention in New Orleans (Goodsell, 1989).

An unnamed source informed Caradori that King had purchased a ticket to attend the fundraiser. This source also disclosed to Caradori that when the Secret Service discovered King's plan to grace the fundraiser, they either ushered him to the federal courthouse or demanded that he make haste to the federal courthouse. Either way, King appeared at the federal courthouse in the early afternoon of February 7, 1990 before U.S. Magistrate Richard Kopf (Bryant, 2009, p. 134). (In the U.S. federal court system, a magistrate judge is a judge appointed to assist a U.S. District Court judge in the performance of his or her duties.)

At the hearing, which Magistrate Kopf called for without a motion from the prosecution or defense, Kopf ordered King to undergo an immediate "mental health evaluation" at the U.S. Medical Center for Federal Prisoners in Springfield, Missouri, even though sources close to King reported that he was not suffering from psychiatric impairment (Associated Press, 1990a). King waived a hearing on Kopf's unorthodox ruling, and that day he found himself en route to Springfield, Missouri in the custody of two U.S. marshals. After King's "mental health evaluation," a U.S. District Court judge remanded him to a federal psychiatric hospital as a pretrial detainee, and King would be at the federal psychiatric hospital for the next five months. King would remain at the federal psychiatric institution as the state and federal grand juries investigated the child abuse allegations.

Vis-à-vis the analogy with DID, if King were not suffering from a psychiatric impairment that would have necessitated his hospitalization, but, rather, if his hospitalization was a ruse to shield him from the grand juries, the abuse disavowing "alter personality" suppressing the evidence of child abuse has now expanded to include the deceit and complicity of two federal judges.

After King was put in a federal psychiatric institution, FBI agents at the Omaha field office began a series of interviews with Alisha Owen, Troy Boner, and Danny King. Owen and King told me that FBI agents vehemently pressured them to recant their allegations of abuse, and Boner would submit an affidavit corroborating Owen and Danny King about being subjected to FBI harassment.

Following Owen's initial statement to Gary Caradori, she was conspicuously harassed in the warden's office at York by two officers of the NSP, which incited rumors among York's inmates that Owen was an informant (Bryant, 2009, p. 131). Six weeks after her meeting with the NSP officers, three inmates attacked Owen in the York shower. In response to the attack, prison officials placed Owen in solitary segregation. Once Owen was in solitary, FBI agents interviewed her several times, and, according to Owen, attempted to force her recantation of the child abuse allegations, but she refused to recant her abuse. Owen was kept in solitary confinement for nearly two years.

After FBI agents initially interviewed Danny King once in February, they conducted a series of interviews with him starting in March of 1990. Danny King initially stuck to his story, but, after repeated interviews, he eventually recanted the statements he had made to Caradori and decided to be what the FBI report described as "totally honest" (Mott & Culver, 1990a). According to an FBI debriefing, after Danny King became "totally honest" (Mott & Culver, 1990a), he stated that Boner visited him in Omaha the night before Boner and Caradori visited Danny King's apartment (Mott & Culver, 1990a). The FBI report stated that Danny King said Boner told him of his upcoming visit with Caradori the next day, and Boner told Danny King that he needed to fabricate stories about his two interstate plane trips with Lawrence King.

Though Danny King pledged to be "totally honest" with the FBI, he evidently was not able to remain consistent with the narrative that was now required of him. For example, during a later FBI debriefing, Danny King said that Boner imparted the fabricated stories to him as Caradori filled his tank with "gas" when they were en route to Lincoln (Mott & Culver, 1990b).

The FBI's final debriefing of Danny King was essentially a cut-and-paste of the debriefings after King became "totally honest," but it contained a new, innovative twist: King denied Boner visiting him on the eve of his initial contact with Caradori and also denied Boner explaining the fabrications to him as Caradori filled his gas tank. The FBI report stated that:

> Caradori and Ormiston left Danny King and Troy Boner in King's hotel room while they returned to Caradori's room, because Boner told Caradori that he and King were going to take a swim for about an hour. After Caradori and Ormiston left the room, Boner and King went to the bar in the hotel where they drank alcohol and talked for approximately one hour. It was during this hour long meeting at the bar in the Residence Inn where Boner first told Danny King what he Boner wanted King to tell Caradori (Culver, 1990).

Boner was then subjected to FBI interviews, and he, too, recanted his abuse allegations at the hands of Lawrence King et al. in a nine-page handwritten statement he composed at Omaha's FBI Field Office. According to Boner's handwritten statement, the day Caradori and Ormiston met Boner, they drove Boner to Caradori's Lincoln, Nebraska office. Caradori then phoned Owen, and handed the phone to Boner. Boner claimed that Owen told him to cooperate with Caradori, because Caradori would help them become rich by suing the men that they named as perpetrators.

Boner's FBI statement indicates that over the next 20 minutes, Boner committed to memory all the "places, locations, people, dates, times, and parties" that Owen disclosed in her videotaped statements to Caradori (Bryant, 2009, p. 153). Boner then claimed that Caradori talked to him and showed him pictures for the next three hours. Boner asserted that he did not recognize a "picture of Larry King" until Caradori pointed him out (Bryant, 2009, p. 153). Boner then gave his videotaped statement to Caradori.

Though this sequence of events would suggest that Boner's recantation is a tissue of lies, his inconsistent statements are not irrefutable proof of prevarication. However, the phone records for Caracorp, Caradori's security firm, on the day Caradori interviewed Boner clearly show that no Caracorp phone calls were placed to York, Nebraska or received from York, Nebraska on that day; and Caradori, like the vast majority of Americans, did not have a cell phone in 1989. The phone logs from York prison also show that Owen did not place a single call on the day Boner alleged to have talked to her (Bryant, 2009, p. 154).

As the FBI was in the process of interviewing Owen, Boner and Danny King, in an apparent effort to force them to recant their accounts of abuse, the *Omaha World-Herald* started to publish articles disparaging Owen and Boner. One article, "One Accuser was Guilty of a Felony," reported that a 21-year-old victim videotaped by the Franklin Committee was incarcerated at York for a bad check felony (Dorr, 1990). The article also detailed that a second videotaped victim had been the "subject of legal proceedings" in the Douglas County juvenile court (Dorr, 1990). The *Omaha World-Herald* would publish additional articles undermining the victims' credibility (Bryant, 2009, pp. 141–142).

As leaks and newspaper coverage chipped away at the victims' credibility, Caradori was not prepared for his investigation's next surprise: his 21 hours of victim testimony was leaked to Omaha TV stations. In the second week of April 1990, Owen phoned the television station whose on-air personality, Mike McKnight, was the first to acquire the leaked tapes, and she consented to an "off the record" meeting with McKnight—York's Visitor's Register confirms that McKnight visited her on April 12. In a quid pro quo, Owen offered to make particular disclosures to McKnight if McKnight revealed who had leaked the tapes. According to Owen, McKnight said that FBI personnel had not actually leaked the tapes to the TV station—they had sold them to the TV station. Though McKnight would eventually be subpoenaed to give an account of how he acquired the tapes, the subpoena would be quashed.

The videotapes became quite a spectacle on Omaha's nightly news. The newspaper articles and leaked tapes sent a resounding message to victims who might have the temerity to step forward: they would be telling their deepest and darkest secrets to the greater Omaha area and also risk being maligned in the print media. The leaked tapes were a catastrophe for Caradori, because he now found it nearly impossible to coax victims from the shadows, even though he would identify approximately 60 alleged victims.

At this point, as mounting evidence pointed to the FBI proactively discrediting the victims and using the media to convince the body politic that the child abuse allegations were spurious and no child abuse was perpetrated, the once nascent "alter" that was protecting the alleged child molesters was becoming the society's dominate personality with regard to Lawrence King-related child abuse allegations.

After the recantations of Danny King and Boner, the media's negative representation of the victims, and the leaked tapes, Caradori managed to videotape a fourth alleged victim named Paul Bonacci in May of 1990 (Caradori, 1990b). The 22-year-old Bonacci was incarcerated at the Lincoln Correctional Center. In November of 1988, within weeks of Franklin's fall, he had been charged with two counts of sexual assault on a child.

After Bonacci's arrest, the court appointed a psychiatrist to determine if Bonacci was a "mentally disordered sex offender" (Bryant, 2009, p. 155). The psychiatrist interviewed Bonacci six times and concluded in a report that Bonacci was not a mentally disordered sex offender, but, rather, that he suffered from "Multiple Personality Disorder" (see psychiatric report; Bryant, 2009, pp. 589–592). By the age of 12, the psychiatrist wrote, Bonacci was heavily victimized by "child prostitution" and involved in drugs (see psychiatric report; Bryant, 2009, pp. 589–592).

Bonacci named the same alleged abusers as Owen, Boner, and Danny King, including Larry King (Caradori & Ormiston, 1990, p. 4), then-Omaha Police Chief Wadman (Caradori & Ormiston, 1990, p. 12) and former *Omaha World-Herald* publisher Harold Andersen (Caradori & Ormiston, 1990, p. 13). He also spoke of similar forms of sadistic abuse that had been described by Owen, Boner, and Danny King. He discussed being repeatedly tied up, whipped, cut by knives, and burned by cigarettes (Caradori & Ormiston, 1990, p. 2).

In addition to corroborating Owen, Boner, and Danny King on multiple victims, places, and perpetrators, Bonacci named several children who attended King's alleged pedophilic parties, including the Boys Town student who Alisha Owen named as having introduced her to Larry King's pandering network (Caradori & Ormiston, 1990, p. 10). Bonacci also claimed to have personally "seen" Owen's abuse at the hands of Chief Wadman (Caradori & Ormiston, 1990, p. 12).

By June of 1990, after the state grand jury had been impaneled for three months, Caradori had been immersed in the "Franklin" case for nearly a year. His investigation included uncovering alleged organized child abuse of an extreme nature, persistent media assaults, and a seemingly concerted effort by state and federal law enforcement and the media to sabotage his investigation. Moreover, two sources had told Caradori that federal and state authorities were in the process of framing him to take the fall for scripting the child abuse allegations (Bryant, 2009, p. 165). Shortly after Caradori realized that he was being "set-up" for an arrest, he wrote a letter to a renowned lawyer noting that the pedophile network he had uncovered extended "to the highest levels of the United States" (Bryant, 2009, p. 166).

The alleged victims Caradori had interviewed and also Shawneta Moore discussed being the victims of child pornography, so Caradori set out to find child pornography of them. He felt that pictures would provide absolute proof of their victimization. Bonacci informed me that one of his final conversations with Caradori revolved around pictures, and Bonacci told Caradori that Rusty Nelson was his best source for the pictures. Bonacci mentioned that Rusty Nelson was a child pornographer when he was initially interviewed by Caradori and Ormiston (Caradori & Ormiston, 1989d, p. 19). Alisha Owen had also singled out Rusty Nelson as an alleged photographer for Lawrence King during her videotaped interviews (Caradori & Ormiston, 1989a, p. 6). Caradori commenced a hunt for Rusty Nelson.

Nelson maintains that Caradori contacted him through a family member when he was in New Mexico, and he agreed to meet Caradori in Chicago and slip him incriminating pictures that would exonerate the victims and expose the perpetrators (Bryant, 2009, p. 170). After Caradori reportedly made contact with Nelson, he flew his 1984 single-engine Piper Saratoga from Lincoln to Chicago. Caradori, accompanied by his eight-year-old son Andrew James (A.J.), ostensibly made the jaunt to attend the July 10 Major League Baseball All-Star Game.

After Caradori and A.J. landed at Chicago's Midway Airport, Caradori's hour-by-hour activities are unclear prior to the game, but four sources—a newspaper reporter in Washington, D.C., Sandi Caradori (his wife), Loran Schmit, and Donna Owen (Alisha Owen's mother)—say they received phone calls from him (Bryant, 2009, p. 170). His conversation with the newspaper reporter in Washington, D.C. was quite candid—Caradori unequivocally told him that he was on the verge of acquiring pictures and other materials that would corroborate the victims' stories (Bryant, 2009, p. 170).

Caradori's call to his wife cryptically conveyed to her that his Chicago trip had been a "success" (Bryant, 2009, p. 170). He also had a pithy conversation with Schmit that the latter relayed to a reporter: "Loran, we got them by the shorthairs" (Bryant, 2009, p. 170). Caradori, having talked to Alisha Owen's parents on various occasions since initially interviewing their daughter, felt terrible about the horrors that had befallen her, and he told Donna Owen that she would be extremely happy upon his return from Chicago.

Caradori and his son flew out of Chicago's Midway Airport around 2:00 a.m. on July 11 (Stern, 1990), and his plane crashed in the Lee County, Illinois cornfield of Harold Cameron. After Cameron heard the sound of a plane and then an explosion, he drove around his property, looking for the crash site. But it was dark, and the four-foot-high corn obscured the wreckage. The plane was spotted at daybreak by a medical helicopter, and deputies from the Lee County Sheriff's Department were the first responders to the crash site, where they found the remains of Gary and A.J. Caradori. Parts of the plane were scattered up to 1,800 feet from the fuselage, and the National Transportation Safety Board (NTSB) stated almost immediately that Caradori's plane broke up in flight, because it was strewn over such a vast area, but the "exact mechanism" for the plane's breakup was unknown.

The personal effects of Caradori and his son salvaged by the NTSB were eventually returned to Sandi Caradori. A.J.'s little backpack and Caradori's 35-millimeter camera were relatively undamaged, but the film in Caradori's camera had been taken out and returned inexplicably developed. Caradori's sturdy leather briefcase, a birthday present from his wife, was never returned. Ormiston told me that the briefcase was virtually an extension of Caradori—it almost "never" left his side throughout the Franklin investigation. If Caradori had acquired pictures in Chicago, she felt they definitely would have been in his briefcase.

Caradori's last statement to Senator Schmit was "We got them by the shorthairs," and Schmit never bought the explanation that Caradori's plane mysteriously "broke up" in flight. After the crash, Schmit stated in an affidavit that he had been warned that Caradori's life was in danger. He also wrote a letter to the NTSB regarding the backseats of Caradori's plane that were never recovered, because he thought a bomb had been used.

The NTSB released its final report on the crash two years after the fact. The report determined that the crash occurred at 2:21 a.m. The report also concluded that Caradori lost control of the plane "for an unknown reason," but it cited "pilot fatigue and probable spatial disorientation of the pilot and/or an instrument malfunction" as likely causes for Caradori's loss of control (see report; Bryant, 2009, p. 560). As Caradori attempted to recover from "uncontrolled flight," the report continued, the wings on his Piper Saratoga snapped off due to an "overload" of stress (see report: Bryant, 2009, p. 560).

Five sources, including Rusty Nelson, corroborate that Caradori acquired what he was seeking—pictures—during his sojourn to Chicago, and the anomalies and inconsistences involved in the official account of the deaths of Gary Caradori and his son are too numerous to explicate in this chapter (Bryant, 2009, pp. 172–174). Either Caradori's death was an oddly timed freak accident that caused his plane to fragment in mid-air or he was murdered. If Caradori and his son were, in fact, murdered, it shows that the "alter personality" impeding the normal continuity of a society from protecting its children against child abuse is willing to maintain the homeostasis that no Lawrence King-related child abuse has occurred by murder.

THE STATE AND FEDERAL GRAND JURIES

One of Gary Caradori's ultimate objectives was to move the Franklin Committee's child abuse investigation beyond the margins of provincial law enforcement and into a grand jury. As I've already mentioned, after the Committee submitted Caradori's videotaped statements of Alisha Owen, Troy Boner, and Danny King to Nebraska's Attorney General, Douglas County's district judges convened and called for a grand jury to investigate the Franklin-related child abuse allegations.

Though Caradori initially welcomed the impaneling of a grand jury, he also realized the inherent flaws of the grand jury process, which makes the initial decision to indict (formally accuse) a criminal defendant to stand trial. Unlike a trial, a grand jury proceeding is private, and there is no cross-examination or presentation of the defense's case. The special prosecutor calls the witnesses, questions the witnesses, and selects the evidence that is shown to the grand jurors, who are ordinary citizens. Generally, only witnesses and evidence deemed relevant by special prosecutors are pursued by grand juries, and special prosecutors are in a unique position to be able to twist grand jurors' judgments in a particular direction. A former Chief Appellate Judge of New York State once quipped that a special prosecutor could persuade a grand jury to "indict a ham sandwich" (Kramer & Lombardi, 1985).

The Douglas County judges ultimately appointed Samuel Van Pelt as the grand jury's special prosecutor. After Van Pelt was appointed to be the special prosecutor of the grand jury probing the child abuse allegations, he dispensed quotes to the *Omaha World-Herald* about the case: "The integrity of the system is being challenge," said Van Pelt (Dorr & Cordes, 1990); "I feel the system needs to work. The grand jury system is the one process that can work now" (Dorr & Cordes, 1990). The tall, lean, 53-year-old Van Pelt grew up in Lincoln, Nebraska and was a graduate of the University of Nebraska Law School (Dorr & Cordes, 1990). In 1972, Nebraska's governor appointed him as a district judge in Lancaster County, but he concluded that being a judge was an "unpleasant job" and resigned after eleven years on the bench (Dorr & Cordes, 1990).

Though some Nebraskans gave Van Pelt a lukewarm appraisal, others viewed him with contempt. Their feelings about Van Pelt centered on an investigation he had directed five years earlier—they claimed he covered up the shooting death of a Nebraska farmer by a NSP SWAT team (Associated Press, 1990a). Shortly after Van Pelt's appointment had been announced, 43 Nebraskans sent a letter to the Speaker of the Legislature charging that Van Pelt was merely a "hired gun for the state" (Associated Press, 1990a).

Prior to his death, Caradori made two appearances before the grand jury overseen by Van Pelt. Though his first appearance was brief, Caradori had concluded that the grand jury was utterly corrupt and the process was a fait accompli. After his first appearance before the grand jury, a forlorn Caradori kissed his wife that night and told her, "It's all over" (Bryant, 2009, p. 229). Following Caradori's first appearance before the grand jury, he formed the opinion that only pictures would save him from the Douglas County grand jury and federal prosecution.

Troy Boner also made two appearances before the Douglas County grand jury. Though Boner's testimony was littered with discrepancies and contradictions, he had passed an FBI polygraph (Bryant, 2009, p. 229). Van Pelt was quick to point out that Boner had passed an FBI polygraph, and it was a point that was not lost on the grand jurors.

At the outset of Boner's testimony, Van Pelt took him through his initial meeting with Caradori and his videotaped statement. Boner maintained that Caradori and Ormiston brought him back to the offices of Caracorp, where, over the phone, he conversed with Owen for 20 minutes, and she told him to fabricate specific allegations of abuse, so they could gain untold riches by suing the alleged perpetrators (transcript of testimony, Douglas County grand jury, 1990). But, as noted earlier, according to Caracorp's phone records, the phone call that Boner pinned the entire "hoax" on never happened.

Boner's description of the alleged phone conversation with Owen at Caradori's office was littered with numerous contradictions. He told the grand jury that Owen fed him "85%" of the content that was contained in his seven-hour videotaped statement to Caradori (transcript of testimony, Douglas County grand jury, 1990). He initially testified that he jotted down dates, times, and places after talking to Owen. However, during his second appearance before the grand jury, Boner maintained that he did not take any notes, but Caradori helped him "over the hump" by giving him "hints" throughout his videotaped statement (transcript of testimony, Douglas County grand jury, 1990). In complete contradiction to his FBI statemen,t and earlier testimony before the grand jury in which he said that he had only one call with Owen, he stated that he had multiple phone calls with Owen to craft the hoax during his second appearance before the grand jury.

Boner initially testified to the grand jury that he briefed Danny King, at King's apartment, for five minutes on the fabricated story that he wanted Danny King to tell Caradori. He then testified that he briefed King for 20 minutes at King's apartment; but during his second appearance at the grand jury, he claimed that Danny King had several calls with Owen too.

Danny King would be called before the grand jury only once—shortly after Boner's first appearance. Boner told the grand jury that he imparted the hoax to Danny King in the latter's apartment while Caradori waited outside, but Danny King testified that Caradori drove Boner and him to Lincoln's Residence Inn, where Boner gave him the low-down on the hoax in the hotel bar over beers. Lincoln's Residence Inn did not even have a bar. The following Q&A is between Van Pelt and an apparently confused Danny King (transcript of testimony, Douglas County grand jury, 1990):

> VAN PELT: And is that true, is that what went on and what went through your mind the night you were visiting with Troy in the bar at the motel?
> DANNY KING: Yeah.
> VAN PELT: And is that why you decided to do this?
> DANNY KING: Yeah.
> VAN PELT: And was any of this true at that time?
> DANNY KING: Any of what true?
> VAN PELT: Any of the business about the basis for suing these people, the parties with all these people? Anything about . . . Larry King, any of those people true at that time?

DANNY KING: Yeah, so I wasn't really—
VAN PELT: I beg your pardon?
DANNY KING: Yeah, I was—I wasn't really making nothing up about any of the persons.

After Danny King's latter statements, Van Pelt walked Danny King through his conversation with Boner at the bar, but King still had considerable difficulties staying on track.

When Boner and Danny King appeared before the grand jury, they recurrently contradicted themselves—I've mentioned a rather limited litany. Both Boner and Danny King would later admit to covering up grave abuses during their grand jury appearances.

In contrast to Boner and Danny King, Alisha Owen never recanted her accounts of abuse, even though she was confined to solitary at the Nebraska Facility for Women at York. She spent two days in front of the grand jury that subjected her to numerous affronts on her character, especially regarding her sexual history. One of those affronts was made by a grand juror remarking, "I can't imagine Alisha being around a man and not having gone to bed with him" (transcript of testimony, Douglas County grand jury, 1990). Testifying before the grand jury, Owen attempted to explain that her teenage sexual history was the result of her sexual abuse: "I had absolutely no concept of what sex . . . was supposed to mean because my sexual experiences started in such a warped way" (transcript of testimony, Douglas County grand jury, 1990).

A few weeks before Owen made her appearance before the Douglas County grand jury, a distinguished Omaha-based attorney by the name of Henry Rosenthal agreed to represent her. Owen's mother had arranged for Rosenthal to represent her daughter, because she felt that Owen's previous attorney was working in collusion with the FBI to sabotage her daughter. Her former attorney would later admit to having an extramarital affair with one of the FBI agents who was attempting to coerce Owen into recanting her accounts of abuse at the hands of Larry King and others.

By the time Senator Schmit made his first appearance before the grand jury, Van Pelt had called selected witnesses who either portrayed the senator in an unfavorable light or severely ravaged his credibility. One witness in particular commented on Schmit's "paranoia," testifying that he was not "well physically or mentally" (transcript of testimony, Douglas County grand jury, 1990).

Schmit was of the opinion that Van Pelt had neglected to address numerous pertinent issues during his appearance before the grand jury. So he requested that he appear before the grand jury a second time, and his request was granted. Between Schmit's first and second appearance before the grand jury, he reported to have heard murmurs that Alisha Owen would be indicted for perjury and Caradori for obstruction of justice.

During his second appearance, he read a prepared statement and gave an impassioned plea for the grand jury to carefully consider all the evidence. Schmit said that "based upon the evidence the Committee has heard, we are convinced that certain prominent citizens have abused children, are abusing children, and will abuse children in the future" (transcript of testimony, Douglas County grand jury, 1990). He also discussed what he viewed as law enforcement's unwillingness to act and its hindrances: "Too many unanswered questions, ladies and gentlemen, too many leads not followed and too many roadblocks placed in the way of the investigation" (transcript of testimony, Douglas County grand jury, 1990).

Van Pelt eventually called a man to the stand who was clearly psychologically disturbed, and he admittedly had no knowledge of the child abuse allegations. He told the grand jurors that the Russian "KGB" had infiltrated the U.S. Food and Drug Administration, and he wanted the grand jury to take action. The latter epitomizes the chaotic proceedings of the Douglas County grand jury, which lasted four months.

During the third week of July 1990, television newscasters and radio talk show hosts tingled with excitement as they quoted sources in the know who whispered that the Douglas County grand jury was in the homestretch of its deliberations. Van Pelt had pledged to restore "integrity" to the system, and his grand jury had ostensibly worked unremittingly to that end for month after month. Finally, the community hoped that all the confusion and uncertainty would be cleared up—criminals would be indicted and the innocent cleared.

On July 23, 1990, within two weeks of Gary Caradori's demise, the Douglas County grand jury released its 43-page report (Flanagan, 1990). The *Omaha World-Herald* bore a banner headline: "Grand Jury Says Abuse Stories were a 'Carefully Crafted Hoax.'" A subheadline stated: "Three Indicted; Many Rumors Debunked" (Dorr & Stern, 1990).

The first page of the Douglas County grand jury's report discussed its thorough deliberations: convening for 82 days, reviewing 395 exhibits, issuing 136 subpoenas, hearing from 76 witnesses, and watching over 30 hours of videotapes (Flanagan, 1990, p. 1). The first page of the report also included an introductory comment: "Two of the victims recanted their video statements and testified that a third victim, Alisha Owen, was perpetrating a hoax for personal gain" (Flanagan, 1990, p. 1).

The grand jury declared that all Lawrence King-related child abuse allegations were a "carefully crafted hoax" (Flanagan, 1990, p. 15), but the grand jury report never specified who concocted the hoax (Flanagan, 1990). Even the report's first page had inaccuracies, because it is not true that the grand jurors reviewed 395 exhibits. On July 23, the very day that the grand jury foreman Michael Flanagan signed off on the grand jury report, grand jury documentation demonstrates that Van Pelt introduced 87 exhibits into evidence. However, 62 of those 87 exhibits were given the same number—"exhibit 394." So it ultimately appears that Van Pelt only introduced 26 exhibits on the grand jury's final day of deliberations.

And among those 87 exhibits introduced on July 23 was a review of Caracorp's phone records. An NSP investigator had picked up a copy of Caracorp's phone records on May 23, and they were not introduced into evidence until July 23, the final day of the grand jury's deliberations when Van Pelt introduced 87 exhibits into evidence. Thus, Van Pelt seemed to possess evidence that the phone call where Owen clued Boner in on the "hoax" never existed.

The grand jury overseen by Van Pelt indicted Alisha Owen on eight counts of perjury, and it indicted Paul Bonacci on three counts of perjury. Owen's perjury indictments pertained to her statements about being molested by then-OPD Chief Robert Wadman and Omaha Judge Theodore Carlson, and also regarding statements about Lawrence King and then-*Omaha World-Herald* publisher Harold Andersen molesting children. Bonacci's perjury indictments pertained to him witnessing OPD Chief Robert Wadman molesting Alisha Owen and him being molested by then-*Omaha World-Herald* publisher Harold Andersen.

Each count of perjury carried a maximum sentence of 20 years, so Owen was looking at 160 years in prison and Bonacci had to contend with 60 years in prison. Alan Baer, whose name emerged on Caradori's videotapes and during the grand jury as one of the alleged wealthy pedophiles in King's network, was indicted on two counts of adult pandering. His charges were reduced to a misdemeanor, and he was fined "$500" (Bryant, 2009, p. 436).

Shortly after the *Omaha World-Herald* published the Douglas County grand jury report, it published an editorial, "Franklin Committee a Disgrace to Nebraska," excoriating the Franklin Committee and a deceased Gary Caradori (*Omaha World-Herald*, 1990, p. 16). The Nebraska legislature rescinded its financing for the Franklin Committee, and it was disbanded in January of 1991.

The federal grand jury investigating the Franklin Credit Union was initially impaneled in September 1988, and it issued indictments against Larry King in May of 1989 for his financial crimes. The federal grand jury would then shift its focus from Franklin-related financial improprieties to Franklin-related child abuse, and be given a six-month extension in April of 1990 to continue exploring the allegations; so it was ultimately impaneled for two years. The FBI served as the investigative entity for the federal grand jury.

Alisha Owen alleges that one of the federal prosecutors pilloried her with threats at the federal courthouse before she took the federal grand jury's oath. She said that he was "livid and discharging spittle" as he shouted that she would suffer grave consequences if she did not recant her prior statements to Caradori, but Owen still refused to recant (Bryant, 2009, p. 272). In the federal grand jury, like the Douglas County grand jury, Troy Boner was a key witness to impeach Owen.

In September of 1990, the federal grand jury released a three-page report stating that it found absolutely no evidence of interstate transportation of children for illicit purposes, and also indicted Alisha Owen on eight counts of perjury. *The New York Times* published an article on the federal grand jury's findings—"Omaha Tales of Sexual Abuse Ruled False" (Associated Press, 1990c).

THE STATE OF NEBRASKA V. ALISHA OWEN

Thus far, in the Franklin case, my investigation has established that state and federal authorities have disrupted the normal continuity of a society that seeks to protect its children from sexual abuse. Initially, the disruption was of omission (e.g., ignoring the abuse allegations), and as the allegations persisted with mounting evidence, the disruption included acts of commission by the OPD, NSP, FBI, and the Nebraska state judiciary and the federal judiciary. The reporting by the local and national media also compounded the state and federal government's disruptive process. The escalating cover-up was also accompanied by the society omitting the reality of the child abuse from the collective memory of its citizens.

But the cover-up in Nebraska was confronted by a pair of wild cards: Alisha Owen and Paul Bonacci—they would have to be found guilty of perjury in a court of law in order for the "carefully crafted hoax" to become the official story. The Douglas County judiciary elected to prosecute Owen first. As Owen lingered in solitary segregation at York throughout the fall of 1991, girding herself for her upcoming trial, her 16-year-old brother, Aaron, stole a car. Although he was a juvenile, Douglas County opted to try him as an adult. The judge sentenced Aaron Owen to between four and seven years in prison.

Shortly thereafter, Aaron Owen hanged himself in his cell. He had slash marks on both wrists, a bone-deep gash on his forehead, and a large bruise under his left eye. The official account essentially found that Owen succumbed to extreme masochism before he decided to hang himself. Aaron Owen signed the alleged suicide note "A.J." He had never referred to himself as A.J. before. The Owens felt that Aaron Owen writing A.J. on the suicide note was a clear sign that he had been murdered in retaliation for his sister's refusal to recant her abuse. Approximately two and a half months after Aaron Owen's death, Troy Boner's younger brother, Shawn, shot himself in the head allegedly playing "Russian roulette."

Since both state and federal grand juries had disavowed the existence of Larry King's pandering network, the state of Nebraska and the United States had vital vested interests in the guilt of Alisha Owen. Although FBI agents had coerced Owen, Boner, and Danny King to recant their accounts of abuse, they were not called to testify before the Douglas County grand jury, but at Owen's trial they would be called as witnesses to impeach Owen's integrity. The *Omaha World-Herald* would play an integral role in underscoring the state's case, and the Columbia Broadcasting System (CBS), the national television network, would also underscore the state's case. So Alisha Owen and her attorney, Henry Rosenthal, found themselves squaring off against the state of Nebraska, the United States government, and the local and national media.

Rosenthal had been an attorney for over 30 years, and he was appalled by the miscarriages of justice he had witnessed against Alisha Owen during her appearances before the Douglas County and federal grand juries that indicted her for perjury, so he consented to represent her pro bono at her trial (Bryant, 2009, p. 325).

Owen's trial was tried in the Douglas County Courthouse, the same site where Van Pelt pledged to restore "integrity" to the system, and Rosenthal was determined that it would not be the scene of a second flagrant miscarriage of justice against Alisha Owen. He managed to have her trial postponed until May of 1991, and he put in 16-hour days backtracking on Caradori's investigation and the Douglas County grand jury. He spent enormous out-of-pocket sums to finance his defense of Owen. As Rosenthal immersed himself in Owen's case and Caradori's investigation, he shared Caradori's views about the perfidious power of state and federal law enforcement to fluently twist truth into lies and vice versa (Bryant, 2009, p. 334).

Alisha Owen's perjury trial turned out to be one of the longest criminal trials in Nebraska history. The state of Nebraska pulled out all the stops and spared no expense: her trial represented much more than a simple case of perjury. If Alisha Owen was found guilty of perjury, the grand jury reports would be validated. But if she were found innocent, their findings would be called into question.

Just as Samuel Van Pelt had been plucked out of judicial retirement to lead the Douglas County grand jury, retired 77-year-old jurist Raymond "Joe" Case would be brought forward to serve as the judge in the Owen trial. Case was originally appointed a judge in Nebraska's rural Cass County in 1950. His tenure as a Cass County judge lasted 40 years, and he retired in 1990. After Case retired from the bench, he went into private practice. Nebraska law prohibits practicing attorneys from serving as judges, but Case was appointed Owen's trial judge nonetheless. Whereas appointing Van Pelt was ostensibly a collective decision of the Douglas County District Court judges, Case was chosen to oversee Alisha Owen's trial by the highest court in the state—the Nebraska Supreme Court.

Douglas County Deputy Attorney Gerald Moran stepped into the ring to represent the state and its vast supporting cast. Moran was a youthful looking 43 years old. Moran had spent the 1970s practicing criminal law for an esteemed Omaha law firm before signing on with the Douglas County Attorney's office in 1981.

Prior to Owen's trial, Rosenthal presented Judge Case with a series of motions that delineated various improprieties by the Douglas County grand jury and also by FBI agents when they questioned Alisha Owen at York prison. Sitting at the bench, Case peered at what he called Rosenthal's "bunch of motions," and he said that Rosenthal had missed the deadline for submitting the motions (Nebraska v. Owen, 1991, p. 6). But the week that Case set the deadline, Rosenthal had been hospitalized for a heart condition; so he had phoned Case, explained his medical predicament, and requested two additional days to file his motions. Case reportedly agreed to Rosenthal's timetable, and instructed Rosenthal to notify Moran about the deadline being pushed back. In accordance with Case's decision, Rosenthal called Moran and explained his quandary.

Shortly after Case brought up Rosenthal's "bunch of motions," Rosenthal reminded him of their phone call in which Case extended the deadline for his motions. Case told Rosenthal that he remembered the phone call, but he could not recall that the crux of the conversation was an extension of his deadline to submit the motions. Rosenthal then said if Case had not issued an extension for the motions, he would have filed the motions on time by hook or by crook. Moran quickly interjected that Rosenthal had not notified him of the extension until after Rosenthal submitted the motions. But Rosenthal disagreed and remarked, "That's absolutely a false statement to the Court—I notified that man and certainly, judge, I would not be in violation of your order" (Nebraska v. Owen, 1991, p. 6). Judge Case now recalled his conversation with Rosenthal, and he said that he explicitly stipulated that Moran had to be in agreement with the extension. It was the first time in Rosenthal's lengthy legal career that an opposing counsel instead of a judge had essentially succeeded in rejecting motions he had submitted. It quickly became evident to Rosenthal that he was not trying Alisha Owen's in an impartial courtroom.

In Rosenthal's opening statement to the jurors, he focused on the state's star witness: Troy Boner. Rosenthal said that it was absurd to believe that Boner's nearly seven-hour statement to Caradori was supposedly gleaned from a 20-minute phone call to Owen. He said that Boner's videotaped statement specified times, places, names, etc. Rosenthal stated that even if Boner had mastered shorthand to the tune of "5,000 words a minute" he could not have jotted down everything he articulated in his videotaped statement to Caradori from one 20-minute phone call (Nebraska v. Owen, 1991, p. 618). Rosenthal told the jurors to carefully scrutinize the videotaped statement of Boner and decide for themselves if Caradori had acted deceitfully, and he remarked on the alleged phone call: "Because if you don't believe the phone call, and if you don't believe the phone call was made, then the cookie crumbles" (Nebraska v. Owen, 1991, p. 618).

By the time Moran called Boner to testify at Owen's trial, his story had been considerably hemmed and hedged. For example, in front of the Douglas County grand jury Boner gave conflicting accounts of imparting the hoax to Danny King: Boner testified he conveyed the hoax to King the night before he and Caradori went to King's apartment, and he also testified that the hoax was transmitted while he and Danny King were alone in King's apartment for 20 minutes. Danny King told Van Pelt and the Douglas County grand jury that Boner had imparted the hoax to him over beers at the Residence Inn. Evidently, the state preferred Danny King's version of events, because Boner's testimony now incorporated King's version. Upon cross-examination, Rosenthal would ensnare Boner in numerous lies. When the state called Danny King to testify, Rosenthal would entrap King in numerous lies too upon cross-examination.

As Rosenthal cross-examined the state's witnesses, Moran barraged him with objections—Rosenthal was consequently kept on a very short leash concerning the questions he could ask the witnesses called by Moran. Conversely, court transcripts demonstrate that Case gave Moran considerable latitude when he cross-examined the witnesses called by Rosenthal.

Owen's trial wended for five weeks, and the trial transcript is over 4,000 pages. A more complete discussion of the miscarriages of justice that constituted the perjury trial of Alisha Owen is included in *The Franklin Scandal.*

On Friday June 7, 1991, after three weeks, 35 witnesses, and scores of exhibits, Moran and the state rested their case. The following Monday morning at 9:00 a.m. Rosenthal met with Moran and Judge Case in the judge's chambers. Rosenthal had prepared a long list of reasons for Judge Case to dismiss perjury charges against Owen or, at the very least, declare a mistrial. He also had a newfound revelation that he thought would ensure a mistrial. But before Rosenthal unfurled his newfound revelation to Moran and Case, he offered the following reasons for Judge Case to declare a mistrial after the state presented its case (Nebraska v. Owen, 1991, pp. 2837–2841):

- The state's use of confidential material plundered from Owen's Social Services records.
- The state's use of confidential material plumbed from Owen's Presentence Probation Report.
- The Court's refusal to accept the motions Rosenthal submitted to Case on May 1.
- The vague wording of Owen's grand jury indictments.
- Misconduct on the part of Van Pelt and the grand jury that "destroyed the impartial administration of justice."
- Misconduct by Owen's previous attorney who provided state and federal law enforcement with various communications—both written and verbal—that were unlawful for the state to use against Owen, because Owen had at no time waived her attorney-client privilege.
- The state's use of information obtained by the NSP and FBI that was involuntary, coerced, and obtained without a competent counsel, violating Owen's right against self-incrimination.

Judge Case was unmoved by any of Rosenthal's arguments, and he dismissed Rosenthal's rationales for a mistrial. Rosenthal then told Case that the Caradori videotapes that were shown to the Douglas County grand jurors had been "altered," and the corroborating statements between Owen and Boner had been edited out (Nebraska v. Owen, 1991, p. 2842). Rosenthal told Judge Case that he wanted to demonstrate to the jurors at Owen's trial how the tapes shown to the grand jury had been doctored, but Moran objected and Judge Case supported Moran.

Rosenthal and Owen felt that Case's refusal to allow the jurors to see that Caradori's videotaped statements of Owen and Boner had been doctored when shown to the Douglas County grand jurors proved that the trial of Alisha Owen was not concerned about whether or not child abuse had occurred—it was only concerned with putting Owen in prison for perjury.

When Rosenthal presented Owen's case to the jurors, he called a number of witnesses who discussed how Boner had told them that the FBI forced him to lie before the state and federal grand juries, and that Boner had lied throughout Owen's trial.

Owen's jurors deliberated her fate for nearly three days. Owen's fate still hung in the balance as her jurors left the Douglas County Courthouse after their first full day of deliberations. The day before, Judge Case had told the jurors that the CBS program *48 Hours* was to be telecast on the following night at 9:00 p.m. Case mentioned that the program may pertain to Owen's trial, and he instructed the jurors not to watch it.

Dan Rather hosted *48 Hours*, and the episode on that particular night was entitled "Accusing Prominent People of Sex Crimes" (Bryant, 2009, p. 428). And the fourth segment of the show began with a shot of Troy Boner, who said that he had falsely accused prominent men of abuse to the *48 Hours* reporter. The *48 Hours* episode demonstrates that the media's portrayal of the Franklin Case as a hoax now extended to primetime, national coverage, and it was aired at an opportune time for the parties executing the cover-up.

According to a juror affidavit, "almost all, if not all" of Owen's jurors opted not to heed Case, and they tuned into *48 Hours* that night (see affidavit; Bryant, 2009, p. 567). The juror's affidavit further stated that the *48 Hours* episode "impacted the decision" of the jurors who watched the program (see affidavit; Bryant, 2009, p. 567).

A second juror's affidavit also discussed "almost all, if not all" of the jurors watching the program, and it had a highly prejudicial impact on Owen (see affidavit; Bryant, 2009, pp. 565–566). In addition, the juror's affidavit alleged that fabricated evidence had been planted in the "jury room," during the jurors' deliberations, that was extremely prejudicial to Owen (see affidavit; Bryant, 2009, pp. 565–566).

The jury ultimately found Owen guilty of perjury, and Case sentenced 22-year-old Alisha Owen to between nine and 15 years in prison.

The following day, a *Omaha World-Herald* editorial entitled, "Prosecution Crushed Lies With Avalanche of Truth," showered accolades on Moran just as previous editorials had praised Samuel Van Pelt (*Omaha World-Herald*, 1991, p. 16).

Shortly after Owen was found guilty, the Douglas County Attorney dismissed the perjury indictments against Bonacci. Owen's trial almost resulted in a hung jury, as evinced by the jury's protracted deliberations, despite the efforts of Case and Moran and the aforementioned misconduct cited by the jurors during their deliberations. If Bonacci were to be found innocent, Owen's conviction would have been jeopardized and, perhaps, even overturned.

Alisha Owen's case would be appealed on multiple acts of misconduct concerning the judge, prosecution, and jurors. The following are appeals alleging the misconduct of Judge Case (Bryant, 2009, pp. 442–443):

- Judge Case erred in refusing to dismiss the charges against Owen based upon the misconduct of the Douglas County grand jury.
- Judge Case erred in refusing to declare a mistrial of Owen's case based on prosecutorial misconduct during the course of the trial.
- Judge Case erred in committing judicial misconduct during the course of Owen's trial.
- Judge Case erred in refusing to grant Owen a new trial based upon the misconduct that occurred during the jury's deliberations.

- Judge Case erred in admitting into evidence, over Rosenthal's objection, contents of a presentence investigation.
- Judge Case erred in admitting into evidence, over Rosenthal's objection, testimony from an employee of Social Services.
- Judge Case erred in allowing the prosecution to introduce irrelevant, immaterial, and prejudicial evidence regarding Owen's character.
- Judge Case erred in allowing the prosecution to admit into evidence statements of Owen's made while she was in custody without having been notified of her Miranda rights.
- Judge Case allowed Wadman to testify about the results of genetic blood testing by means of hearsay and without establishing a proper "foundation and custody" that demonstrated the blood tested was, in fact, from Wadman, Owen, and Owen's daughter. Thus the question of whether or not Wadman was the father of Owen's daughter was never satisfactorily established.
- Judge Case had improper contact with the jury—the appeal cited Case's verbal directions to the jury concerning "reasonable doubt" and also an Allen charge.
- Judge Case erred in overruling Rosenthal's pretrial motions.
- Judge Case's quashing of subpoenas deprived Owen of a fair trial.
- Judge Case improperly limited Rosenthal's cross-examination of witnesses.
- Judge Case repeatedly allowed "hearsay evidence" to be used against Owen.
- Judge Case repeatedly allowed "prejudicial and irrelevant" evidence to be used against Owen.

Despite the numerous miscarriages of justice that were cited in Owen's trial and the subsequent appeals they fostered, the Nebraska judiciary refused to declare a mistrial on Owen's behalf. But Owen and her appellate attorneys were given hope for corrective legal remedies when Troy Boner came forward and submitted an affidavit whereby he confessed that he "lied" before the grand juries and also at Alisha Owen's trial (see affidavit; Bryant, 2009, pp. 524–537).

Boner's affidavit is 14 pages long, but the first page offers a succinct rundown of both his motives for the affidavit and the wrongful acts he committed against Owen:

> I, and my mother and my family, are exhausted from living in fear of death or injury as a result of my personal involvement in the Franklin matters which ended up in my testifying at the Grand Jury hearings as well as at the Alisha Owen trial. I lied at the Grand Jury hearings, and I lied at the Alisha Owen trial. I lied when I 'recanted' my original statement to Gary Caradori. I lied because I truly believed and still do believe that it was a situation where I must either 'lie or die' . . . (see affidavit; Bryant, 2009, pp. 524–537).

His affidavit further stated that he had balked at testifying against Alisha Owen at her trial, and he felt his brother's death via Russian roulette was a murder that was designed to ensure that he testify at Alisha Owen's trial. Boner's affidavit explicitly mentioned delivering Alisha Owen to OPD Chief Wadman, and it exonerated Gary Caradori of any improprieties.

An appellate hearing that had the potential to secure Owen a new trial was set for December of 1994 at the Douglas County Courthouse, and Boner was to testify that he had lied before the grand juries and at Alisha Owen's trial. As Alisha Owen, Owen's parents, Troy Boner, and Owen's appellate attorney walked through the Douglas County Courthouse towards the courtroom where the hearing was to be held, they saw Douglas County Deputy Attorney Robert Sigler, and then they noticed a handful of men conspicuously milling around Sigler. Owen thought the men were either Douglas County Deputy Sheriffs or NSP officers. Alisha Owen, Owen's parents, and Owen's appellate attorney witnessed the men around Sigler abruptly approach Boner, snatch him, and drag him into a vacant room. After the men, Sigler, and Boner disappeared into the room, its door was locked, and Alisha and her party heard screaming emanating from the room.

A terrified Boner eventually emerged from the room, and he pointblank told Owen's appellate attorney that he would invoke his Fifth Amendment right against self-incrimination when called to testify at Owen's hearing; Boner said that if he did not take the Fifth, he would end up in prison just like Owen.

In the Franklin saga's previous disruptions of a society that seeks to protect its children from sexual abuse, the disruptions generally occurred behind closed doors (e.g., meetings among law enforcement and the judiciary, law enforcement's meeting with victims, the secrecy of grand juries, etc.), but Owen's trial and subsequent hearing with Troy Boner were hijacked in a public forum. The government and the media had publicly trumped the laws and mores of the body politic to protect its children in the case of Lawrence King-related child abuse, and it was now functioning much like a powerful abuser-aligned alter within the larger psyche of an individual with DID, in that both disavow child abuse.

Alisha Owen was paroled from prison in 2000.

THE WASHINGTON, D.C. CONNECTION

The extreme power described above that was deployed in Nebraska to eradicate the slightest vestiges of Lawrence King-related child abuse is nearly impossible to comprehend without understanding King's relationship to Washington, D.C., the epicenter of America's political authority.

When Senator Schmit proposed Legislative Resolution 5, which called for the formation of the Franklin Committee, he reported that he was anonymously warned against the Committee's investigation, because it would lead to the "highest levels of the Republican party." Gary Caradori also informed a renowned attorney that the pedophile network he uncovered in his investigation extended "to the highest levels of the United States."

The alleged warning to Senator Schmit and the information relayed by Gary Caradori implies that the alleged child-pandering network of Lawrence King extended beyond the geographical confines of Nebraska. Earlier, I mentioned the accounts of Eulice Washington, Alisha Owen, Troy Boner, Danny King, and Paul Bonacci, all of whom stated that they had been flown to various states where Lawrence King had pandered them as underage sex workers. I also mentioned Gary Caradori collecting accounts of underage children accompanying Lawrence King on chartered flights, and King renting charter planes on an almost weekly basis—his favored destination was Washington, D.C.

According to five sources cited in *The Franklin Scandal,* including a police detective (Bryant, 2009, pp. 307–308) and a newspaper reporter (Bryant, 2009, p. 284), King's partner in pedophilic pandering was Craig Spence, a Washington, D.C.-based lobbyist and powerbroker. An article featured on the front page of the *Washington Times*, "Power Broker Served Drugs, Sex at Parties Bugged for Blackmail" included extensive corroboration that Spence's home was bugged for audio-visual surveillance (Hedges & Seper, 1989a). Craig Spence also confessed to being a CIA asset (Hedges & Seper, 1989b), and *Washington Times* reporters corroborated his claim (Bryant, 2009, p. 287). Spence later confessed to *Washington Times* reporters that "friendly" intelligence agents had bugged his home (Hedges & Seper, 1989c).

According to credit card vouchers salvaged by the *Washington Times*, Craig Spence spent up to $20,000 a month on male escorts from an escort service operated by Henry Vinson (Hedges & Seper, 1989d). As the credit card vouchers demonstrated, Vinson dealt with Spence prolifically over the course of two years. I conducted an extensive investigation of Lawrence King and Craig Spence, and their relationship to Henry Vinson. Vinson told me that Spence eventually introduced him to Lawrence King, and Vinson alleges that King and Spence were involved with not only pedophilic pandering but also pedophilic blackmail. Vinson also indicates that Spence personally showed him the blackmail equipment that was scattered throughout Spence's home.

Vinson also alleges that both King and Spence attempted to coerce him into providing them with "children," even though his escort service only provided consenting adults, and he refused to be a party to pedophilic pandering. According to Vinson, he continued to refuse to cooperate with Spence on child pandering and other crimes, and a high-ranking officer in the Justice Department pressured him to cooperate with Spence or be subjected to legal ramifications. Spence had told Vinson that he provided this particular high-ranking officer with "adolescent boys."

Vinson said he did not succumb to the pressure, and shortly thereafter the U.S. Secret Service raided his home. During the raid, the Secret Service garnered evidence that Vinson was running an escort service, and the U.S. Attorney for the District of Washington, D.C. eventually impaneled a federal grand jury to investigate Vinson's criminal activity and the criminal activity of his accomplices. *The Franklin Scandal* addresses various improprieties that occurred in that grand jury's deliberations.

The Washington, D.C. grand jury exonerated Spence of any crimes, including solicitation of prostitution, but Vinson was charged with a 43-count RICO indictment, and he was facing 295 years in prison. RICO is an acronym for the Racketeer Influenced and Corrupt Organizations Act, and it was originally designed to dismantle the Mafia, as RICO allows for mob bosses to be tried for crimes that were sanctioned on their behalf.

Vinson viewed the RICO Act in his case as prosecutorial overkill by the federal government. Vinson told me that he feels the federal government's prosecutorial overkill was designed to leverage his cooperation and ultimate silence. Facing a 295-year sentence, Vinson ultimately cooperated with the federal government, and he entered into a plea agreement of 63 months of incarceration.

At the onset of his cooperation, government agents debriefed Vinson, and Vinson claims that he told the debriefing agents about the interstate pedophile network operated by King and Spence. However, federal officials in Washington, D.C. never publicly acknowledged the purported network, and they sealed Vinson's evidentiary file, which may include Vinson's statements to federal officials about a King and Spence pedophile network and whether or not these allegations were investigated. The

Washington Times attempted to unseal Vinson's evidentiary file twice, but the government rebuffed each attempt.

Readers of *The Franklin Scandal* are confronted with a quandary concerning Vinson's revelations: should they believe Vinson, a convicted felon, whose statements are partially corroborated by the *Washington Times*? Or should they believe the federal government, which refuses to unseal the documents in his case? Absent of any evidence to the contrary, it seems plausible that the government was protecting Vinson's customers and perhaps Spence and King's pedophilic enterprise as it protected King from child abuse charges in Nebraska.

Throughout the course of investigating *The Franklin Scandal*, the names of eminent politicians and powerbrokers have emerged as alleged child molesters, particularly in Washington, D.C. Given the names that have surfaced in my investigation, a major political scandal may have erupted without an immaculate cover-up of King's alleged pedophilic pandering—a political scandal that may have had the seismic impact of Watergate.

King was ultimately sentenced to 15 years in a federal prison for his financial crimes, but he would not be charged with a single count of child abuse, and Spence committed suicide in 1989.

Although Lawrence King was not charged with a single count of child abuse, Paul Bonacci and his attorney filed 16 civil lawsuits in federal court against people Bonacci accused of molesting him, including Lawrence King, or of covering up his abuse, and the lawsuits contended that these individuals had deprived Bonacci of his civil rights. U.S. District Court Judge Warren Urbom declared Bonacci's allegations were unsubstantiated and "bizarre," and he dismissed 15 of the lawsuits. Larry King was incarcerated for his financial crimes when Bonacci's lawsuits were filed, and he opted not to contest the allegations, so Judge Urbom granted Bonacci a default judgment against King in 1998. Bonacci's attorney then requested a separate hearing on the single issue of damages, and called Bonacci to the stand along with other witnesses who partially corroborated Bonacci's accusations. After Judge Urbom listened to the testimony, he awarded Paul Bonacci a one-million-dollar judgment.

Urbom's one-million-dollar judgment discussed the scope of Bonacci's allegations against King, which included "repeated sexual assaults, false imprisonments, infliction of extreme emotional distress, organized and directed satanic rituals . . ." (Bonacci v. King, 1999, Memorandum of Decision). The judgment also addressed Bonacci's suffering because of King:

> He has suffered burns, broken fingers, beating of the head and face and other indignities by the wrongful actions of the defendant King. In addition to the misery of going through the experiences just related over a period of eight years, the plaintiff has suffered the lingering results to the present time.

King appealed the judgment, and then withdrew his appeal after Bonacci's attorney made "motions for depositions." Judge Urbom awarded Bonacci the one-million-dollar judgment in 1999, but Bonacci has yet to receive any remuneration from King.

CONCLUSION

The Franklin Scandal documents the existence of an apparent nationwide pedophile network that pandered children to the power elite of the U.S., and it was covered up by both state and federal authorities. The extraordinary power that was deployed to orchestrate the cover-up of the Franklin story, and the striking aberrations it created in the state and federal judiciaries, is deeply disturbing. The media's participation in the government's cover-up of child abuse is also deeply disturbing. The Franklin story is a cautionary warning for the United States, because it demonstrates that the government and the media, working in conjunction, have the potential to transform fictions into facts and facts into fictions regarding the most heinous of crimes that are anathema to the laws and mores of the American body politic.

The events delineated in *The Franklin Scandal* are analogous to DID in the respect that a nascent abuse disavowing "alter personality" initially emerged to disrupt the normal continuity of a society to protect the Webb children from abuse, and accompanying that alter personality was a disavowal of the abuses. As the cover-up of child abuse effected by multiple institutions and agencies intensified and proliferated, the child-protective laws and values of the body politic and citizenry were thwarted, much as abuse-denying, abuser-aligned "alter personalities" can thwart lift-affirming, self-protective functions in individuals with DID.

REFERENCES

American Psychiatric Association. (2013). *Diagnostic and statistical manual of mental disorders* (5th ed., text rev.). Washington, DC.

Associated Press. (1990a, April 5). Judge orders King to hospital, finds him unable to stand trial. *Omaha World-Herald*, p. 11.

Associated Press. (1990b, March 3) Group says Van Pelt a 'hired gun' for the state. *Lincoln Journal*, p. 7.

Associated Press. (1990c, September 27). Omaha tales of sexual abuse ruled false. *The New York Times*, p. A15.

Bryant, N. (2009). *The Franklin Scandal.* (Paperback Edition) Walterville, OR: Trineday.

Caradori, G. (1989a, October 30). Investigative Reports. 89–1204.

Caradori, G. (1989b, October 11). Investigative Reports. 89–1204.

Caradori, G. (1989c, November 25). Investigative Reports. [Notes]. 89–1204.

Caradori, G. (1989d, December 2). Investigative Reports. 89–1204.

Caradori, G. (1990a, April 13). Investigative Reports. 89–1204.

Caradori, G. (1990b, May 10). Investigative Reports. 89–1204.

Caradori, G., & Ormiston, K. (1989a, November 7). Interview synopsis. Alisha Owens (sic).

Caradori, G., & Ormiston, K. (1989b, November 25). Interview synopsis. Troy Boner.

Caradori, G., & Ormiston, K. (1989c, December 3). Interview synopsis. James Daniel King.

Caradori, G., & Ormiston, K. (1990, May 14). Interview synopsis. Paul Bonacci.

Carmean, I. (1988, July 5). Child Pornography (Information Report). Omaha Police Department. 62913-A.

Carpenter, A. (1985, December 18). Request for Juvenile Petition. Freemont Offices, Department of Social Services, State of Nebraska.

Carpenter, A. (1986, February 7). Request for Juvenile Petition. Freemont Offices, Department of Social Services, State of Nebraska.

Culver, W. (1990, March 21). FD-302 of James Daniel King. Federal Bureau of Investigation, Omaha Field Office. OM 31C-OM-35967.

Dalenberg, C. J., Brand, B. L., Gleaves, D. H., Dorahy, M. J., Loewenstein, R. J., Cardeña, E., Frewen, P. A., Carlson, E. B., & Spiegel, D. (2012, March 12). Evaluation of the evidence for the trauma and fantasy models of dissociation. *Psychological Bulletin*. Advance online publication. doi: 10.1037/a0027447

Dorr, R. (1988, December 1). Franklin deposits now estimated at $39 million. *Omaha World-Herald*, p. 1.

Dorr, R. (1990, February 2). One accuser was guilty of a felony. *Omaha World-Herald*, p. 1.

Dorr, R., & Cordes, H. (1990, February 7). Former judge is prosecutor in franklin case. *Omaha World-Herald*, p. 1.

Dorr, R., & Stern, G. (1990, July 25). Grand jury says abuse stories were a 'carefully crafted hoax.' *Omaha World-Herald*, p. 1.

Flanagan, M., (1990, July 23). Douglas County Grand Jury Report. Michael Flanagan, Foreman.

Flanery, J. (1989, June, 17). Sen. Schmit told of pressure to halt probe. *Omaha World-Herald*, p. 1.

Goodsell, P. (1989, January 8). Purpose of King group questioned. *Omaha World-Herald*, p. 1.

Hedges, M., & Seper, J. (1989a, June 30). Power broker served drugs, sex at parties bugged for blackmail. *Washington Times*, p. A1.

Hedges, M., & Seper, J. (1989b, November 13). In death, Spence stayed true to form. *Washington Times*, p. A1.

Hedges, M., & Seper, J. (1989c, August 9). Spence arrested in N.Y., released; once-host to powerful reduced to begging, sleeping in park. *Washington Times*, p. A1.

Hedges, M., & Seper, J. (1989d, November 13). Spence as much an enigma in death as he was in life. *Washington Times*, p. A11.

Hoch, M. (1988, May 10). Possible Child Pornography. Omaha Police Department. 50001-A.

Keary, J. (1998, December 15). Nebraska joins probers of GOP high-roller King. *Washington Times*, p. A4.

Kramer, M., & Lombardi, F. (1985, January 31). Abolish grand juries & let us decide. *New York Daily News*, p. 3.

Mott, M., & Culver, W. (1990a, March 5). FD-302 of James Daniel King. Federal Bureau of Investigation, Omaha Field Office. OM 31C-OM-35967.

Mott, M., & Culver, W. (1990b, March 8). FD-302 of James Daniel King. Federal Bureau of Investigation, Omaha Field Office. OM 31C-OM-35967.

Nebraska v. Owen (1991). Trial transcript. The District Court of Douglas County, Nebraska.

Omaha World-Herald (1990, July 31). Franklin Committee a Disgrace to Nebraska {Editorial}. *Omaha World-Herald*, p.16.

Omaha World-Herald (1991, June 22) Prosecution Crushed Lies With Avalanche of Truth {Editorial}. *Omaha World-Herald*, p. 16.

Robbins, W. (1988, December 18). A lurid, mysterious scandal begins taking shape in Omaha. *New York Times*, section 1, p. 30.

Rutledge, K. (1988, December 20). Spire, Wadman deny lack of action on child abuse. *Lincoln Journal*, p. 7.

Sar, V., & Öztürk, E. (2009). Psychotic presentations of Dissociative Identity Disorder. In P. Dell & J. O'Neil (Eds.), *Dissociation and the Dissociative Disorders: DSM-V and Beyond* (pp. 535–545). New York, NY: Routledge.

Stern, G. (1990, July 12). Caradori faced criticism of probe Utah firm. *Omaha World-Herald*, p. 1.

World-Herald Bureau. (1988, November 19). Lawmakers order state to investigate failed credit union. *Omaha World-Herald*, p. 1.

Index

Page numbers in *italic* refer to tables